# Women Under Fire:
## Abuse in the Military

### SARAH L. BLUM
### Foreword by Retired Colonel Ann Wright, US Army

Brown Sparrow Publishing Olympia, Washington

# Copyright © 2013

Library of Congress Cataloging-in-Publication Data

Blum, Sarah L.
Women Under Fire: Abuse in the Military/ Sarah L. Blum

ISBN – 13: 978-1-62822-000-1 paperback
1. History – military
2. True Crime
3. Sociology
4. Women's Studies



Printed on recycled, acid-free paper

Manufactured in the United States of America

# Table of Contents

- Sally Griffiths
- Shannon
- Sherrye
- Carolyn Cummings Favreau
- Colleen Mussolino
- Nancy Lilja
- K.H.
- Beckie Wilson
- Laura Sellinger

# Dedication

This book is lovingly and respectfully dedicated to Irish Bresnahan, a U.S. Army Captain, who served from1971 to 1977. Without Irish, this book may never have been started. It was Irish who believed in me and the stories that needed to be told. It was Irish who began the connections with women who had served in the military and who had stories to tell. Since Irish could not sleep and was up on the east coast at three in the morning, and I was up writing at midnight on the west coast, we talked together for hours.

Irish knew and helped many women veterans file claims for disability and get the medical services and other resources they needed. Her own claim for disability did not come through before we lost her.

Irish was exposed to mustard gas added to the tear gas in the gas chamber at Fort McClellan, AL and developed big blisters on her wrists, head, neck, and mouth, which required her to be hospitalized. She was also exposed to Agent Orange sprayed on the training grounds. Within a year, she dropped thirty-five pounds and had excessive saliva. She was sent to Walter Reed Army Medical Center for studies and was diagnosed with irreversible, progressive, demyelinating neurological disease, and multiple chemical sensitivities. She also had excessive uterine bleeding with clots the size of grapefruits. The doctor told her it was from her exposure to toxic chemicals, specifically mustard gas and he was not concerned.

She continued her service for several years and received the Army Commendation Medal with Oak Leaf Cluster and was ultimately given a medical discharge due to her progressive and debilitating nerve and bone diseases, which caused her severe pain. She had also developed slurred speech and peripheral neuropathy.

Irish expressed her despair that she was once healthy, fit and strong, then was reduced to not even being able to care for her own basic needs. She was angry that she and other veterans were treated with such disdain by the Veteran's Administration. She died March 11, 2009. Here are her own words typed by her hands into an email to me.

"I GUESS MY QUESTION WAS HOW MUCH LONGER THIS PAIN AND SUFFERING WILL CONTINUE BEFORE OUR VOICE IS HEARD AND THE AMERICAN PEOPLE WILL KNOW HOW VETS ARE TREATED. I'VE BEEN AT THIS FOR 36 YEARS.

I CAN GIVE YOU NAMES AND ADDRESSES OF MY VET FRIENDS WHO HAVE ALSO BEEN FIGHTING THE VA SYSTEM. MANY ARE SICK AND DYING FROM CHEMICAL EXPOSURE ON ACTIVE DUTY. WE ARE ALL DYING FROM EXPOSURE, SOME FASTER THAN OTHERS. I PLEAD WITH YOU TO ACT QUICKLY BEFORE ONE MORE OF US DIES.

I SAY NOW, NOT LATER, HEAL OUR WOUNDS, AND THE WOUNDS OF TODAY'S MEMBERS OF THE ARMED FORCES OF THE UNITED STATES."

# Acknowledgements

There are many people to acknowledge and thank for supporting me in writing this book, working through my doubts, learning about writing, editing, publishing, how this industry works, meeting agents and editors, securing an agent contract and a publisher, plus all that goes into a published and promoted book.

First and foremost my immense gratitude to the Divine for guiding me through this experience, loving me through my doubts and setbacks, and opening the doors wide for this book to reach the public and fulfill its mission to bring justice to our women under fire.

My gratitude to Virginia Essene who brought forth the message to write this book and the reminder that it was my soul's mission to not only to bring healing to others but to also bring justice. For a long time I did not have a clue how to go about bringing justice into our world, as one small person in this very large world, and through Virginia I was shown the way.

My gratitude to Bente Hansen whose vision of my success with this project helped me keep going at those moments when I was not sure I could do it.

My gratitude to Julie Cooper whose vision of the outcome, support and friendship in accomplishing my mission helped me over many a moment of doubt. I express my deep gratitude to Julie for being there for me through the editing process and introducing me to Tawn Holstra, my amazing publisher.

I give my gratitude and a salute to my friend Irish who listened to me late into the night, believed in me, trusted me and introduced me to many women veterans whose stories lead to this book.

To all the courageous women veterans who spent hours with me telling me their painful stories and allowing me to include them in this book. And for those who gave and then withdrew their stories.

Thank you to Linda J. Shepherd who was another great gift from the Divine. I met Linda in the kitchen during a potluck at a drum circle and discovered that she was a published author, an amazing writer and editor and it was Linda who, not only told me about the Pacific Northwest Writer's Conference, but invited me into her long established writing group. I have undying gratitude for Linda guiding me on the path to where I would be educated, supported, guided, helped to grow in my writing skills, accepted and given constructive appreciated feedback, and celebrated. Great gratitude for you Linda, and to Brian Herbert, Bruce Taylor, Roberta Gregory, and Cal Lawson, my writer's group, for supporting me in writing this book and helping me learn.

I have great gratitude for Pam Binder, the president of the Pacific Northwest Writer's Association for being on the other end of the phone when I made my first call to find out about the conference in 2008. Pam was so gracious and patient and lead me through all the things I needed to bring to be prepared to make the most of the conference including how to do a pitch, planning for meetings with agents and editors, and to create and bring a book proposal. I did all of that and met so many positive and supportive writers, agents, and editors, all of whom gave me great responses and feedback about my book. Before that conference was over I was offered an agent contract and I felt like I was on my way with Women Under Fire.

In 2009 after attending my second PNWA Conference I sent my book off to an editor that I found listed in the conference brochure to get his feedback. It turns out that he absconded with my $500 and did not provide the services I paid for. I contacted Pam Binder to let her know what had happened and after investigating she found someone else to perform those services and PNWA paid for it. I will be eternally grateful to Pam and for that experience because it lead to the book you are holding right now. Pam arranged for Jason Black to read over my book and give me feedback. I have immense gratitude for Jason and his detailed, honest feedback, which took me through deep grief to clarity and a new vision (detailed in the Preface) Thank you Jason for helping me develop the laser focus on the culture of abuse in the military and to the fulfillment of my mission to bring justice to our women under fire.

All along the way since I began this writing, the guiding hand of the Divine has been there and was evident to me every step of the way. In February of 2012 after completing the book, the door to getting it published seemed closed to me. I was sitting in a church in Seattle at the Women Of Wisdom Conference when I felt the Divine touch and inspire me. I was looking over at Jean Houston thinking how youthful and fabulous she looked, when the inspiration came through to talk with her about my book. I was attending her workshop the next day and realized what a great idea that was, and one I never would have thought of on my own. The next morning I went early and Jean was open and available. She listened and said to email her and she would put me in touch with someone and she did. Great joyful thanks to Jean Houston for being open and connecting me to Bill Gladstone at the Waterside Agency and for reading and writing an endorsement for my book.

Great gratitude to Bill Gladstone of the Waterside Agency, for responding to my email so quickly and signing me to a contract, and for David Nelson my agent who believed in me as an author and in the book.

My great love and appreciation to many women veterans who shared news articles and videos with me about military sexual assault and for Gary Noling, father to Carri Goodwin, who did the same.

Special thank you to Susan Avila-Smith who, more than any woman I know, has lead the charge to help female service members who were assaulted in the military to get to safety, find housing, and file claims. Thank you to Susan for believing in me and inviting me to her retreat where I met survivors of military sexual assault and had the honor to support them in their healing and be accepted as one of them. Gratitude to Susan and all my wonderful sisters who attended the retreat on Whidbey Island and for the healing it brought me.

More gratitude for the opportunity to be part of the filming of the Invisible War Movie, and to meet and work with Kirby Dick, Amy Ziering, and their fabulous film crew and for the opportunity to speak at several of the Seattle showings of their academy award winning documentary.

Deep gratitude to my dear friends who have always been silently behind me believing in me, and my mission: Connor Sauer, Deanna Turner, Mary Shakelford.

Grateful thanks to Barbara Turner-Vesselago for teaching me how to write from my heart and for showing me that I can write.

Thank you Deanna Turner for the cover art that took my breath away and gave me chills and that will touch many. Thank you to Chris McLeod my attorney friend who has advised me all along and crafted the release form.

With joyful heart I acknowledge and give gratitude to Tawn Holstra who matched my passion for this book and was willing to publish it. Thank you Tawn for you, and for bringing this book to the world.

# Foreword

A
fter almost a century of enduring sexual assault and abuse when they join the U.S. Military, over the past ten years hundreds of women have bravely come forward and talked about the horrific experiences they have endured. Their stories have finally been heard by members of the United States Congress, first women members of Congress and later by men in the Congress. Sarah Blum's Women Under Fire: Abuse in the Military is an encyclopedia of the crimes that have plagued women in the U.S. Military.

The Congress has now forced the chiefs of the U.S. Military services to acknowledge that criminal acts are being committed against women (and men) in the military by others also in the military. The latest Department of Defense statistics reveal, that probably there were more than 26,000 cases of sexual assault in the military in 2012, up from 19,000 estimated assaults in 2011.

Women Under Fire is a very difficult book to read because it's hard to comprehend that all of these women that Sarah Blum has interviewed and thousands more each year, are raped in our military and then are unable to have the crimes investigated and the perpetrators brought to trial.

Congressional attention on senior levels of the military is not yet sufficient to guarantee that these crimes will end. In fact, the rates of sexual assault have not gone down—but more women and men are willing to come forward to tell what has happened to them.

I spent 29 years in the U.S. Army and Army Reserves and retired as a Colonel. I did not realize how pervasive sexual assault was in the army until long after I retired. When PFC Suzanne Swift and her mother Sara Rich began talking publicly about the repeated rapes on her in Iraq by a senior non-commissioned officer who held life and death control over her, I began to talk with other women about their experiences in the army—and was stunned to hear from many women that they had been sexually assaulted.

In 2006 and 2007, I organized several small groups of women to come to the U.S. Congress and talk with individual Congress persons about the trauma they suffered. Now 7 years later, women and men have spoken in front of full Congressional committees and senior military leaders have had to testify also to these committees. The Chairman of the Joint Chiefs, the Secretary of Defense, and the President of the United States, have now spoken publicly condemning the sexual violence in the U.S. Military and promising to end it.

In May, 2013, President Obama told U.S. Naval Academy graduates that the plague of sexual assaults in the military threatens to undercut the public's trust in the armed forces. The military's newest leaders must follow an 'inner compass' and do what's right, because: "The misconduct of some can have effects that ripple far and wide. Those who commit sexual assault are not only committing a crime, they threaten the trust and discipline that makes our military strong," Obama said.

Now that the crimes have been exposed, the next step is prosecuting the perpetrators, giving them dishonorable discharges from the military and placing their names on the national sex crimes register. Steps that are not being done with regularity at this time.

Women Under Fire: Abuse in the Military, should be required reading by those considering joining the military and by the friends and relatives who encourage young women and men to join the military. These stories stand as warnings to think carefully about joining an organization that has a long history of protecting criminals who commit sexual crimes.

*Ann Wright*

**Ann Wright is a 29 year U.S. Army/Army Reserve Colonel. She also served 16 years in the U.S. Diplomatic Corps. She has written many articles about sexual assault in the military and is the co-author of <u>Dissent: Voices of Conscience</u>.**

# **<u>http://www.voicesofconscience.com/</u>**

# Preface

I began this book in the fall of 2006 to share the stories of women veterans. I had no idea how to write a book or how I would find the women veterans to interview, but I began. I sent out requests everywhere I could think of and gradually made contact with different organizations and women veterans. I followed each and every lead. As I said in the dedication, when I found Irish she opened the floodgates to many women veterans, after she grilled me on what I was doing and why. She made sure I meant no harm to any of the women, and that I would treat them and their stories with respect and care. As we came to talk more, she sent more women vets my way. Some were willing to tell me their stories and some were not. Some decided not to have their story in the book.

I did most of the interviews on the phone. They took from 90-120 minutes each; some took several hours. I supported each woman through the interview emotionally, and would stop to deal with any feelings that came up. I felt very connected to each one of them through the process. Gradually I began to hear more and more stories of sexual assault and retaliatory responses to women who reported those assaults. Hearing those stories created a passion in me to bring them justice, and positive change to the systems that were so unjust and hurtful to them.

I was also learning how to write a book and how the editing and publishing industry worked. In that process, I decided to turn over what I had already written to an editor for feedback. In 2009, I turned what I had written over to Jason Black. The title of the book that he read was Women Under Fire: Their Stories, Their Words, which included stories of respect; prejudice, service, pride, basic training, mustard gas, military sexual trauma, and post-traumatic stress disorder. Jason said it was too diffuse and lacked focus. In his wisdom and skill, he pointed out the distressing stories of sexual assault and suggested I narrow the focus to the culture of abuse in the military. I was not emotionally prepared to do that and was distressed about all the women whose stories did not fit into that narrow focus. I did not want to betray the women who gave me their stories. I went through three months of grieving and did not know what to do. I gave in to the grief and confusion until I came to clarity. I am a deeply spiritual woman and rely on that spiritual connection to guide me. I felt that was where the original motivation to write the book came from and was aware that I had a spiritual mission for justice, but did not know how to fulfill it. Once I released all my feelings and could be calm again, I was able to listen to the inspiration coming to me. It was then, that I realized I had two books, not one, and that the stories that did not fit into the two books could go on the website www.womenunderfire. net. The first book Women Under Fire: Abuse in the Military is what you are now reading. The second book Women Under Fire: PTSD and Healing will follow when I complete it.

It is my sincere desire to help bring justice to the many women in our military who have been treated so unjustly by the Military Service Corps, in which they served proudly and with dedication. I offer this book as a way to begin that. I will go to the halls of Congress and talk with as many legislators as I can about the issue of military sexual assault and what needs to be done to respond more humanely to women who report those assaults and to bring them justice. I ask you the reader, to do what you can to support our women under fire by letting your Senators and Congresswomen know your feelings and ask that they read the book and do what it suggests.

# The Shame
# of Our Military

olleen Mussolino, an Army cook in the 1960's, details being gang-raped by four soldiers who took her into the woods. Colleen fought and screamed as they held her down and raped her. The soldiers' knees were on her arms to keep her from fighting. They beat her unconscious and gang-raped her. When she regained consciousness she was bruised on her neck, head, jaw and arms, and was bleeding down her thighs. Colleen ran to the road for help and some MP's (Military Police) stopped and took her to the hospital. She was taken to the CID (Criminal Investigation Division) and interrogated from 7 a.m.-4 p.m. five days a week for six weeks. They threatened her with a dishonorable discharge if she did not sign a paper saying she would not prosecute. "I felt betrayed and made the criminal.

I felt like a prisoner of war instead of a woman soldier who was gang-raped!"*

Sharon Mixon, a twenty-one year old decorated combat medic in Desert Storm was devastated by her experience of being gang-raped while waiting to process out of Dhahran, Saudi Arabia in 1991. Someone in line with her offered her a drink, which she accepted.

"The next thing I remember is waking up face down on a cot. Somebody was on top of me, penetrating me. I was being held down. And there were six men taking turns raping me. They were U.S. Soldiers, and they told me that if I told anybody that they would kill me. But I went to the MP's anyway. And they told me the same thing. They laughed and said, "We will always know where to find you, and if you open your mouth, you know what's gonna happen."[1]

Sharon Mixon was silent for ten years and continued her military career until she began showing symptoms of PTSD/MST (Post Traumatic Stress Disorder/Military Sexual Trauma) and was hospitalized. She said of the military, "I had been awarded a medal for valor in combat and went from being a standard-setting soldier to being something that they wanted to hide in a closet."

"Women in the U.S. Military are more likely to be raped by a fellow soldier than killed by enemy fire in Iraq."[2] Our women have been under fire in our military for a long time. They experience the fires of hostility, hatred, contempt, rape, sexual assault, and violence from those who outrank them and serve side by side with them in combat and non-combat assignments. Combat, yes indeed, women serve

-----------------------------------------------------------------------

*From an interview with Colleen in June 2007.

[1]"Army Rape Accuser Speaks Out," *60 Minutes,* CBS, 20 February 2005.

[2]Jane Harmon, "Rapist in the Ranks," *Los Angeles Times,* 31 March 2008.

in combat; they serve proudly and effectively. This book is about women who were abused while members of the U.S. Armed Forces. There is no question that women are and have been under fire in combat on behalf of the United States of America, just as there is no question that many women have been under fire from the good old boys network that demeans, degrades, and derides them through extreme hostility, and misogyny.

The system is broken! Now that women serve beside men and are as competent and able as their male counterparts, the attitudes and behavior in the command structure must change to accommodate the highest and best functioning at every level of the military. Women are as necessary to our current military as men. Women serve as proudly and proficiently as men. Women deserve the same level of respect as men. Women need the same opportunities as men for advancement. Women must have the same equality of justice as the men.

It is an enormous shame that this great nation, the United States of America, and our military, have chosen to do nothing about the rampant sexual abuse toward women that has been going on for decades. From Tailhook to the latest news of rapes at Lackland AFB (Air Force Base), our Congress, our Military, and our Commander-in-Chief, have done nothing more than poke a pencil at the problem. There are few in Congress who have been concerned and raised the issue, but it has gone nowhere. Leon Panetta, as Secretary of Defense, did acknowledge the issue, gave it serious attention and started to make minor changes before he left office. Unfortunately our American Military is disrespectful, demeaning, demoralizing, and downright hostile toward women. This culture of abuse in our military needs to be brought further into the light and changed. That is my mission.

I know that what I am writing about in this book does not apply across the board to all soldiers, doctors, military police, or commanders.  Those of you who are and have served alongside women respectfully, I thank you and enlist your support again, to back them up on this horrendous issue.

My own experiences were mild compared to what you will read in this book, yet I think it important to describe them to you here, because they are part of the culture of abuse and the entitlement men in the military live by. When I was stationed at Letterman General Hospital for five months in the operating room course for the Army Nurse Corps, I was sexually molested. When I was the scrub nurse for an open-heart surgery case, the heart surgeon, a colonel came around behind me and put his gloved hands under my scrub dress and over my breasts. I was shocked and angry. I told him, "Take your hands off me now, or I will break scrub and report you." He did and I was never allowed on one of his cases after that. It seems to me the message was either you allow me to do as I please with you, or you won't be on my cases. After my five months at Letterman I was sent to the 12th Evacuation Hospital, in Cu Chi, Vietnam as an operating room nurse. After being there about two months, I was sent along with other nurses, to a general's party. It was for a general with the 196th Light Infantry Brigade. While the party was nice and I had excellent food, what happened after eating was very telling. I was talking with the general who commanded the First Infantry Division, called 'Big Red One.' He had obviously been drinking a lot and his speech was slurred. He was very large and I was five feet tall and weighed about ninety-eight pounds. We were in a large room with people all around. He was putting cigarettes into his nose and ears, trying to be funny. Then he suddenly pulled me onto his lap and said, "I want you to be my girl. I will send a helicopter for you whenever I want you. I will tell your chief nurse." He was disgusting and I was completely grossed out.

I was trying to figure out how to get away from him without making a scene. I told him I needed to go to the ladies room (no such thing in a war zone, but we were at a hospital in Bien Hoa and they had a real ladies room). I slipped off his lap and went. I considered my options and how I could get out of there. I waited until he was distracted and ran for the door and outside. I got away from him and that situation. My entire story will be told in my next book, Women Under Fire: PTSD and Healing. This general believed an army nurse would be 'his girl,' who he could call whenever he had the need or desire to 'have her.' If he expected that and he was the general of an entire division, that is what every soldier would expect, in one form or another. Nurses were professionals there to help the wounded, not to 'service' our soldiers or commanders sexually.

I knew there was more sexual harassment and even attempts to molest women, since I had experienced that myself, but I was truly unaware of the rampant sexual assault that exists in the military until I began this project. A 2003 survey of women veterans showed that twenty-eight percent were sexually assaulted during their career. A 2005 study reported by The *Associated Press* and *NPR*, revealed that half the women serving in the national guard or reserves were sexually assaulted. At the same time, a Pentagon report stated that hostile attitudes toward women persist in both the Army and Naval Academies. In 2007 the Miles Foundation reported a ten to fifteen percent increase in date-rape, gang-rape and serial offenders per quarter.[3] *ABC news* announced that 60,000 women serving in Iraq and Afghanistan had been sexually assaulted. Of the women seeking health care from the VA, seventy-one percent said they were sexually assaulted or raped while serving. In their sample of women, the rate

-------------------------------------------------------------------------

[3]"Reported Cases of Sexual Assault in Military Rise," *All Things Considered,* NPR, 4 October 2007.

was almost two to three times higher than civilian women seeking psychiatric care.[4] One in three women were sexually assaulted while serving in the military and between 80-90 percent were never reported. The latest estimate (2011) is there are 19,000 sexual assaults each year in our Military.

The Tailhook scandal hit the news in 1991 describing navy pilots raping women naval officers at a convention. Then in 1996 army trainees at Aberdeen Proving Ground were forcibly raped and even sodomized by their higher-ranking teachers. In 2003 the Air Force Academy was accused of looking the other way when female cadets were being raped. The Senate Armed Services Committee panel concluded that since 1993, the highest levels of air force leadership have known of serious sexual misconduct problems at the academy, but failed to take effective action.

In 1992, an article by Melissa Healy, blasted a probe into the Tailhook scandal, stating the navy has been indulgent toward such sexual misconduct in the past. The navy allowed demeaning behavior and attitudes toward women to prevail.[5]

When female trainees at the Army's Aberdeen Proving Ground, charged their male drill sergeants with sexual assault, an investigation ensued which resulted in six charges against the sergeant major of the army, the highest ranking enlisted soldier in the army. The ten-month

-------------------------------------------------------------------------------

[4] Poulsny M.Murdoch, J.Hodges and N.O'Brien, "Prevalence of In-Service and Post-Service Sexual Assault among Combat and Noncombat Veterans Applying for Department of Veterans Affairs Posttraumatic Stress Disorder Disability Benefits," *Military Medicine* 169 (May 2004):392-395.

[5] "Pentagon Blasts Tailhook Probe, Two Admirals Resign," *Los Angeles Times,* 25 September 1992.

review and report stated clearly that the army has a problem with attitude and leadership. Emphasizing women are discriminated against and not treated with respect.[6] The military investigators, led by Major General Richard S. Siegfried, said the army's written policy had failed in practice. The report affirmed, "Sexual harassment exists throughout the army crossing gender, rank, and racial lines. Victims are re-victimized by the system." The report exposed the fact that commanders are perceived as having little interest in enforcing the rules or policy re: sexual harassment/assault and a breakdown in trust occurred between soldiers, both men and women. Forty percent of the women and thirty seven percent of the men polled in the investigation concurred that army leadership was more interested in their own careers than the well being of the soldiers. *That is quite an indictment. Why isn't Congress or the President doing something about it? This report is sixteen years old.*

This negative attitude toward females is evident to many in the military and people hearing women veteran's stories." Women are discriminated against and not treated with respect;"[7] documented in a ten-month report on the army. That review and report stated clearly that the army has a problem with attitude and leadership. It called for action, specifically for women soldiers to be treated with dignity and respect. Army Chief of Staff General Dennis Reimer told the *U.S.A. Today* Editorial Board, that the issue at Aberdeen was abuse of power. Former Marine Corps, Lance Corporal Stephen Funk, recounted that during training, his drill sergeant said in rousing rhetoric, "This is the reality of war. We marines like war. We like killing. We like raping

--------------------------------------------------------------------------

[6]"Army's Leadership Blamed in Report on Sexual Abuse," *The New York Times,* 12 September 1997.

[7]*The Secretary of the Army Senior Review Panel Report on Sexual Harassment,* vol. 1, July 1997.

females. This is what we do!"[8]

It is? I always knew the marines were good at what they did, but I never knew they liked killing and raping.

As I read articles and reports, the discounting evident in the armed forces and in our government increasingly angered me. There was a panel review of the sexual misconduct at the Air Force Academy and in their report was this; "The Panel is also concerned about the seeming inability of the air force to adequately investigate itself [and highlighted] the ineffective oversight by Air Force Academy Leadership."[9] It went on to recommend the "Department of Defense and Inspector General, conduct a thorough review of accountability of the academy and Air Force Headquarters Leadership for the sexual assault problems over the last decade."

The last decade! Who has been minding the store? The report addressed many specific problems including command supervision and oversight, organizational culture and character, and character development. What happened to all those recommendations? Who or what is in charge of follow through? Who has oversight on the air force?

Women soldiers are held at knifepoint and raped in Iraq. They won't drink water after dinner for fear they will be raped on the way to the latrine. Their screams will not be heard, because of the sound of the generators.

---------------------------------------------------------------------------

[8]Aimee Allison, "An Excellent Reason Not to Join the Military," *Alternet,* 5 May 2006
[9]*Report of the Panel to Review Sexual Misconduct Allegations at the U.S. Air Force Academy,* September 22, 2003.
http://www.defense.gov/news/Sep2003/d20030922usafareport.pdf

Doctors taking liberties with women who come to them for exams, and commanders or high ranking officers forcing and coercing lower ranking women to have sex with them. Women, like men, are taught they must obey the commands of those of higher rank.

In 2007 Colonel Janis Karpinski reported that in 2003, "Three female soldiers had died of dehydration in Iraq," rather than risk rape by their brother soldiers near the latrines and generators. Colonel Karpinski was in the room when the doctor gave his briefing to the deputy commander saying, "These women died in their cots." Worse yet, she heard the deputy commander, "Tell him [the doctor] not to say anything about it, because that would bring attention to the problem."[10] Perhaps more than attention to the problem, it would bring attention to a **military corps' failure to deal with a problem.** In addition to having a culture of abuse, the military is choosing to cover up what is happening to our women soldiers. When women are raped and come forward to report it they are punished, ostracized, treated as traitors and often discharged without benefits, while rapists are free to do as they please and are often promoted.

There is a **"good old boys network"** in the military. It is alive and well. This good old boys network includes the military police, Military Justice System and their courts. They protect their own, male soldiers of all ranks, and punish the women who have the audacity to report rape. From the perspective of the good old boys, reporting risks the careers of soldiers and officers and the image of the army, navy, air force, marines or the coast guard. Each commander decides whether or not to investigate, how to carry it out, what the approach or attitude will be, what to do with the information, and whether or

---

[10]Helen Benedict, "The Private War of Women Soldiers," *Salon* 7 March 2007, http://www.salon.com/news/feature/2007/03/07/women_in_Military

not to stop the investigation or to prosecute. That is a lot of power in one commander who is being asked to reveal something potentially damaging to him or his unit. Miles Moffeit and Amy Herdy, in their special report for the *Denver Post* in 2004 wrote about the 1999 National Academy of Public Administration Panel's urgent concern of, 'command interference' in sexual assault cases. That panel called for the DOD (Department of Defense) to put an end to it. That has not happened! There is also the 2001 Cox Commission Report, which stated, "The greatest barrier to operating a fair system of criminal justice [is the] far reaching role of the commanding officer. Even serial offenders are allowed to resign with administrative punishments and they can slip back into the civilian world with no criminal record." [11]

The Miles Foundation received over 1000 reports of rape and sexual assault in Iraq and Afghanistan between 2002 and July 2008. [12] Most of those were attacks by other soldiers, their brothers in arms. A survey conducted by the VA in 2005 assessed sexual assault at thirty percent of female veterans and fourteen percent of those were gang-raped, while twenty percent were raped more than once. [13] The military is widely recognized as having a distinct subculture in which rape conducive norms abound." [14] The DOD report shows almost ninety percent of rape victims are junior ranking women with an average age of twenty-one and most assailants are non-commissioned officers or junior men with an average age of twenty-eight. [15]

-------------------------------------------------------------

[11] Miles Moffeit and Amy Herdy, "Betrayal in the Ranks: A Special Report," *The Denver Post,* 2004 http://extras.denverpost.com/justice/tdp_betrayal.pdf
[12] Kimberly Hefling, "Female Soldiers Cite Sexual Assaults," *MSNBC.com,* 21 July 2008.
[13] "Military Culture and Gender," *The Miles Foundation,* 15-16 September 2005.
[14] Ibid.
[15] Moffeit and Herdy, "Betrayal in the Ranks."

The latest data from the Pentagon shows a nine percent increase in the number of sexual assaults reported in the 2008/2009 fiscal year and a twenty-five percent increase in sexual assaults to women serving in Iraq/Afghanistan. "The chilling fact is that, as the Pentagon readily admits, the overwhelming majority of rapes that occur in the military go unreported, perhaps as many as 80%."[16] So we know the percent of increase is far larger than nine percent. Most of the perpetrators of these attacks receive little or no punishment and are not held accountable. "The military's record of prosecuting rapists is not just lousy, it's atrocious."[17]

I began my research and interviews with women veterans in the fall of 2006 just after the news reports of Suzanne Swift's case. Suzanne had been, "Sexually harassed repeatedly by three of her superiors throughout her military service beginning in Kuwait, through much of her time in Iraq and following her return to Fort Lewis."[18]

On her first day Suzanne appropriately asked where she was to report for duty. Her sergeant's inappropriate response was, "On my bed naked."

Suzanne followed protocol and reported this experience to the designated equal opportunity representative. This same sergeant, her squad leader, coerced Suzanne into having sex with him for four months. He would come to her door late at night and demand intercourse. Suzanne, like most young recruits, feared not following the orders of her sergeant and feared retaliation if she refused. She

-------------------------------------------------------------

[16]Bob Herbert, "The Great Shame," *The New York Times,* 21March 2009.
[17]Ibid.
[18]Sara Corbett, "A Woman's War," *The New York Times Magazine,* 18 March 2007.

told Sara Corbett of *The New York Times,* "If your sergeant tells you to walk over a minefield, you're supposed to do it."[19]

Gene Fidell, President of the private group, National Institute of Military Justice, vehemently states that people in the military are intensely trained to follow orders from a superior so there is little place for a 'No'. "It is a rigid hierarchy. You're talking about people who are used to doing what they are told." [20]

When Suzanne Swift finally had the courage to say "No," to her squad leader sergeant, she experienced what she had feared; his retaliation! She was forced to march all alone at night in full battle gear from one side of camp to the other and she was repeatedly humiliated in front of her fellow soldiers. The squad leader was ultimately moved to another unit and was **promoted!** That is our military culture at work! Suzanne's mother an M.S.W. (Medical Social Worker) told Amy Goodman of NPR, that she was shocked by the blatant and rampant sexual abuse by male soldiers and that when a woman reported it, she was treated as a traitor to her unit and her country. Sara Rich, Suzanne's mother, implores, "Why in the world are our federal elected officials not stopping this?" [21]

Suzanne was a Humvee driver who worked sixteen hour shifts, was hit nightly by mortar attacks and during her tour of duty at Camp Lima, had a close friend injured by a car bomb and lost another to friendly fire. She came home with nightmares, crying fits, anxiety, numbness, and she was detached, demoralized, and depressed. What distressed her the most was the memory of her squad leader forcing

------------------------------------------------------------

[19]Corbett, "A Woman's War."

[20]Marie Tessier, "Sexual Assault Pervasive in Military," *Alternet,* 2 April 2003.

[21]Corbett, "A Woman's War."

her to have sex with him. Command rape occurs when sex is forced or coerced by someone of higher rank, usually several ranks above their prey. MSA (Military Sexual Assault) is a deep wounding betrayal that occurs when a soldier is sexually assaulted by a fellow soldier or superior. Women are told they can rely on these men to protect them in combat. These are the men they're told they can trust to 'have their back'. Women are drilled on this in basic training to rely on their buddy soldiers and commanders. Male soldiers of all ranks who assault their sister soldiers are proving that they cannot be trusted and they are not protecting female soldiers. They are betraying their trust, they are hurting them deeply and they are attacking them unnecessarily. This means they are not trustworthy in battle either and that does affect military preparedness, outcomes in armed conflicts, and ultimately reflects on the military corps. It must STOP!

Suzanne filed her report one year before she went AWOL and refused to be re-deployed to Iraq. It was only when she was AWOL that any investigation into the charges was begun. How does an investigation one year after the fact, have any merit? In Suzanne's case and many others where sexual abuse, sexual harassment, trauma, or coercion are reported, the outcome is the same, **the charges could not be substantiated, because of lack of evidence.** Of course they could not be substantiated, it was a year after the fact, it happened at night and everyone there was in the middle of a war that could, at any moment, take their life.

Marciela Guzman, age 21, had her first ever sexual experience when she was molested by a commanding officer during boot camp. She was on watch dispersing laundry and while going through a dark room full of sleeping soldiers was grabbed from behind and molested. She could tell from his badge as he was leaving through the back door, that he was a commander. The next day she was reprimanded for,

"Not following proper procedures while on duty, and from then on, she remained silent." [22] It is common for officers and NCO's (Non Commissioned Officers) to come up with a reprimand, or complaint of some type against the women they have harassed or assaulted. They are following the approach: the best defense is a good offense. It offends and shocks the women because they know they have done nothing wrong, and it shifts the focus away from what actually took place.

Aimee Allison, a medic in the army reserves, received a, "Demeaning and uncomfortable pelvic exam during her induction physical."[23] The doctor did not wear gloves. This type of experience is all too common. Aimee described being too intimidated to speak up for herself.

Dorothy Mackey was a 21 year-old college student at the University of Ohio, in the ROTC program for the air force, when she was sent for her induction physical and a colonel was very rough and violent to her during the pelvic exam." He put his finger in my vagina and it was so traumatic that I dissociated and could not speak."[24] Later in her career as an officer she went to an OB/GYN clinic and had another traumatic experience of a doctor sodomizing her with his fingers during the exam. She again dissociated and could not speak. "They want to brush it under a rug. They want it to go away,"[25] Marine Lieutenant Tara Burkhart, told Steve Kroft of *60 Minutes.* Tara served

--------------------------------------------------------------

[22]Celina DeLeon, "For Female Soldiers, Sexual Assault Remains a Danger," *Alternet,* 5 January 2007.

[23]Allison, "An Excellent Reason."

[24]Kari Lydersen, "Rape Nation," *Alternet.* 2 July 2004.

[25]"Army Rape Accuser Speaks Out," *60 Minutes,* CBS, 20 February 2005.

as a public affairs officer in Kuwait during Operation Iraqi Freedom. She was raped by her sergeant and was silent until charges were brought against her. Her attorney immediately contacted the command and yelled, "This is crazy, my client was raped!" Tara's command said she was lying and they would prosecute her. "She's gonna go to court-martial," retorted her command. Tara was charged with nineteen counts including sexual misconduct, making false statements and disobeying orders. These charges would have sent her to prison for twenty-six years.[26] That is our Military Justice System following protocol to indict the women and protect the men. It is outrageous and must be *stopped.*

The sergeant who raped Lieutenant Burkhart was accused of another rape while they were investigating her case and he was never prosecuted. Tara told *60 Minutes*: "There [have] never been any charges brought against him. He was given immunity to testify against me."[27] She was acquitted of the most serious charges but served thirty days for violating alcohol policies and disobeying orders. That too is typical of the system.

"The military as a whole has wished this issue would go away," said Scott Berkowitz, Founder and President of the Rape, Abuse and Incest National Network, which runs the largest rape hotline in the country." Three out of every one hundred women say that they were sexually assaulted. That compares to the equivalent civilian rate for women that age, which is three in one thousand. The problem in the military could be as much as ten times the civilian problem." [28]

------------------------------------------------------------------

[26]"Army Rape Accuser Speaks Out," *60 Minutes.*
[27]Ibid.
[28]Ibid.

Jennifer Neal, a navy petty officer was raped June 14, 2001, at the Naval Training Center in Great Lakes, Illinois. Jennifer was near the top of her class in engineering and was attending a cookout at the training center. A fellow petty officer, Jessie R. Capers, asked her to get him a beer from his room. As she entered the room he, "Grabbed her by the throat, pinned her to the bed, and raped her." [29]

Neal reported the rape immediately and "Went to the hospital where doctors collected DNA evidence and investigators took photos of her bloody torn clothing and the bite marks that covered her chest and neck. Despite all those steps, Neal was threatened, intimidated, and deprived of basic assistance from the military." [30]

After Capers was arrested, he was released to roam free on base while Neal was afraid to leave her room. She asked to talk with her supervisors and one of them threatened to have her put on a psychiatric ward. This is your military in action  mistreating women in service. This is what they do. This is protocol. It is not justice. A woman in the military who is raped and reports it, deserves to be heard and given appropriate services to meet her needs. Christine Hansen, Director of the Miles Foundation, has seen thousands of cases like this and says there is no justice for these women in the military. I completely agree. That is the reason for this book, to highlight that fact, and call for action to create a more just system for them.

Dorothy Mackey, who experienced the inappropriate pelvic exams related previously, became an air force officer and was gang-raped during her service. She began her air force career in 1983 and by 1987; she had been promoted to captain and had 450 soldiers in

---

[29]Moffeit and Herdy, "Betrayal in the Ranks."
[30]Ibid.

her unit. In Spain, with her group on a training mission, Dorothy was playing volleyball and became thirsty. She asked her first sergeant, whom she trusted, to get her some water. She drank the water and realized immediately that something was wrong. She had taken two large gulps of water and started to stagger and lose her balance. She stumbled inside and began to vomit violently. While she was in that state, her first sergeant was standing in the doorway laughing. When the vomiting stopped she passed out and later awoke in her first sergeant's room where four guys were playing cards and laughing. She passed out again and when she came to consciousness the second time, her first sergeant was on top of her penetrating her. She told him "NO," and passed out again. She did not regain consciousness until there was a loud knock on the door and someone who was concerned about her was asking how she was doing. She saw her first sergeant hiding behind the door naked with a full erection. She knew she had to get out of there. Using all her determination, since she had no energy, she rolled off the bed and got herself up and was helped back to her room. When she tried to file a complaint no one would listen to her. [31]

Dorothy Mackey, along with other women veterans, attended the National Summit of Women Veteran Issues held in Washington, D.C., June 19th and 20th, 2004. Many women came to her and told her about the abuse and rapes they suffered by officers, doctors and fellow soldiers. Many of the attacks involved the use of drugs or alcohol given to women intentionally to render them helpless.[32] There was agreement among the women that our military fosters a culture of sexual violence and contempt for women.

---------------------------------

[31]Lydersen, "Rape Nation."
[32]Ibid.

Dorothy began studying the law while in the air force and was motivated by her experiences to do something. In 1994 she filed a civil lawsuit in district court, Dayton, Ohio against the man who assaulted her and the superiors who abused her when she tried to report it. The Justice Department decided to represent the defendants so the case was moved to federal court. Eventually it was thrown out when the Department of Justice attorney said bringing the case to trial constituted a threat to national security and would disrupt the order and discipline of the military. Sexual assault in the military is already disrupting the order and discipline. The case was a threat to the *status quo*; to the way the military mistreats women and *continues to get away with it*. This case made it all the way to the Supreme Court, which refused to hear it.[33]

"It's in all the services and it's a pervasive part of the culture. Sexual assault is considered a rite of passage in the service, and [the women] are treated like the black sheep of the family when they ask for accountability."[34] That quote is from Christine Hansen, the Executive Director of the Miles Foundation, a victim service and advocacy agency for casualties of sexual and domestic violence in the military. She goes on to say that any report to a nurse, doctor, counselor or police officer within the military must be communicated to the commander.

"It is difficult for any victim of sexual assault to come forward, even in the best of circumstances, especially if it means the information is going to their commander. [In the military all] decisions about investigations and prosecutions are made within the chain of command, not by an adversarial outside agency like a prosecutor's office. This

-----------------------------------

[33]DeLeon, "Sexual Assault Remains a Danger."
[34]Tessier, "Sexual Assault Pervasive in Military."

leaves commanders with an inherent conflict of interest: on the one hand they are responsible for seeking justice for crimes; and on the other, they are bound as leaders to protect the soldiers and sailors they value and maintain good morale in their units. There's an inherent conflict of interest that may seriously deter them from holding offenders accountable."[35] It seems to me that many commanders make clear in their decisions and actions regarding sexual assault, that they value the perpetrators more than the victims.

An army Chaplain at Fort Benning, Georgia, was being prosecuted for molesting a fifteen year-old boy. The prosecutor, James Willson was confident of a conviction, but Delbert Spurlock halted the case. Spurlock was Assistant Secretary of the Army at that time, and was concerned about negative publicity. He told the commander to, "Let him resign."[36] Decisions like these discount the crime committed, prevent full accountability and do a disservice to the victim, the perpetrator, and the military. This decision confirms that the military is more interested in their image than being effective or demonstrating leadership. If our military is not interested in being effective or in modeling excellence in leadership, what is their intention? This compromises the mission of our military and may be cause for serious concern by Congress and our Commander-in-Chief. I would think any leader would want to model honesty and accountability and expect that from their subordinates. Perhaps there is more to investigate than sexual assault. This indicts the entire premise of leadership in the military.

Myla Haider has investigated dozens of rape cases as a CID (Criminal Investigation Division) investigator with the Military police.

---

[35]Tessier, "Sexual Assault Pervasive in Military."

[36]Moffeit and Herdy, "Betrayal in the Ranks."

Myla said there is a pervasive attitude toward the victim that guarantees the cases will fail. Haider said investigators look for lies, not truth, and work together interrogating victims until they relent and won't pursue the charges. CID training does not focus on evidence collection for acquaintance rape and therefore it is not taken seriously. [37]

Helen Benedict in her article, Why Soldiers Rape, says, "Platoons are enclosed hierarchical societies, riddled with gossip, so any woman who reports sexual assault has little chance of remaining anonymous. She will probably have to face her assailant day after day and put up with resentment and blame from other soldiers who see her as a snitch. She risks being persecuted by her assailant if he's her superior, and punished by any commander who considers her a troublemaker. Because [the] military culture demands that all soldiers keep their pain and distress to themselves, reporting an assault will make her look weak and cowardly."[38]

"The military is one of the most highly controlled environments imaginable. When there are rules that the Pentagon absolutely wants followed, they are rigidly enforced by the chain of command. Violations are not tolerated. The military could bring about a radical reduction in the number of rapes and other forms of sexual assault if it wanted to, and it could radically improve the overall treatment of women in the armed forces. There is no real desire in the military to modify this aspect of its culture. It is an ultra-macho environment in which the overwhelming tendency has been to see all women, civilian and military, young and old, american and foreign solely as sexual objects.

--------------------------------------------------------

[37]Jessica Pupovac, "Raped and Silenced in the Barracks," *In These Times,* 3 March 2008.

[38]Helen Benedict, "Why Soldiers Rape," *In These Times,* 13 August 2008.

Real change, drastic change, will have to be imposed from outside the military. It will not come from within. Rape and other forms of sexual assault against women is the great shame of the U. S. Armed Forces, and there is no evidence that this ghastly problem, kept out of sight as much as possible, is diminishing." [39]

Twenty-year-old Marine Lance Corporal Maria Lauterbach, reported being raped by Corporal Cesar Laurean, and obtained a military order of protection, yet was still forced to stay on the same base and attend the same meetings with him. She was on her way to one of those meetings on December 14, 2007 at Camp Lejeune, N.C., when she disappeared. This was shortly before she was due to testify against him. On January 11, 2008 Maria's charred body was uncovered in a shallow grave behind the Laurean home. That same day Corporal Cesar Laurean failed to show for questioning at the county sheriff's office. Laurean's wife told investigators that he had gone to Mexico and left a note for them. The note said Maria had slit her own throat and he buried her. The autopsy showed that Lance Corporal Maria Lauterbach died of blunt force trauma to the head. The media took the story and challenged her character and credibility and questioned the slow response by the marine corps. Susan Avila Smith, a former army linguist and founder of Vet WOW, Women Organizing Women, assists women in the military who have been sexually assaulted. She responded by saying that the handling of Maria Lauterbach's case is typical and epitomizes the failure of all branches of the military to address sexual assault for the violent crime it is. The system as it exists puts victims on the defense and rape survivors who have the courage to speak out are put at even greater risk than if they had simply, "Accepted the abuse as collateral damage in their military careers."[40]

-------------------------------------------------------

[39]Bob Herbert, "The Great Shame," *The New York Times,* 21 March 2009.

[40]Pupovac, "Raped and Silenced."

A marine brother in her unit raped Corporal, Brittany Thornton, on Christmas Day 2005 in Okinawa, Japan. She reported the rape immediately and pressed charges. Then she was put on antidepressants, removed from her post in weapons maintenance, and assigned to a desk job. The marines even revoked her certification, which she had earned. Brittany was forced to live in the same barracks as her rapist despite repeated requests for a transfer. She told Jessica Pupovac, "I felt like I was being punished. I think it was just a way for them to make things difficult for me because they [the chain of command] didn't believe me."[41] While at her desk job she had access to her file and looked at it. She was appalled at what she read. The CID agent had completely revised her account of the assault so that it had no truth in it and made Brittany sound like she was drunk and having consensual sex with her rapist. Revision of victim reports seems to be protocol for CID investigations. I heard that same account from many women. Brittany's case, like most others, went nowhere and the rapist received no more than a *slap on the wrist.*

Private S. Clark said, "My CID wasn't an investigator, he was an interrogator. The thing I remember is him leaning over the desk with his cigarette breath screaming at me, "Why don't you admit that it was rough, consensual sex between two drunken adults?"[42] Private Clark, who did not give her first name, said that her attacker had beaten her so badly that she began to have seizures. Her doctors said the cause of her seizures was cranial tearing. She also stated that one of the most painful parts of her experience was being deserted by those she considered brothers. They turned on her and showed their contempt and hatred outwardly as though she had done something horrid to them. These are her brothers in arms who supposedly will

---

[41]Pupovac,"Raped and Silenced."
[42]Ibid.

take a bullet for her in combat, but instead now turn their back on her and call her a whore, because she was raped. Is this truly the culture we wish to foster in our military? How will this help us defend our country? *It will not.* When brothers at arms do not support their sister soldiers, our military is not ready nor will it be effective.

Clark said the CID agent, "Made me feel as if I had dishonored my army, and my country by speaking out against another soldier."[43] There it is again, another soldier. It is not another soldier; it is a violent rapist! Wasn't the rapist speaking out against another soldier by his actions? If a co-worker rapes you or a woman you care about, is it wrong for you or them to speak out against the rapist? You would be speaking out against another co-worker. Are we supposed to allow anyone in the military to do anything they wish with another soldier, if that soldier is a woman? Do we really expect and accept that the leadership in the Armed Forces of the United States of America looks the other way when its female soldiers are assaulted? Do we want to send our sons into a military that will teach them to devalue, demean, hate and rape the women they serve with?

Myla Haider, the former CID agent, said, "The law enforcement responses make it so that victims don't want anything to do with the investigation anymore."[44] Military investigations seem to be another form of punishment to women who have the courage to report a sexual assault. They are grilled for hours at a time in disrespectful ways and treated more like a criminal than victim. My belief is the military police or CID does that to break them down and get them to sign away their rights rather than follow through. How do we make a broken

-----------------------------------------

[43]Pupovac,"Raped and Silenced."
[44]Ibid.

military that discounts its women soldiers become accountable for what happens on the job? What would happen in the civilian world if a large corporation/employer allowed male employees and supervisors to rape, assault, sexually harass, coerce and humiliate women employees?

How do we respond as human beings and Americans when we hear of a twenty-one-year-old female soldier who shot herself with her M-16 rifle two weeks after filing a rape charge against a fellow soldier and two days after being diagnosed with MST? What do we do when the army tells us their investigation failed to substantiate the rape claim? We can no longer be quiet about this! We can no longer collude with the military and the corporate media in keeping all this under wraps. We can no longer allow the military to investigate themselves. They are far too self-protective. It is time for independent unbiased investigations into sex crimes and the handling of those crimes in the military. Our Congress is the oversight body and must take its rightful place and do its job. I am calling for unbiased <u>thorough</u> congressional investigations into all the military services NOW! Examine what leaders at every level are saying and doing as they lead. Research how leaders are trained and that includes what is communicated non-verbally and with laughter. Do a thorough evaluation at every level of how reports of abuse by women are handled, how protective orders are managed, and how the system applies accountability and justice, if at all.

Imagine that you have a daughter who is now a senior in high school and recruiters come to the school to do presentations on their branch of the military, showing all the opportunities available to students when they sign up. This recruiter appears as a good-looking male in uniform appearing as father/friend/guide to young women, someone they can trust. Many young girls become victims of sexual abuse even before they take the military oath. An *Associated Press* investigation showed that in 2005 there were over two hundred recruiters punished for harassment and abuse. The army by itself had 722 recruiters accused of rape and sexual harassment by 2007. The investigation pointed out that recruiter sexual misconduct occurs in the recruiting station, government vehicles and in the recruiter's apartment. Would you want your daughter or anyone's daughter to fall prey to a military recruiter?

Did you know that men are also the targets of sexual abuse in the military? It is largely ignored by the media yet does take place. These are the least acknowledged casualties of military service. A Pentagon study showed that greater than nine percent or over 2000 sexual assaults were to men serving in Iraq between 2002 and 2003. It is important to acknowledge that sexual assault toward men does occur in the U.S. Armed Forces, even though that is not the subject of this book. For a man to step forward and say that he was sexually assaulted while serving his country in the military is even more humiliating and shaming than for women. Whatever is done to change the culture of the military will also benefit men who are victims or would be victims.

In 1997, Major Elsbeth Ritchie, Assistant Chief of Outpatient Psychiatry at Walter Reed Health Care System testified at a trial against a drill sergeant from Aberdeen Proving Ground. She described a hierarchical structure so powerful that a victim reporting a rape would find her superiors closing ranks and protecting one another, instead of the victim. That was 1997, and sixteen years later the situation is worse than ever. Women are kept silent through coercion, while male perpetrators are protected at all costs. Our military is designed that way. It is their creed. A woman in civilian life has the power to resign from her job if her boss makes a sexual advance; women in the military do not. Major Ritchie said, ''If you are in the military, you cannot just leave, you can't go AWOL.''[45]

Nancy Alexander, a former air force nurse was assigned to the ICU (Intensive Care Unit) at the SAC (Strategic Air Command) in Oklahoma, when an airman assaulted her in 1969. She did not report the rape for fear of repercussions. She believed that she would have been blamed and lost her career. Her roommate had reported an assault and was discharged. That is how sexual assaults to military women were and are handled.

A psychologist serving as a sexual assault counselor at the Veteran's Outreach Center in White Plains, New York, said that it is common practice in the military for women to be blamed for sexual assaults against them. They choose not report them for fear of the reprisals; which is a double trauma for women. Dr. Yael Margolin-Rice, a psychologist at the Franklin Delano Roosevelt Veterans Hospital Center in Montrose, New York told Kate Stone Lombardi of *The New York Times*, that the social ostracism by both male and female comrades was very debilitating for young women in the military, who had never before been away from their families. Both Dr. Margolin-Rice and her colleague, Dr. Kathleen McNamee said that these women had symptoms of post-traumatic stress disorder similar to those of soldiers with battle trauma, including nightmares, flashbacks, and emotional numbing. These women are accosted by their commanders with the attitude, "What is it that you did that caused this to happen?" Dr. Margolin-Rice described a woman who

-------------------------------------------------------

[45]Elaine Sciolino, "Military Women are Vulnerable to Abuse, Psychiatrist Says," *The New York Times,* 16 April 1997.

was brutally raped by an officer and reported it to a female supervisor who assumed her client was lying and put her in solitary confinement for three weeks. That was doubly traumatic for someone who was brutally raped. The trauma goes much deeper when a female superior colludes with the old boys network.[46]

Dr. Margolin-Rice reported joining the army when she was a young adult. She saw that the rules and regulations gave women a false sense of safety because they learned quickly that those rules don't apply to them. She also said it is difficult for women to come to the VA for treatment because it is still so male dominated and if they were sexually traumatized in service they don't want anything to do with the military. Why would they return to a system that victimized them? If they do come in, they are surrounded by male veterans, any of whom could be a perpetrator. Women also do not volunteer the information that they were sexually assaulted. It usually comes out when they see a doctor for symptoms and the assault is later revealed as the cause. The women do not make the connection themselves and are often numb and have blocked it out. [47]

Lieutenant Jennifer Dyer, appeared on a *60 Minutes* episode and revealed that she was treated like a common criminal after she accused a fellow officer of raping her in early 2004. Lieutenant Dyer immediately reported the rape to CID and was then taken to a civilian hospital for a rape kit where CID held her in seclusion for the next three days with no counseling and no medical treatment. The CID agent, "Threatened to prosecute her for filing a false report."[48] Her command announced her reported rape to the entire unit, while she was in seclusion. When she finally returned she was, "fearful for her

-------------------------------------------------------

[46]Kate Stone Lombardi, "Female Veterans Find Help for Assault," *The New York Times,* 26 January 1997.

[47]Ibid.

[48]Allison, "An Excellent Reason."

health, safety, and sanity."[49] The rapist was roaming free on base and was acquitted of any crime. Lieutenant Dyer was a law enforcement officer in civilian life and was willing to risk criminal charges rather than go back to where her rapist was walking around unrestricted. [50]

"I think most of these women will tell you, the rape was bad enough. How the military treated me was worse," said Representative Loretta Sanchez of California. She is the ranking female on the House Armed Services Committee and one of the strongest advocates for military victims of sexual assault." If you talk to a lot of them, they'll tell you, "I'm the one that was, you know, drummed out of the military. I'm the one that suffered from this. All they did was move him to a different unit. He's still out there. In case after case."[51]

Sanchez has been working to get the Pentagon to update its archaic statutes on sexual assault that were written fifty years ago. She wants to bring them in line with current civilian laws and changing attitudes. The Pentagon chooses to stay in the past. Sanchez passionately says, "They want the subject to go away. It's not going away!" [52]

December 2, 2007, *The Seattle Times* reported the army attempting to court martial First Lieutenant Elizabeth Whiteside, for a crazed PTSD (Post Traumatic Stress Disorder) inflicted gunshot wound. Whiteside had seven years of exemplary service in the army reserves, yet faced the possibility of life in prison. She had been a high

----------------------------------------------------------

[49]Allison, "An Excellent Reason."

[50]"Army Rape Accuser Speaks Out," *60 Minutes.*

[51]Ibid.

[52]Ibid.

school soccer player, wrestler and valedictorian. One of her higher-ranking officers, Captain Joel Grant wrote, "This superior officer is in the top ten percent of officers I have worked with and must be promoted immediately, ahead of all peers."[53] So what happened?

Iraq 2006, Lieutenant Whiteside ate only one meal a day and slept in two four hour shifts in the barracks, inside the prison where she worked seven days a week. She was a platoon leader of the 329th Medical Company (ground ambulance) at Camp Cropper detainee prison near Baghdad airport. Her commander, Lieutenant Colonel Darlene McCurdy, wrote in her evaluation, "She has produced outstanding results in one of the most demanding and challenging combat zones."[54] Even though she was doing an outstanding job, one of the company's male officers had been blocking promotions for women officers, and had on several occasions undercut Whiteside's authority. As all of that intensified, Lieutenant Whiteside began to have panic attacks and could not sleep. She began to self-medicate with Nyquil and Benadryl and did not seek help through the mental health clinic because she feared the army would send her home. Many of these women were very dedicated to their mission, strong minded, strong willed and when troubled, would push through it in any way they could.

On December 30, 2006, the U. S. took Sadaam Hussein from his cell (for execution) at Camp Cropper. "The next day thousands of [Iraqi] inmates rioted, and the military police used rubber bullets, flash-bang grenades and tear gas to restore order."[55] Lieutenant Whiteside

--------------------------------------------

[53]Dana Priest and Anne Hull, "Army Charges Iraq Vet over Self-Inflicted Gun Wound," *The Seattle Times,* 2 December 2007.

[54]Ibid.

[55]Ibid.

took charge of all that, and the next day she encountered the male officer who had been harassing her and undermining her authority. They argued. That was her tipping point. There are many stories of extremely effective women officers serving in combat who are harassed by male peers who perceive the women officers as challenges to their own advancement. Women soldiers and officers have demonstrated their competence and effectiveness to the point that men feel threatened by their very presence and their personal power. The culture and pervasive attitudes in the military create circumstances that are not safe or healthy for them or their units.

Elizabeth Whiteside succumbed to the full intensity of her PTSD symptoms and was described as 'freaking out.' Another soldier went for help. A mental health nurse, Major Ana Luisa Ramirez found Lieutenant Whiteside sitting on her bed mumbling and visibly stricken. The nurse left to get some medication and before her return saw the Lieutenant in a, "Dark hallway with her sweatshirt hood pulled over her head and her hands in her pockets." The nurse saw dried blood on Lieutenant Whiteside's neck and hands and when she came closer to look, Lieutenant Whiteside, "Pointed an M-9 pistol at her and told her to move away."[56] The nurse tried to take the gun but the lieutenant fired two rounds into the ceiling and the nurse began to yell. As armed soldiers approached, the lieutenant slammed her door and shot herself in the stomach.

Lieutenant Whiteside was taken to Walter Reed where she was treated for her physical and emotional wounds. Major Stefan Wolfe, the prosecutor, argued that Lieutenant Whiteside could be court-martialed.

---

[56]Priest and Hull, "Self-Inflicted Gun Wound."

Colonel George Brandt, Chief of Behavioral Health Services responded with outrage saying, "I am here out of genuine concern for a human being that is breaking and that is broken. She has a severe and significant illness. Let's treat her as a human being for Christ's sake!" [57]

January 28th, 2008 while waiting to hear if she would be court-martialed, Lieutenant Whiteside took a handful of her antidepressants and other pills and wrote a note about her disappointment with the army and her hope that other soldiers would fare better than she. She was taken to the emergency room on the 29th and was stabilized. The next day she learned that the charges against her were dismissed.

Suicide and attempted suicide have become almost epidemic in the military. The latest data is that there are 17.5 suicides for every 100,000 Soldiers. In 2012 the Army reached an all-time high of 30 suicides per 100,000 active-duty soldiers, up fifteen percent since 2011.[58] That too is an issue that the military must deal with, and it is another form of violence that comes out of despair and helplessness.

What drives sexual violence? Many say it is unabashed hatred of women, misogyny, expressed in words like "pussy, dyke, or bitch." "Misogyny has always been at the root of sexual violence in the military."[59] Janet Meyer in a seventeen-page synthesis of theories of root causes of sexual violence concludes that research shows a combination of characteristics within the individual and our culture. That is the best explanation at this time.[60]

--------------------------------------------------------------

[57]Priest and Hull, "Self-Inflicted Gun Wound."

[58]Greg Zaroya, "Army Navy Suicides at Record High," *USA Today,* 18 November 2012.

[59]Benedict, "Why Soldiers Rape."

[60]Janet Meyer, "Root Causes of Sexual Assault," *Colorado Coalition Against Sexual Assault,*2000.

It has been shown that alcohol increases chances that friendliness will be misperceived in a way that gives the perpetrator license to be sexually aggressive; emphasis on the misperception. Alcohol affects judgment and therefore any sign or signal by a potential victim can be misperceived and misunderstood as an opening for the perpetrator to act. Research acknowledges that perpetrators are more aggressive and victims less effective at setting boundaries and defending themselves, when drinking alcohol.

Some of the research showed that culturally traditional men are more likely to accept abuse of women. In other words, men who believe that they should be heads of households exclusively are the most accepting of men abusing women. Sexually aggressive men are more likely to believe the myth about rape, that the use of interpersonal violence is an effective strategy for resolving conflict. [61]

There is research that clearly stated sexual assault is more about power and anger than sexual desire. Some studies in colleges showed men did not believe it was wrong to rape their dates. Men had a sense of entitlement when they dated a female; they felt they deserved to have what they wanted, since they paid for the date.

From a panel on violence against women, it was noted that men raised in patriarchal family structures, in which men are the decision makers and women subservient, are more likely to become violent adults, to rape women acquaintances and to batter their intimate partners, than men raised in more egalitarian homes. Culturally, we tend to encourage men to feel superior, entitled, and ready to initiate sex in their relationships with women, while our sexual expectations teach women to feel responsible for setting the pace of sexual contact

--------------------------------------------------------------------------

[61]Meyer, "Root Causes of Sexual Assault."

in their relationships with men, and the sexual limits.[62] The role of media was also explored in the research. The media is filled with images of violence against women while the pain and suffering of a victim and her community tend to be invisible and the offenders suffer no consequences for their actions. As in the military the women are silent or silenced, and the perpetrators have no consequences. Could it be said that our culture has created the environment to support sexual assault against women?

Marion Hood graduated from army basic training in 1987 and celebrated with girlfriends at a local motel, near Fort Dix. The other girls went shopping and Marion was in the room. Shortly after they left she heard a knock on her door and opened it thinking they had forgotten something. It was not her girlfriends; it was her drill sergeant. He smashed the door into her face bloodying her nose. Behind him were four other men in fatigues, all of whom pushed their way into the room. They each took turns raping and sodomizing her. They beat her, kicked her, broke her right knee, nose, spine and right cheekbone. Then they urinated on her, burned her with cigarettes, split her lip and spit on her while threatening to kill her. Marion is a black woman. She dissociated during the attack and was detached watching what they were doing to her, nonetheless, her body was experiencing all of it and suffering greatly. Dissociation is a common response to overwhelming unremitting trauma. The men turned the room inside out taking money and traveler's checks then dumping Marion in a tub they filled with water. Before they left, on the sergeant's orders, they dunked her head under the water.[63]

Hours later her girlfriends returned and called for an ambulance. At the hospital a nurse told the doctor she thought Marion had been raped. The doctor responded by saying, "Oh, we have girls come

---

[62]Meyer, "Root Causes of Sexual Assault."
[63]Moffeit and Herdy, "Betrayal In the Ranks."

in all the time and claim this. She probably just got into a fight with her boyfriend." Doctors are sworn to do no harm. This doctor made an assumption, which can be construed as racist as well as, a blatant lie. Part of the protocol in the military is to discount and deny rape, and then create a lie in the form of a believable storyline that does not require any accountability. This physician has perpetrated a lie that will cause a lifetime of harm. He has violated his Hippocratic Oath.

The military police came and looked at Marion saying they would return the next day. They never returned. The doctor's fabrication prevailed. Why do our armed forces discount at this high level denying truth and evidence? How can our military believe they are honorable and teach honor, when what they say and do repeatedly, is act dishonorably? If it were possible to give our military a dishonorable discharge and disband them—that might be the best action. The Military of the United States is behaving in completely dishonorable ways in relationship to women and abuse. They are behaving in ways that are unbecoming of officers and gentlemen. They make it clear by their behavior, that honor and truth are not important to them in these situations. What would happen to our military if everyone serving knew this? When I was a lieutenant and later a captain in the Army Nurse Corps in Vietnam, I often said, *"Even an act of Congress or an act of God, cannot make a gentleman out of you,"* to many of the male officers.

The military police did not return to Marion's room, but her drill sergeant did. He arrived carrying daisies for her and told Marion, "If you tell, no one will believe you."[64] Marion was rightfully, distraught.

---

[64]Moffeit and Herdy, "Betrayal In the Ranks."

Miles and Herdy of the *Denver Post* contacted a senior officer at Fort Dix, who did not return their inquiries. Marion was hospitalized for two months and then called her mother to say she was coming home. Marion's mother had been in the army herself and had not wanted Marion to enlist. It is believed that Marion's mother was also raped in the army.

During basic, Marion's drill sergeant had pressed her for sex incessantly and each time, Marion refused and reported him. Her supervisor told her she was delusional and gave her extra duty. She said no to him repeatedly and her punishment was to be gang-raped. The army's response was to tell her she was "Delusional." Marion believed that through the army she could be all that she could be. That belief changed after the rape. When she was ready to leave the hospital she was given a bus ticket and discharge papers. She never told her mother what happened to her. Marion has had four surgeries on fractured vertebrae that cause severe pain in her legs from pressure and she has seizures from a blood clot in her brain, rectal problems and scars on her lip and body. She has four daughters ages 4, 7, 9, and 14. She wrote a will in which she tells them they will not get any money from her if they join the military.[65]

Why did the DOD (Department of Defense) take three years to name a fifteen person civilian task force to examine the allegations of sexual assault in the military? Chairmen Henry Waxman of the House Committee on National Security and Foreign Affairs, along with Representative Elijah Cummings, asked serious questions about nineteen year old Army PFC LaVena Johnson's death in Iraq. The army is calling her death a suicide. Dr. John Johnson, LaVena's father, is an army veteran with a twenty-five year history as a civilian employee of the army and who has counseled veterans. He is investigating his

---

[65]Moffeit and Herdy, "Betrayal In the Ranks."

daughter's death and a multitude of discrepancies in the army reports compared to the evidence. Dr. Johnson has spent two and a half years relentlessly pursuing the truth through the Freedom of Information Act and through congressional offices. He eventually was given the CD showing photographs of his daughter's body showing that she, "Had been struck in the face with a blunt instrument, perhaps a weapon stock. Her nose was broken, her teeth knocked backwards, one elbow was distended. The back of her clothes had debris on them indicating she had been dragged from one location to another."[66] Her disrobed body showed multiple bruises, scratch marks and teeth imprints on the upper part of her body and her genital area showed massive bruising and lacerations." Corrosive liquid had been poured into her genital area, probably to destroy DNA evidence of sexual assault." Despite all that, "Her body was found completely dressed in a burning tent and there was a trail from outside a contractor's tent to where her body was found." Initially the army investigators assumed her death was a homicide, but later a decision was made at the command level to stop the investigation and call her death a suicide. Johnson said the pictures and documents show conclusively that his daughter was brutally raped, beaten, shot and set afire.[67] LaVena Johnson, like Marion Hood was a black woman soldier.

The family of Army PFC Tina Priest and Congressmen Henry Waxman and Elijah Cummings, like the Johnsons, are looking for answers. Tina was twenty years old when a fellow soldier raped her in February of 2008, at Camp Taji, Iraq. The army called her death

---------------------------------------------------

[66]Ann Wright, "Is There an Army Cover Up of Rape and Murder of Women Soldiers?" *CommonDreams.org,* 28 April 2008, http://www.commondreams.org/archive/2008/04/28/8564

[67]Ibid.

a suicide eleven days after her rape. Her family disputes the notion that she shot herself with her M-16 rifle. Rape charges against the rapist were dropped a few weeks after her death, even though his sperm was found on her sleeping bag. Members of the House Committee have asked for hearings on these and other deaths that were called suicide. While congressional representatives on the House Oversight Committee seek information and answers, and DOD officials avoid subpoenas, the navy relieved two senior officers of duty on the U.S.S. Washington, because of injuries to twenty-three sailors, and seventy million in ship damage caused by a smoking violation. [68]

There are many more stories to be told of women who were sexually assaulted during their military service. There is much to be done to shed light on the abuse and the military's response to reports of abuse. In the chapters to follow it is my intention to provide as complete a picture as possible of what is happening and how it can be changed to benefit the women and the military. The stories in the following chapters came from my direct interviews with women who agreed to share their experiences with me. I did not begin expecting to write this book. I began expecting to tell you about the many different kinds of experiences women had while serving. It did not take long for me to realize how many devastating traumatic experiences occurred and to decide to write this book focusing on the culture of abuse in our armed forces. It is because these repeated abusive experiences have been kept hidden for so long, that they need to be revealed. It is because our military has been so hurtful to these women that we need to bring healing and change. It is because of the injustices to women who report sexual assaults, that **justice** and **accountability** must now be our priority.

------------------------------------------------

[68]Ann Wright, "Is There an Army Cover Up of Rape and Murder of Women Soldiers?" *CommonDreams.org,* 28 April 2008, http://www.commondreams.org/archive/2008/04/28/8564

These stories include graphic detail and some readers may find it difficult to continue to read them. If that happens for you I ask that you look at my writing in italics to learn more without the distress, and perhaps read only a few stories in each chapter and the entire last chapter. If you are a survivor of MST know that these stories are likely to trigger you. I believe reading what has happened to other women may be validating and yet, depending on how active your symptoms are, all of the full stories may be too triggering for you. Take care of yourself as you go through and read what you can but be sure to read the entire last chapter.

My voice will now be in italics and the women's voices will be in regular type until the last chapter.

# Rape and Reporting

## Sally Griffiths – Gulf War Era

*Growing up, Sally was always patriotic. At age seventeen, right after high school, she decided to join the marines. Her parents were not very happy about her decision, yet supported her when they saw her determination. She started boot camp in the summer of 1992, at Parris Island, South Carolina.*

Basic training was very challenging; it was a positive, confidence instilling experience for me. I left Parris Island believing I could conquer any obstacle in my path.

My first assignment was to "A" School for a Military Occupational Specialty (MOS) in administration. I spent fourteen weeks at Camp Johnson, North Carolina. That's when I had my awakening. I was in my barracks with my two roommates, when the duty NCO knocked on the door and said the staff duty wanted to see me at staff barracks. I asked if I was in trouble. He said, "If staff duty wants to see you, you're always in trouble." I asked where he was and he told me to go to staff barracks. My roommates were hearing all that. I put on my uniform, hat and jacket, and went. The building was across the grass. He was at the door waiting for me and invited me in. I told him I did not feel comfortable going in and needed to go back. He said, "You need help studying for your final exam, I have the answers, why don't you come in." I reiterated that I was not permitted to fraternize with my instructors and told him I was leaving and ran back to my barracks. My roommates told me to report it, I didn't want to because I did not want to be put on a legal hold. I was afraid, because I had seen what happened to other women who had reported. My roommates did report it and when I was questioned by the company commander, I lied and told him that never happened. Two weeks later I graduated with my class.

My first duty station was in Okinawa, Japan where I did administrative work for the company commander. I was at Camp Schwab for about eight months and was one of six women on the whole base. We were labeled whores and dykes. *(The same names given to me/the author and the other nurses I served with in Vietnam.)* A few of the men treated us like sisters, looking out for us and treating us with the respect we deserved as fellow soldiers yet from the moment I got there, my superiors hit on me.

In the next room from us was Sergeant W, who was good friends with my roommate. He flirted with me. I never returned any of his flirts. One day he came in and laid down on my bed and put his hands down his pants and said, "I know you probably want some of this and I would give you some, but you'd probably tell everyone." I was shocked! He was close to forty years old, and I was eighteen and away from home in a foreign country. That was not right. Another day he followed me into the women's restroom and cornered me up against the wall, then tried to kiss me. I slapped him and told him to back off.

He looked shocked and walked out. I went back to work and he acted as if nothing happened. I went to my gunnery sergeant, Sergeant W's superior, and reported the incident. I filed charges against him. They brought out an independent investigator and interrogated me for about two hours. They told me my perception was wrong and reprimanded me, telling me I was insubordinate. Nothing was done to either of us. I was threatened with an article 15 (non-judicial punishment given by commanding officer for minor offense).

Between those two instances, Sergeant W did an impromptu inspection in my room and flipped over my mattress, threw apart my wall locker and then said my room was unsatisfactory. I was mad and knew that was not right. I went and did the same to his room. I am sure that is what they meant when they said I was insubordinate. They never did anything to him or me.

I had a hard time at work with him in the same office. I think they put us in there at different times. They also let me move my barracks room to a different floor from his room.

When I had to clean my weapon, even though I never fired it, and no matter how clean it was, it was never good enough. I always had to redo it over and over. That was also true in my work; that I had to redo it over and over until they thought it was satisfactory. This is the typical way they deal with women.

There was one guy, an acquaintance I occasionally exercised with and who went jogging with me one night. It was July 29, 1993. He came to the barracks to visit a group of us and said he wanted to spend some time with me; he told me his unit was scheduled to deploy next week. I told me I was going running and didn't want to hang out with him. He said he didn't want to run. Later I went running and had to cross a bridge. He was waiting for me there. I stopped and asked him what he was doing there? He said he decided to jog with me. His name was Joseph Holquin. I told him I was going to jog at the beach. It gave me comfort to jog there, because when I was little my dad would take me to the beach. Being alone in Japan without my family, the beach by the water gave me comfort. It was starting to get dark so Joseph went up to the barracks to get a flashlight. I followed him up the hill and thought we were going to jog on the beach. He came back with a flashlight and we ran for a while. Then I stopped by a rock to rest. He sat down next to me and started kissing me on my neck. I said, "What are you doing?" He was only an acquaintance. He said, "We are going to make love." I said, "NO, I don't want to." He threw me down on the sand and got on top of me and held me down. I was wearing my physical training (PT) clothes and he pulled them to the side and stretched them out. He raped me right there. I was scared to death, I didn't know if he was going to kill me or what! When he was done he said, "I'm sorry, give me a hug." I got up and ran as fast as I could to the barracks. I had to run up a million stairs and past the duty officer. I took a shower right away and I could not stop crying. My roommate came into the bathroom. She was there with her boyfriend. She saw me screaming and hysterical and she knew. She said, "Oh my God!" I told her, "Please don't say anything." She said, "I am going to report this!" I screamed at her, "DON'T." Her boyfriend got my big white teddy bear and he sat there with me. Then the company commander came with the gunnery sergeant and staff on duty. They all came into my room. The CO looked shocked and concerned. He said, "You're going to the hospital." I said, "I don't want to, I don't want to report it." I felt like I was hyperventilating. They took me into a small clinic. There was a navy corpsman sitting there with a smirk on his face. He was a complete asshole. He thought it was funny and did not believe me. He called an MP (Military Policeman) from the base. He came in and asked me to draw a map of where it happened. I told him the best I could remember. *Because of what happens in the brain during a severe trauma, a victim is literally unable to describe details of what happened or the sequence of actions. She does not have access in her brain to the kind of information she is being asked to give.*

They had to call another base to get transport to get me to the hospital. The navy corpsman was laughing while he was asking me questions. I told him to fuck off. It was just he and me there. I had to lie down in the back of the ambulance for a one-hour ride to the hospital. They took me to Camp Kadina.

The hospital duty sergeant and nurse were arguing that there was no room for me and I would have to wait out there. Only later I realized the rapist was in the next room. I was not told, but I remember them not letting me go to the bathroom because the rapist was next to it. The nurse was not friendly or supportive. She was angry she had to do a rape kit and didn't know how. She even said, "You sure did a number on his back," referring to the scratches I left on his back while trying to fight him off. They took about eight tubes of blood. I never gave my consent and I was angry. Finally a woman civilian advocate came in and held my hand. After the exam she left and I never got to thank her or know who she was.

They took all my clothes for evidence. A bitchy lady from the Naval Criminal Investigation Service (NCIS) showed up and gave me a morning after pill and wanted me to talk to her. I explained to her that I did not want to press charges and I did not feel like speaking with her at that time. I did not want to press charges because I had seen what other women have gone through who did report. It was three to four a.m. by now and she was interrogating me while someone else was interrogating Joseph Holquin. They would compare notes with each other even while I was with her. She'd ask me a question detail and then she'd tell me, "Well he said that is not what happened." She drove me back to base the next morning. All I wanted to do was go to sleep. I remember everyone looking at me weird and later found out that the CO, Major N, had told the whole formation in the morning before I got back. I was given twenty-four hours off and slept when I could. Major N seemed to believe that twenty-four hours was sufficient time to recover from being raped. He said that the sooner I returned to duty the better off I would be. Approximately two days later, Major N summoned me to his office; he sat me down and asked how I was doing. I responded "Fine sir." Inside I wanted to scream, sir, considering I was raped two days ago and returned to find out that you took the liberty of informing the entire company; I think I am doing pretty damn well to be sitting here calmly, sir. In reality my body ached. Physically I was sore. Mentally I was detached. Major N told me that I needed to, "Be a marine and carry on." I was told that the NCIS agency would be in touch.

I had to talk to another NCIS agent, a man. He questioned me every day and took me to the beach where it happened. We did this for a week. Two weeks later the gunnery sergeant came to me to ask how long it would take me to pack my things. He told me I was being transferred to Camp Hansen. He told me not to talk to my roommate again, or call her and he drove me to Camp Hansen. I called my roommate and she said, "You know I can't talk to you." and hung up the phone. *This is another part of the protocol in the punishment of women who report rape, to isolate them and cut off all connection to support.*

I was put to work in the battalion commander's office, but there was no work for me. I just sat there. No job, no title, no one to talk to. One day the chaplain came to talk to me, asked me how I was doing and asked about the rape. I didn't tell him anything because I always saw him talking to the base commander and didn't trust him.

The 'Article 32' hearing was all mockery. The courtroom was full of men and I was not allowed to have an advocate there. *Why is it that the rapist had an attorney advocate and the victim had no one?* Holquin's attorney purposely stood behind him because I refused to look at the rapist. I was told I had to look at the attorney, so I had to keep seeing my rapist. The attorney held up my clothes from the rape. When I found out later that <u>they had all the evidence and his confession</u>, I was so very angry. **Why did they put me through all that?**

That was when I started cutting myself. When my feelings got so strong and intense and I could not talk about it, and had no support, that was all I could do. The physical pain was a relief from the emotional pain. I had no control over the situation and I did have control over my pain and my body. I did this for years after all that, when my feelings came up intensely.

*Trauma results in feeling out of control and seeking some means to feel in control. Cutting often can provide that, as can compulsive behavior.*

Another day I was fingerprinted by two NCIS men who told me I was being charged with lying and making false statements. They said my roommate gave a sworn statement saying I lied to her about it. It looked like her handwriting. I don't know because I did not get to talk to her. I went ballistic! I screamed, "When are you going to stop fucking with me," and I turned over a chair. That day I was physically and emotionally distraught. That was when a woman sergeant major in my office called me in and said, "Close the door I just want to tell you something; be strong, hang in there. Personally if it was me, I'd take an M-16 and blow his balls off, but I am not telling you to do that."

Through this experience the only man that showed a single ounce of compassion was my attorney, Major A. He sat at his desk leaned across and asked me to look him in the eye. He said, "Listen, I don't care if you ran across his squad bare naked, no one has the right to do what he did to you."

That night I took all the pills I could find and tried to kill myself. Someone found me, took me to the hospital where they pumped my stomach and then sent me to the psych ward. NCIS came to visit and brought my bags of clothes from the night of the rape. He was releasing the evidence to me. When I got out of the hospital I went back to work and was told to watch the phone when others went to lunch. I found a filing cabinet with NCIS files and found the keys. I looked through and found the file for my case. I saw the confession from Holquin and his polygraph test. I took it to the copy machine. When the CO came in I stood at attention, saluted and said, "Good afternoon Sir" and kept going to copy it. I put it in my pocket and mailed it to my dad the next day. The confession happened on the first interrogation and I was never told.

I called my attorney and he told me all the charges against Holquin were being dropped. I later learned that Mr. Holguin received several promotions and served an additional six years in the marine corps.

*The values held by the marine corps: they would rather promote and protect a rapist, than acknowledge the rape and provide support to the victim, who was also a marine. Can they truly feel proud of a marine corps that honors rape and rapists?*

My parents took all the documents to Senator John McCain's office and within days I was sent home from Okinawa. I was told about the treatment program at Palo Alto, but I just wanted to forget and move on. I went to the Balboa Naval Hospital while I waited for my discharge and then went home to Arizona.

I was given a medical discharge with PTSD related to MST (Military Sexual Trauma) and I was given fifty percent disability. When I reported to sign the paperwork for my medical board, I was greeted by an old man who said, "You can't be in the military. Damn, when I was in the navy, I didn't have shipmates that look that good," as he groped me with his eyes. I felt violated all over again. I was there to sign the paperwork allowing me to receive an honorable discharge and I was experiencing the same harassment I was subjected to during the term of my enlistment. Approximately ten years later in September of 2003, I had an opportunity to speak with a reporter, Miles Moffeit, for a series in the *Denver Post,* called "Betrayal in the Ranks." During the process of opening up about my experience after nearly a decade of silence I started to cut again, as the feelings were so intense. I volunteered to go the VA hospital to get help. I was placed in the psychiatric ward and awoke to a man standing over me saying, "You sure are a pretty one." After that I realized that this was not a place I could receive the help I so desperately needed, and checked myself out the next morning. I eventually had counseling for a brief period at the local Vet Center and was later awarded seventy percent disability for PTSD as a result of military sexual trauma.

In the summer of 1994, I tried to get a job as a camp counselor and I couldn't do it. I had flashbacks of the rape, being mistreated in the military and I could not stand the man in charge of the camp. I went to the Arizona State University to study nursing and changed my major, because I could not handle the man in charge or working for men. At the vet center, they had no female counselors, so I never got help. I changed my major to education and moved to Houston Baptist University, a small private Christian School and got a BA in education and an MBA at LeTourneau University, another small private school. I got married and had one stillborn daughter named Hannah, in 2002. Hannah is the one who gave me the strength to begin the healing process. Her birth and death was equally traumatic. I was home by myself and she started to arrive before the ambulance could get there. I delivered her at the hospital with my husband at my side. We had an opportunity to hold her and tell her goodbye. She was so beautiful; it was almost as if God had sent an angel as a vessel to allow me to heal. At her funeral I received strength from the warm embraces of my friends and family. As her casket was lowered to the ground I walked away with a renewed strength in the steps that she will never take. I was able to grieve and had support for that, and never had support for the trauma I received in the military. One year later, my husband and I adopted two baby girls through a private agency.

The military was not all negative, but much of it was. I decided to forgive Joseph Holquin for raping me, but I still have flashbacks, and I am hyper vigilant and don't sleep well. I have a really hard time relating to men and I have panic attacks. It's hard for me to respect men, because of the lack of integrity I saw in my superiors in the military. My God, they turned the other cheek when I was raped and acted as if it were my fault!

*Now Sally teaches fourth grade at an inner city school, is a team leader, and works with mostly women, where she does very well. She was awarded ESL teacher of the year, this past year. She no longer does hurtful things to herself. She has kept in touch with*

*Miles Moffeit, who befriended her and confronted Joseph Holquin, as Moffeit was writing the Denver Post series. He told Sally the results of his confrontation and for Sally it was some relief and gave her some closure.*

*Two years later she agreed to speak with Miles, to a group of 500 people in Washington, DC, at a conference for victims of crime. Sally's story was also featured on 60 Minutes, along with three other courageous veterans who lived similar nightmares. For Sally, sharing her story has become a source of continual healing, and she does so, with the hope of encouraging others to take the steps toward wholeness. Sally has done volunteer work with her local area women's shelter, and hopes to one day see changes in the way the military deals with sexual assault. She wants women to know:*

It is my hope that one day women seeking to give their lives in service to their country will be treated with the dignity and respect they deserve as soldiers. Meanwhile, I will continue to assist those returning broken, ashamed and experiencing the tremendous weight of self-blame, to move forward realizing that there is nothing they could have done differently. It is not your fault.

*Sally's experience could have been less traumatizing to her and she could have continued to serve proudly as a U.S. Marine if her rape and its aftermath had been handled more respectfully, professionally, and compassionately.*

1.  *If she knew to begin with that she would be both safe and supported by the marine corps when she reported the rape because it was the protocol and it has been done that way repeatedly in rape cases.*

2.  *If she had a safe place to go to report the rape, be examined, express her feelings, and she was given details of what to expect.*

3.  *If she was not taken to the same area of any clinic/treatment facility as her rapist.*

4.  *If all personnel working with her through the process were specifically trained in compassionately, professionally, and respectfully dealing with sexual assault.*

5.  *If the commanding officer held all information about her and her rape, in confidence with respect and compassion, while only those in the chain of command who need to know were given the information. All who were informed had a contract to hold the information in strict confidence.*

6.  *If Sally was given at least five-seven days recovery time, which included a minimum of three one to one therapeutic counseling sessions, before her return to duty.*

7.  *If roommates, confidants and specific support personnel to Sally remained available for contact, in their current location, position/job, throughout the legal and therapeutic processes, and there is never an attempt or action taken to prevent ongoing contact and communication.*

8.  *If questioning and investigations are done in professional, compassionate and respectful ways using the protocols developed by Russell Strand and an advocate for Sally is present at all times who can call time-out, ask for a break, and/or reschedule. No questioning will go on for more than two hours without a break and there are no more than two, two-hour sessions in any one day.*

9.  *If, in hearings and legal proceedings, Sally is only required to identify her rapist and is never required to make eye contact with or look at her rapist.*

10. *If Sally was told immediately when Joseph Holquin admitted to the rape.*

11. *If Sally had a personal and legal advocate with her to consult with throughout the investigation and legal processes all the way to completion.*

12. *If all legal proceedings related to the rape are handled professionally, compassionately, and respectfully, by all parties.*

13. *If the highest level of accountability is required and expected of all participants throughout the processes.*

## Shannon–Persian Gulf Era

*Shannon graduated in the top ten of her class from college and then went to basic training at Fort Dix, New Jersey. While on leave from basic, she was sexually assaulted by an army recruiter.*

I was at home on my 22nd birthday when the army recruiter came by. It did not seem unusual, because when I was in high school my boyfriend's army recruiter came by to see him several times. When he said he was passing by and stopped in, I was not alarmed.

*Shannon is six feet eight inches tall, very athletic, and especially good on track and high jump.*

I was wearing sweat pants and a sweatshirt. He made sexually derogatory remarks about me, and guys in the military. He acted like he was going to hit on me, so I told him to leave. He did not leave, so I walked in front of him to open the door and he grabbed my ponytail, snapped my neck and knocked me to the ground. *Shannon blacked out or dissociated because her next memory is the recruiter on top of her.*

I was face up and he was raping me. I felt something pointy under my chin and thought, what the hell is going on? I felt frozen as he took my pants off. I couldn't move or speak. How could this be happening?

He was married and had three kids. I could not believe he was doing this. He laughed before he left. I took a shower, a very long shower. I don't remember what happened the next day; it is a blank. I was in shock, full of rage and felt helpless. I did not know what to do. The next day I called Maxwell Air Force Base, which is near where I lived. I talked with five different people. One guy threatened me and my family and said, "You gave me your name and I know where you live. If you press this, I'll come after you." So I gave up after that.

*Another tactic used to frighten women into not reporting is to intimidate and threaten them to preserve the image of the corps, whether army, navy, air force, or coast guard. In this military culture of abuse they protect what is disgusting, demoralizing, and disrespectful to all they profess to represent, such as honor, courage, and integrity. This military response does not demonstrate honor, courage, or integrity, rather it shows dishonor to all involved, unwillingness to be accountable or to expect accountability. I believe this exemplifies a failure of leadership.*

The army is the best place for a rapist because there is an unspoken rule that it is tolerated even with the zero tolerance protocol. If you come forward to report it, they won't keep it confidential; they harass you and give you shit.

*Her command violates her confidentiality so that she must endure even more shame and humiliation than the rape induced. Instead of protecting her and her vulnerability, they dishonored her and themselves by piling on even more abuse to their wounded soldier. Everyone was encouraged to shun her. How can this be called leadership? Women are trained to be soldiers to serve beside their brothers at arms, who in this culture, can behave like barbarians and get support for that behavior from their leaders.*

*Shannon muddled through her leave and then reported to the Defense Language School at Fort Ord, in Monterey, California. During a soccer game a guy accidentally stepped on her foot causing severe pain. She had a bone sticking out of her foot but when they x-rayed it, they found nothing wrong and she was sent back to duty with crutches. They would not allow her see the doctor. The platoon sergeant discounted her pain and injury and said she was malingering. She went to the medical liaison and was then sent to a podiatrist who said to her, "You can't fake a bone sticking out of your foot!" He said she would need surgery.*

*In the meantime, she had been experiencing harassment from a lieutenant colonel student in her class. She did not say or do anything about it, but several other students, both enlisted and officers saw and heard what was being done to her, and they reported it to the sergeant who then reported it to the captain in charge. Shannon was removed from the class. Nothing was said or done to the lieutenant colonel who was harassing her.*

*These themes of women being raped, being threatened and intimidated to not report, losing their position in a class or job, being discounted and disregarded are common because that is the protocol, standard operating procedure, in all branches of our military. It is part of their culture of abuse that men can behave in vicious ways and not only are they not held accountable, they are often promoted, while their victims are re-victimized by losing their careers, their health and their benefits.*

# Sherrye - Bosnia Era

*Sherrye was 19 years old when she entered the military and went to basic training. She describes herself as a "girly girl." She went to Fort Leonard Wood, Missouri for her basic and advanced infantry training (AIT). She tested and qualified for language school and wanted the fastest route so chose a transportation unit where she expected to drive a jeep.*

*The first day of AIT she experienced the men not wanting women there. They were all angry that they had to make separate billets and bathrooms for the women. She and the other women had to do extra push ups, leg lifts and running in place to make up for the extra work being done to accommodate them. Women had to look and sound tough and take what the guys were dishing out, yet still look feminine.*

*Sherrye was sent to Germany for her first duty station after only 30 days in the transportation unit at Ft. Leonard Wood. Her assignment was to stencil numbers on trucks or sweep them. Only the women were given that job, while the men made pick-ups and deliveries. They were told that women could not read maps or follow directions.*

I was in a co-ed barracks and it was okay for the first few days, but then at 3 a.m. one night there was a guy beating my door down. I had no phone, no protection and I am nineteen in a foreign country and I don't know this guy beating on my door. There are two men in each room and maybe there are seventy guys and eight women and no supervisor. Some women were alone and some had female roommates. I called out, "What do you want?" He wanted to borrow some beer, and he went away. Later he apologized and said he was drunk.

One weekend in June when it was hot, one of the girls was making frozen daiquiris and between us we drank a whole bottle. Then we were laughing, being stupid and teasing each other when a guy came by and invited us to his room. He had red hair and was kind of nerdy. We all went to his room to watch a movie together. When I got up to go to the bathroom and came back, no one was there except the redheaded guy. I asked him where Angel and Aaron went. He said they went to get another movie. He had music playing very loud and showed me his stereo system.

In an instant it shifted to violence. He was suddenly on top of me and I was yelling, "No!" He had me pinned on the bed and my head was between the concrete wall and his footlocker. The more I yelled and tried to fight him off, the more he was energized. With each no, he would slam my head between the concrete wall and the footlocker. There was one moment of clarity when he went to get a condom. I was looking at the door and wondering if I could make it. It was too far, not enough time, and I had too much alcohol and I blacked out. The next thing I remember is his roommate Jason, shaking me on the shoulder and asking me if I was hurt. I was nude, there was blood on the sheets and I asked him to get me back to my room. I passed another girl on the way and she asked me what happened. I told her, "He made me."

I have no memory of the rest of the day. Jason said, "I can't believe he did this. He's over in his room drinking beer." I took shower after shower and sat in the shower. I would black out and then wake up and go back in the shower. The next day I never left my room. I bundled up on Monday and went to formation. I used make up to cover the bruises on my head and neck. Another girl took me to the clinic and told me to get checked out or she would call somebody. The doctor asked me, "Did someone hurt you?" I said, "Yes." He said he wanted the doctors at Landstuhl to see me. When I left the doctor's office there were two MP's waiting for me. They took me to Landstuhl and they had a big camera there taking pictures of me. There were big flashes. They were very nice and did a rape check all over, even in my nails and vagina. They said they wished I had not showered all weekend. Then I was sent somewhere else; to Badkneunach, a larger post where I was interrogated. They asked me what I was wearing and what I was drinking. They asked me if I was teasing Kevin (the rapist) about his red pubic hair. I was not allowed to sit; I had to stand at ease in front of the desk. I was told that if I try to leave I would be court-martialed. An interrogator was standing over me screaming, "Why can't you agree this was rough consensual sex by two drunken adults?" I was crying and said nothing. He would not listen to anything I said. Whenever I tried to tell him the details he focused on my drinking and whether I had sex with other guys. I wanted to leave and go home; I was bone-weary tired.

*This, too, is part of the culture of abuse. They have a variety of story lines that they employ and impose on women in these circumstances and they use pressure, coercion and intimidation tactics to get women to agree to the military's made up story- line.*

When I finally got back to the barracks I was told to report to the sergeant. He said, "I want you to know I am sorry for what happened to you and I believe you." I was told I did not have to stay in the barracks and could stay with another girl in the military.

Later I met with a lawyer who was very professional. I told him my story and he said, "In the military we would have trouble getting a conviction, even if you were a lily-white virgin." He told me what the defense would do to me and that there were already two guys supporting Kevin. Where is the accountability?

*There is no accountability. The culture of abuse includes a sense of entitlement for men to do as they please and get away with it. Men support men at every level of the military. Women are non-entities to them and don't belong in 'their military.' The Military Justice System is for men only when it comes to rape and sexual assault. They will mercilessly go after the women who report rape with every intimidation tactic and story they can conjure.*

The company commander said, "If you push it to trial, I'd support you if you want to go home. I will have you home in three days with 10 % disability." I went home. I drank so much and took so many pills for the next three months it was mind-boggling. Pills to sleep, pills to wake up, and alcohol to not think. I just wanted to die. I was scared of my own shadow. I could not go out and be with people. I did not go to a mall for over a year and a half.

*Sherrye's response is typical: to self-medicate and try to avoid dealing with the emotional pain. This is a classic Post Traumatic Stress Disorder (PTSD) and Military Sexual Trauma (MST), which is the subject of my next book:* <u>Women Under Fire: PTSD and Healing</u>*. Sherrye was eventually able to get some therapy and is now able to function better. She was evaluated at the VA in Ashville and given 100%*

*disability because of scarring on the left side of her brain due to the rapist slamming her head into the wall during the rape. Sherrye now has grand mal seizures from the scarring.*

Sherrye told me, "The military will always be male focused. Women are not taken seriously. There is an underlying sense of vulnerability that women feel, and the military exploits that. Sexual abuse, violence and harassment are rampant for women in the military. Many don't report it until thirty days later, if at all."

*Even in these few stories it seems clear that there is no safety among peers, for women who choose to serve in the U.S. Military. Men see the military as theirs and are hostile and resentful of women who invade their territory. Women have to work twice as hard, prove themselves and their competency repeatedly, and still are not accepted or respected.*

*When there was a Women's Army Corps, the women had their own space, training and leaders. They could still work side by side with male soldiers and leaders, with a higher level of respect; inappropriate disrespectful behavior was not tolerated. Had the Women's Army Corps been in place when Sherrye was in Germany, she would have had women's barracks and some external protection; it is doubtful the rape would have occurred.*

*If the military truly took women and sexual assault seriously, there would have been extensive education in basic training regarding sexual assault: how to prevent it and all the protocols and emergency numbers to call if an assault takes place. All personnel would be trained in every detail of dealing with a sexual assault victim from the first contact to the last. Every woman would know that support for her is real and genuine and it is safe to report and seek treatment.*

*The highest level of confidentiality is protocol for all reports of sexual assault. She would know who to call and where to go for help if it is needed. There would be a specific place to go that would be safe and has victim advocates, counselors, nurses and doctors on duty twenty-four hours a day to handle sexual assault. Any female victim would be treated with dignity, respect, compassion, gentleness and with appropriate protocols for someone in crisis. Discounting and disrespect would find no home in this picture.*

*Treatment would always come first and only after that would the military police be allowed to question the victim. Whenever members of the Military Justice System are present with the victim, she has an advocate with her who will support, protect her and advise her on her legal rights.*

*If this were in place, never again would one of our women soldiers be mistreated and forced to agree to a fabricated self-serving story made up by the military.*

## Carolynn Cummings Favreau - Vietnam Era

*Carolynn entered basic training for nine weeks in the Woman's Army Corps at Fort McClellan, Alabama in 1965. She was sick the first week with nausea, severe headache, achy all over and thought it was the flu. She was not yet assigned a company and went to sickbay twice where they told her that she had probably eaten something that did not agree with her, and not to worry. She continued to be sick while at Fort McClellan and the medical personnel continued to discount it.*

In basic training we had to go into the gas chambers. We went through first with our gas masks on, and then we took a deep breath, removed our masks, said our name, rank, and serial number, and walked out of the building before breathing. Some of the women weren't able to do that and ended up breathing in the chemicals. Another time we were told to take a deep breath of air before entering the building (without our masks on) then enter the building, repeat again our name, rank, and serial number before exiting the building and before breathing. In the chamber we were exposed to Sarin and Chlorine gas. I'm not sure what else. This went on for several days in basic training; I don't remember the length of time. I ended up having to go to sickbay because my eyes were itching and burning and I was told it would go away in time. They gave me some eye drops and said, "They are just a little irritated from the chemicals."

The whole time during basic training I slept on a bunk next to pipes that were coated with asbestos, but of course we didn't know back then that breathing asbestos could harm us. They also sprayed a section of Ft. McClellan with Agent Orange, to kill the foliage. They built a Vietnam village in which to train troops for Vietnam duty.

There always seemed to be a strange smell around the base and the town but I never gave it a thought because I came from the country in Michigan, and just figured the air was different in bigger cities. Now, years later, I learned the smells were from chemicals at the Monsanto Chemical Company in Anniston, Alabama.

*While at Fort McClellan, Carolynn met and married a young soldier stationed there. He was being assigned to Fort Benning, Georgia. She wanted to go with him, but was instead sent to Fort Benjamin Harrison, Indiana. She was sent there for three weeks of training in court stenography, even though she asked for medical training at Fort Sam Houston, Texas. Her job at headquarters was to type orders for soldiers going to Vietnam, and process papers for those coming back in body bags. She had a hard time emotionally with the latter when she saw the names and felt responsible for their deaths.*

*Larry, her staff sergeant was always talking with her and seemingly as a good friend. One day he offered her a ride from the office to her barracks and she accepted because there was a bad storm outside.*

As he went out of the gate, instead of turning right to the barracks he turned left, and I said, "Where are you going?"

He said, "Oh I have some errands to run. Have you ever been out to the reservoir?"

"I didn't even know there was one, but I don't want to go there, I have things to do. Please take me back to the barracks."

"Oh we won't be gone long," he said and took me there.

I told him again, "I want to go back to the barracks!"
"I just want to show you the reservoir."

I said, "TAKE ME BACK TO THE BARRACKS NOW!"

His response was,"Let's just walk down to the shoreline. I want to show you a few things."

I told him, "I don't like this. TAKE ME BACK NOW!" The next thing I knew I was down on the ground. I'll tell you how bad it was, he raped me and I was laying on a batch of poison ivy and ended up in the hospital with poison ivy all over my legs, my body and inside me. I was in the hospital for almost a week.

Then when they started talking to me and asked what happened and I told them, they swept it under the rug. I can guarantee there is no report of it; there never is and in my case there never was. They even doctored my medical records so there was no mention of the rape. What saved my case was the severe pelvic inflammatory disease and poison ivy that was recorded.

They had me talk to a psychiatrist who said, "The thing is, you went out with this guy and you were having second thoughts because you were married, and you were afraid he'd find out, so this was your way of telling yourself psychologically that you're not to blame."

*This is an example of a psychiatrist participating in the culture of abuse by fabricating a storyline/lie to shift accountability for the rape to Carolyn, the rape victim.*

They told me as long as I kept my mouth shut and didn't pursue the rape issue I could continue my military career otherwise I would be discharged. I told them, "I just want to get out of here and be at Fort Benning, GA with my husband. Get me off this base." I had done the testing for Officer Candidate School (OCS) and had already put in for transfer to Fort Benning.

The psychiatrist said, "We'll just put in for you to be discharged because you are unsuitable for military service." That is what they did to anyone who reported rape. If I had known then, what I know now, I'd have fought a lot harder. I don't know how it is for the other women in this man's army, but as soon as they report rape they're gone.

*In November 1965, Carolyn found out she was pregnant and in December she had a miscarriage. The doctor told her that the fetus disintegrated.*

The Doctor knew that it was a girl but he said, "The fetus was so badly deformed you could hardly tell it was a fetus. You are actually lucky you lost it." When I asked what he thought was wrong he couldn't explain it but asked me if I had been exposed to any type of chemicals at any time. I never made the connection until he asked the question.

*In February of 1966, her husband was sent to Vietnam and Carolyn had another miscarriage, after being pregnant for six months. She was told that the fetus was only four months in development.*

I knew something was wrong and had another miscarriage after my husband came back from Vietnam. I also continued to have symptoms of nausea, headache and felt achy all over. I requested my medical records, but they have never come.

*Many of the women I interviewed, and others I knew about through veteran advocates, said that obtaining personal medical records was extremely difficult if not impossible and if they did get their records they were often missing critical pages and information.*

I had a hysterectomy at age twenty-five for multiple tumors and had multiple polyps in my colon, fibromyalgia, pernicious anemia, masses on both kidneys, blood in my urine and degenerative spine and joint diseases. Now I believe it was from being exposed to toxic chemicals while at Fort McClellan.

*Carolynn has recently received 70% Service Connected Disability for Post-Traumatic Stress disorder and Military Sexual Trauma (PTSD/MST) and was just approved for un-employability. She will be paid at a 100% rate.*

It took forty-two years for the VA, looking at the same reports, to finally see what was in my military hospital records from Ft. Benjamin Harrison, and to finally admit this happened to me. I figure since I won that battle I didn't need to fight any more about the chemicals, because they will never admit to it anyway.

I don't think it was very fair that I was denied for 42 years and wish I had never quit fighting. I don't think I received enough back compensation for what I went through all those years unable to cope, unable to work around people, being looked down upon because I acted strange around men where I worked and the fact that the US Army took away my chance at a career. It will never be over for me, but I have learned to live with it better than a lot of other women who had this happen to them.

## Colleen Mussolino – Vietnam Era

*Colleen was the National Commander of the Women Veterans of America, helping other women veterans, and died in June of 2009. When Colleen was eighteen she wanted to become an electronic engineer, however she was in college majoring in music. She was looking for a way to become an electronic engineer when she saw the army recruiter. The recruiter told her she could learn to be an engineer in the army. She took the test, aced it, and then in July of 1965 went to basic training at Fort McClellan, Alabama. She thought basic was fun because she was a tomboy and grew up in the country. Her father was strict so she felt free in Alabama.*

*After basic training Colleen was sent to cook school at Fort Dix, New Jersey and was very unhappy and angry with the recruiter for lying to her. The engineer program was not open to women.*

*She was assigned to the WAC headquarters at Fort McClellan in December of 1965 and was lonely and homesick at holiday time. She took the bus to the enlisted men's club where she met a guy that she had seen previously. They had a few beers together and he offered to escort her home.*

I was nineteen years old and the next thing I knew three other guys joined him. They took me out into the woods, where they beat and raped me. I was screaming and fighting but they kept hitting me and raping me. I passed out and when I regained consciousness I ran out to the road and saw a Volkswagen with MP's. They took me to the station to report it, and to the hospital. I had bruises on my jaw, neck, head, arms and I was bleeding down my thighs. The rapists had their knees on my arms to stop me from fighting. At the hospital someone called my Commanding Officer (CO).

She came down and was angry to be awakened for this. I was discharged from the hospital and Monday went before the CO. I was told not to wear my combat boots, and not to wear short skirts or attend any social activities on post. Then I was ostracized and taken to a different area to sleep, and no one was to associate with me. I could go to church, work, and to the mess hall and that was it.

*This was the protocol for women who reported rape. They were ostracized, isolated and set apart from everyone else. Women who reported rape were often set apart through orders to wear tennis shoes instead of combat boots. They became 'marked women.'*

I did go to a lineup and I pointed out two of the guys and then all the guys admitted it. I was taken to the CID and interrogated from 7a.m. - 4p.m., five days a week for <u>six weeks.</u> They threatened me with a dishonorable discharge if I did not sign a paper saying I would not prosecute. I felt betrayed, made the criminal, and not seen as the victim. I felt like a prisoner of war. I signed their paper and told them God would take care of it. After I signed the paper, the mess sergeant still yelled at me all the time. I was eventually relieved of duty and sat in the first sergeant's office for a couple of months because they had no place for me. I read books and did puzzles. Then they put me in supply so they did not have to see me.

*Another theme in these stories is women being interrogated for long periods of time as a punishment for having the audacity to cause the military to deal with their rape. Many were also threatened with harm to themselves or families and dishonorable discharge if they did not sign a paper saying, either it never happened, or they would not prosecute. (It's a crime under both military law and civilian federal law to threaten or intimidate a witness.)*

I reconnected with a high school beau who came back from Vietnam and tried to get a compassionate assignment with him at Fort Eustus, Virginia. They never put through my request. We eventually married and I was discharged in March of 1967. The worst for me was how I was treated after the rape: being interrogated over and over for six weeks and being ostracized.

*When I asked Colleen about PTSD she told me:* I was nervous, jumpy, lashed out angrily and got into fights. I became very nasty after my military experience. I had no benefits; there were no benefits for women until 1973. After about fifteen years I was aware something was wrong with me. I started losing control and I was either violent or crying hysterically. I did not understand what was going on with me.

When my husband died, I was alone and got violent with co-workers; I was broke and had no place to go. My husband and I had been superintendents of the apartments, and after he was gone two weeks, I was thrown out of the apartment. I got legal help and went to New York where it was cheaper. I went fishing a lot and met a WWII Vet. We could talk about our experiences and it helped me a lot. He was like a father to me and he took me through the VA system to get help. He was able to get a congresswoman to help me, and I found out he was with the Disabled American Veterans (DAV). He put my papers through and in 1984 I got 10% disability for PTSD and then in 1994, ten years later, I was given 100% disability with help from my own DAV chapter.

I did get into a woman vets group for counseling at the VA in Brooklyn, N.Y. in 1985. We created a support group for women vets but we were not taken seriously; people did not know women were veterans. From that support group we created a logo and became the Women Vets of America with our motto 'Still Serving Proudly.' We have thirty-two chapters now and about 3000 members who are active duty and reservists. We help women navigate through the VA system to get benefits.

*If Congress had already held investigations into the culture of abuse in our military and positive change had already taken place, Colleen would have reported her rape in a safe private office on post where she had an advocate. She also would have had a compassionate nurse and/or doctor and all the resources she needed to fully examine and care for her, document findings appropriately in her medical record and had an opportunity to talk with a counselor and begin dealing with her rape. Her experience with her advocate would have been safe and supportive and the military police would treat her respectfully, asking only appropriate questions about the details of her rape and her assailants. Breaks were given to her, as she needed them* *throughout the interrogation, which would have been limited to two-hours each session. An advocate would have been present with her at all times and advising her truthfully and accurately of her rights during the process. Additionally, her commander would have been notified and would have visited her at some point and behaved as a compassionate leader concerned for her health and safety as well as, determining who among the soldier's command had done this to her. Her commander would have been resolved to seek full accountability for the beating and gang rape and would also have insisted on attitude checks in the perpetrators unit. It would be the job of her commander to <u>insure</u> that this type of behavior was labeled criminal and adjudicated as such.*

*Colleen would have been able to receive the support she needed on a daily basis, including continuing all her normal contacts and schedule, as she was able. She could go to the dining hall and sit where she liked, with whomever she wanted. Her rape would have remained confidential and known only to those mentioned. Colleen would not have been asked to sign the paper saying she would not prosecute and she would have seen that her rapists were made to be fully accountable under appropriate law. Colleen would have the opportunity to continue to serve, if she so chose.*

## Nancy Lilja – Vietnam Era

*Nancy knew from age seven that she was going to be a navy nurse. In high school she went to visit recruiters and when it was time to leave high school she received a scholarship for a three-year diploma nursing school. The navy wanted her to give up the scholarship. Nancy decided the navy was not as hands-on as she would like, and joined the army student nurse program instead. She graduated in 1967 and went to basic at Fort Sam Houston, Texas for eight weeks.*

I took my mother with me because she had congestive heart failure; we lived off post so I could care for her. She was in the army hospital on and off.

After basic I went to Fort Benning, Georgia. I drove in the heat with my mom to my first duty station. I worked at the Martin Army Hospital on the orthopedic ward. Then in February of 1968 I was sent to Japan to the 249th General Hospital, South Camp Drake. I worked medical, surgical and neurology for two years. The patients were evacuated from Vietnam to us. We always had a high patient count especially during TET (the Vietnamese New Year celebrations). The patients were either returned to duty or sent home to the United States. We had one ward with head-injured patients, one ward with burn injuries, and one with orthopedic injuries. One time a soldier sat up and angrily said, "What am I supposed to tell my wife?" I was shocked out of my shoes. He was an amputee and had wounds all over his body.

I saw everything in my two years and had a well-rounded preparation for being in Vietnam. I gradually got numb to it all: tracheotomies (small opening made in the trachea/throat and stainless steel tube put in to hold it open for breathing), head wounds, missing limbs and body parts. The guys were waking up to what had happened to them and the full awareness of their wounds. I was there to encourage them, be positive and give them clean white sheets and bandages.

When I got to Vietnam I was stationed at the 3rd Surgical Hospital, which was at Binh Thuy, southwest of Saigon. *(The 3rd Surgical Hospital moved during the Vietnam War and was located in different areas. In 1967 it was at Bien Hoa).* I was assigned to the emergency room as a replacement for the departing head nurse. I quickly became proficient at starting IV's (intravenous), doing triage and minor surgical procedures. I had some hairy experiences with doctors. One major would not come when called and said negative things about the nurses in the Intensive Care Unit (ICU). When he started telling me how lousy the nurses were I said, "I've had enough of your shit, the next time you're on-call I will not do any of your work or write your orders for you until you get here and write them down. Furthermore, do not say anything more about the nurses, they are doing the best they can, and don't bring in any more unauthorized Vietnamese patients." We were all glad to see that doctor leave.

I was sexually harassed in Vietnam. A male nurse supervisor would come up to me, look in my eyes and tell me I had bedroom eyes. It made me cringe. He was always trying to force himself on me. I kept saying, "You're married aren't you? I'll tell your wife."

A colonel raped me there. He was a doctor and was banging loudly on my door to talk to me. I got up to tell him to shut the hell up, and he shoved his way into my small room, pushed me down and raped me. I lay there like a lump of clay telling myself this was not happening. He was the chief of surgery, married and very drunk and it was two a.m. I got up the next day and went to work. I did not know what to do. I told no one. He went on leave to meet his wife soon after that and brought back an accordion for me. He made a big production of giving it to me in front of others. I felt like a real schmuck. I never played it and sent it home to a niece. I was not a virgin and I'd had a relationship, so what could I do? It was very demeaning and I felt dirty and bad. I went on to work and never said anything.

One woman was assaulted by an enlisted man and reported it. For that she was given an 'Article 15' (non-judicial punishment). It was probably better that I did not say anything about it because the perpetrators were never given any consequences, but the women were. I did all kinds of things in my mind to guilt myself. I never realized there was any damage to me until the last two years. It made a very confused personal package to take into my marriage later. I could not tell my husband and I always felt I could not give myself fully and that I was hiding something. I also had a problem with endometriosis and I never realized any connection. I had a D and C (Dilatation and Curettage/uterine scraping) while in Vietnam and the condition continued when I came back.

I ended up becoming an alcoholic, suicidal, with PTSD and finally in the last few years got the help I needed.

*Nancy gave me this interview in 2007, thirty-seven years after being raped. She is still struggling with the effects of that on her life, and her marriage.*

# K. H. – Persian Gulf Era

I joined the marines before I finished high school because I thought it would be a cool way to travel the world and grow up. I was five feet tall, weighed ninety-four pounds and was eighteen years old. The marines required the highest test scores, so I thought they had the highest standards and must have a higher class of people there.

They sent me to basic training at Paris Island, South Carolina for twelve weeks. Before joining the marines I was a marathon runner and ran twenty to thirty miles a day. In basic they had me sitting in classes most of the time and I ran only once a week. I started to gain weight and was not happy. There was little physical activity there for me.

From basic I was sent to Quantico, Virginia for Military Occupational Specialty (MOS) training as a computer programmer. For four months I was there with mostly men and only a few women. The guys talked a lot about their sexual conquests with prostitutes and how much they paid. Even the officers were telling the guys that the hookers on one street were better than others.

Next I was sent to El Toro Marine Base in Santa Ana, California as a lance corporal. For two and one-half years I worked as a computer programmer in an airplane hangar for their headquarters. I was the only woman in my unit, among seventy guys, but there were navy women at our base hospital.

*Her supervisors told her many times, "This is a man's corps and women should only have a desk job pushing papers and should not rise above E-3."*

I was passed over for promotion three times and was told I would not advance because I was a woman and did not belong in the marine corps.

When our section went on physical training (PT), I was not allowed to go because, "Women can't handle physical activity." One day the guys did a practice PT and told me I could go with them and directed, "Take the turn off for the half mile run, because women can't run that far, and you can walk back." There were over a hundred guys running the three to four mile course and only three of them beat me back. None of them knew I was a weight lifter and marathon runner.

I was number two in the State of Oregon in cross-country and from that day on I never heard any more about what women could do physically. After that another woman was assigned to my unit.

The barracks were co-ed except for one that was all male. In the coed barracks we had individual rooms that were gender specific. I had two dates with a Non-Commissioned Officer In Charge, (NCOIC), who was a coworker. After two dates he was already planning our wedding so I never dated coworker's after that, wore ugly black glasses to work, and kept my work separate from my personal life.

One day I was walking along the catwalks outside my barracks when a guy grabbed me and pulled me into a room and pushed me down. He demanded that I give him oral sex; he'd already pulled his pants down. When he reached down to pull them off, I ran out of the room. I did not know him. The next day I saw him at the chow hall and told my NCOIC. There was no investigation or anything and no questions. When I told my NCOIC he said he would look into it and the next time I saw the guy I called my NCOIC to tell him the guy was there; he came right over and talked to the guy, wrote down some stuff and I never saw that guy again; he disappeared.

A few months later I was watching TV in the co-ed barracks sitting in the doorway and got up to go to the bathroom. When I came back the door was closed and there were a bunch of guys there. **Seventeen Marines raped me.** They were saying things like, "Oh you know you want it, you've been wanting this for a long time." I started shouting and they turned the TV up real loud. I had seen a couple of these guys at the club when I was dancing, so they were familiar. Three or four of them seemed to be in charge of the gang rape. One even left and came back with other guys. Several grabbed me and threw me on a bed and were taking my clothes off. They turned the lights off, pulled the curtains and raped me. They were saying, "Oh she's hot, you know you like it." Sometimes there was more than one at a time going orally and anally. They stuffed something in my mouth when I was screaming, and they held me down and wrapped sheets around my arms so it wouldn't leave marks. It seemed like they had done this before and knew what to do. They even put me in the shower and made sure I showered before they left. I cried and cried and felt numb and hopeless. They raped me and washed me at the same time. I was pretty limp by then. Afterwards they had me put my clothes on and told me to go. I stumbled back to my room and cried myself to sleep. My roommate was not there.

The next day I went to work and told my NCOIC, the same one who helped me before. I told him I had to see the Officer In Charge (OIC). The OIC told me, "For the betterment of your career and the marine corps, forget the whole thing. If you report this, it will be on your record for everybody to see; it will be a permanent mark on your record." I had been trained to listen to my commanding officer, do what they said and not to think about it or question it. Here I was being ordered not to report being gang-raped by seventeen marines. What could I do?

He asked me if I wanted a career in the marine corps. I told him I did. He said, "Then just forget it ever happened." I was not supposed to question my commander, who told me not to say anything. So I kept quiet.

*This is a serious conflict within the structure of the military. The chain of command has far too much power over individuals along with a conflict of interest.*

*The commander is responsible for each soldier, and the unit, so when faced with a sexual assault by a soldier on another soldier in their unit, that conflict of interest becomes paramount. Because of that conflict of interest and commanders tendency to cover up crimes that would reflect on them as officers, the decision making power and authority over the handling of all sexual assault cases needs to be removed from the chain of command. From the fifty eight interviews I have done, it is clear that commanders almost always choose to side with the perpetrators and not the victims. Why is that?*

*Following orders also brings up the whole issue of accountability. I believe it is correct to refuse to follow <u>inappropriate or improper</u> orders. In the situation described above, it would have been appropriate to report the gang rape and not follow the improper order of her OIC. There are many instances known to the public, where an order is deemed inappropriate and the best action was to refuse to follow the order, such as in the My Lai massacre and Abu Ghraib. When I served on a selection committee for my congressman's appointments to the military academies, I always asked the applicants what they would do if they were given an unethical and inappropriate order. I wanted officers who would think clearly and not take an action, or order their soldiers to take an action that was a violation of their duty, the constitution, or what they knew to be morally correct. Soldiers are trained to heed the orders of those superior to them, and it is important in combat that soldiers do not question orders and carry out what they are ordered to do. Their superiors have more information and know more than they do in those situations, and immediate action is necessary. In basic training each trainee needs to be taught <u>when</u> it might be appropriate to question an order and have a way to check it out. Rape and reporting are instances when questioning is appropriate, especially when the officers clearly have a conflict of interest. Orders to torture or perform illegal or immoral actions also need to be questioned.*

After the rapes my proficiency scores went down. I was drinking more and did not talk to people; I withdrew. Friends noticed this and stopped being friends with me. I was told to forget about everything, not report it and keep my mouth shut. I tried to do that and did not get any help from the marines. Not long after the gang rape, I got sick and found out I had gonorrhea. I told the sick call doctor what happened and he looked at me and said, "Oh you had sex with seventeen marines; you are a nymphomaniac. I can get you out on a mental discharge for that." I told him I was gang raped and held down; the assault was not my choice. He told me they would all say I was a willing participant, therefore it was considered a mental defect.

*Another tactic the military uses, is to twist and distort what women tell them so that it is turned against them. Here is a case where a woman marine is gang raped and when she tells her doctor, he labels her a nymphomaniac and offers to give her a discharge that describes her as unfit for duty so she will not have access to any benefits. Women in this situation do not know this until after it is done. It is vital that women are given information and support, for their health and welfare including victim advocacy so they know what they are being offered or coerced into to signing or agreeing to. Remember this is happening when they are in a state of shock and trauma and cannot think clearly or respond with full access to whole brain function. Documentation is also important so that later when these women need care or when filing a claim, the information in their record is accurate. I have heard countless stories of women whose files have had missing pages or are incomplete. They need all the information in their files to be accurate and complete to successfully file a claim or get the healthcare appropriate to them.*

I tried to forget about the rapes but was not sleeping well. I began drinking more so I could forget. I took double shifts and did things so I did not have to sleep. In 1984, I saw that I was not getting any help and asked to go overseas. They told me I checked into the wrong part of the base, "You are not supposed to be working for us," and they sent me to the other side of the base. They told me I had to be on post one year before they could send me overseas, and they acted as though I had just gotten there.

My boyfriend at the time was from a Catholic family. I never told him what happened because I was afraid he'd see me as damaged goods and wouldn't want me. I never told anyone until 1995. I got a letter from the VA saying there was help available for women if raped or sexually harassed. My PTSD symptoms never really went away. I was screaming at night and kicking in my sleep.

In 1984, I had knee surgery that was not successful. I could not run anymore or march or even stand in formation. I was given a medical discharge and had no medical exam or dental exam. They gave me my records and signed me out with a medical discharge, and I did not have to do anything. They had walked it through and had all the signatures. I kept the records even though there were pages missing.

I married my boyfriend in August of 1985 and got out in December. I buried the rape experience but it made sex very difficult for me. My husband complained that I needed to loosen up, that I was too tense. I was always afraid when he wanted to try something. He became abusive and was hitting me and pushing me around. He punched my stomach when I was pregnant with my third child so I'd have a miscarriage. In August of 1990, I split up with him. After a few years I was diagnosed with fibromyalgia and lupus. It was five years later before I realized how wrong all that was and wished I had not listened to the commander. That is what they taught me, to obey orders, and I did. That is what hurts me now.

In 1995, I told my second husband and in 1998, I filed a claim. The medical review board out of Philadelphia said I couldn't have been raped if I was sexually active. I filed for a re-consideration and it came back denied. My VA records state I have Military Sexual Trauma (MST), but review board won't give me disability for it. It took me nine months to get my personnel file and when I got it I saw many pages missing. They kept telling me there is no record in my file of the rape, and with all the missing pages there wasn't. I went to my congressman and my claim was taken from Philadelphia to Washington, D.C. and it has been there ever since.

*K. H. is still working to get her claim through and to get counseling. She has many health problems including: fibromyalgia, lupus, eosinophilia, and early kidney failure from medications. She found out she was allergic to the jet fuel she was exposed to at El Toro, when the planes would circle the airbase and dump the fuel into the air. She has migraine headaches and a knee injury from the rifle range. She is on welfare and social security. If every one of our military services would put in place a protocol for women that provides a place to report sexual assaults with a nurse, counselor and victim advocate available, plus all the necessary records were detailed and complete. Women like K.H. would be able to get the help they need and continue to serve. She could have had counseling to deal with the rapes and stayed in her job. Then it would be important for everyone who deals with those records to preserve them. I wonder who orders pages to be removed from health records or military service records. Who does the actual removing? Who has oversight over that and how do we get accountability?*

*While there is a cost for the resources that I describe, there is greater cost to the marine corps when they lose the value of the training they have provided and they lose their soldier. Why not preserve the best of every soldier, male or female, and provide the services they need? Protecting rapists and the image of the marines seems paramount to the marines. If that were not the case, then why would the marine corps coerce women into not reporting the criminal behavior of their male soldiers? It seems that they would rather sacrifice one good woman marine for seventeen male rapists.*

## Beckie Wilson – Desert Storm

*Beckie was 24, going from job to job, and met a navy recruiter who talked her into joining. She went to boot camp in Orlando, Florida in July 1974.*

I had a cool company commander and had a good experience. Other girls had commanders who were tyrants and their experience was very different. I did not have to carry a rifle.

After navy boot camp I went to Cryptography Training School (CTR) at Pensacola, Florida, to learn encryption, cryptography, and Morse Code. We learned that we would be stationed in desolate places with marines and that if we were captured, our marine would shoot us. This was during the Cold War. I think they were trying to get the women out of the navy, because the men were never told that. Men felt we were invading their territory and they did not want us there. They wanted us in our place as runners and clerks. I left the school and went to Pax River, Maryland. For the first six months I worked for the Secretary to the Command Master Chief, and then the squad went to Jacksonville, Florida. I was getting ready to go and chose to be an SK- storekeeper, so I could move up in rank. I studied for SK –E3 at Jacksonville and worked in maintenance control providing supplies for planes, matched records, and ordered supplies, boots etc. I made SK-3 and got orders immediately to go to Rosie Roads, Puerto Rico. It was fun. I drove fork lifts, unloaded C 130's and C 140's and loaded them with supplies going to Vietnam.

After six months of doing that they asked me to be the storekeeper for the captain. So I ordered supplies for him and for the post and kept the books. I went to Continental U.S. (CONUS) to get things for him and did that job for one year. Then I went to 'A' school in Memphis for eight weeks and began to teach aviation hydraulics. I was the first female instructor to teach there.

While I was an instructor I was dating the chief of police. Someone made a comment about a gunny sergeant who was ripping off the government and had gotten enough stuff to build a room on his house, including a refrigerator and washer. (I saw the stuff come in but I never saw it go out so I didn't think anything of it.) Then this chief I worked for started stalking me, and came over with bottles of tequila and wanted me to drink with him and sleep with him. He made sexual comments, stalked and threatened me. He told me if I did not sleep with him my evaluations would hit the dirt. He threatened me and forced himself on me four or five times. *Here is more evidence of how the chain of command is rigged in favor of men and sexual assault toward women. It must be stopped and it will take action by Congress to effect change in the abusive culture.*

I told the CO who said, "Boys will be boys" and did nothing. I just took it in and buried it. I said fine, girls will be girls and from then on I made stupid decisions. I wore low cut dresses and became obnoxious for about six months. Then when the case about the gunny sergeant came up I finally stood up to the chief and told him to do whatever but don't expect sex from me anymore.

Because I had the gumption to tell them what I knew, I was sent out of the school to work for the base master chief doing secretarial stuff. He liked me and knew what had been done to me, but there was nothing he could do. He would take me over to the welding shop so I could learn to weld. Then I was transferred to Hawaii for three years.

I was an aviation hydraulics mechanic and the only woman in the shop. Cursing did not bother me but it was high stress to have an airplane in the air twenty-four hours a day. The master chief said all he wanted to see was elbows or assholes. I was an E-5 then and in charge of the tool shed. One guy forgot his tag and I tried to get it to him, but couldn't and then forgot. Master chief did everything he could to get me to cry and I wouldn't. I owned up to having the tag and thought I deserved being chewed out. Later I did cry in the bathroom and the master chief told me he respected me for not caving in and not letting my guard down.

I lived off base and one night someone tried to break in to my place. A young couple next door came to help me. I was hiding in the closet under some dirty clothes because I was terrified. The young marine from next door scared the guy off and came to check on me and called the police. They knocked and said who they were. The marine and his wife became good friends after that.

I felt 99% respected, but the other 1% was harassing me with sexual comments and of course the rape. Once a couple of guys were talking about how long their penises were and I finally got mad and took out a yardstick and said "Prove it," and they backed off.

I was ready to move on after three years. The island was hot and boring. I went to Oak Harbor, Washington and was there about five years doing aviation hydraulics. I met my first love, Jerry who was also in the navy. We both went to Desert Storm 1989/1990.

After five years at Oak Harbor I was transferred to the U.S.S. Samuel Gompers in Alameda, California and I came back up to Washington on some weekends. Jerry was on the U.S.S. Roosevelt and we passed each other. I was going into port Jubail Dubai and he was going out. I was there on ship during desert storm for six months. You think our guys were bad, you ain't seen nothing to those Arabs. A cab driver said to me, "Come back to my house I want to fuck you." We had two women who were blonde with blue eyes who were kidnapped over there. Fortunately we got them back and they were shipped home right away to get the care they needed.

I had taught myself computers and my job on ship was computers. We sailed around for a while and I got off before it went back to desert storm. I ended up in Oakland for two years doing computers. Jerry had a heart attack and I lost him and then retired out of Oakland and moved back to Washington.

I have aches and pains no one can explain and I have had cancer twice. Some mornings I can't get up and I make myself. The VA said they recognize the effect of chemicals but they don't, and they tell us it is nothing and won't acknowledge it. They put us over there, why don't they take care of us? *The military is also good at covering up the effects of chemicals on soldiers whether at places like Fort Drum or Fort McClellan, working around jet fuel, breathing in jet fuel and other chemicals.*

I registered as a Desert Storm Vet and have 30% disability for a hysterectomy at age 30 while in the military. I had precancerous cells. I also have a spot on my lung and fell off an airplane wing once causing damage to my spine. My disability is now up to 50%.

Four years ago I had cancer of the breast, which should have been picked up on mammogram, and was not. I had a mastectomy and chemo at the VA. May of 2006 they found another lump and thankfully it was benign.

# Laura Sellinger– Iraq

*Laura's most prized possession was her grandfather's navy dog tags. He had an internal pride and strength, was like an oak tree and those dog tags were something she valued highly. Her grandfather's navy buddies were like uncles and she called them uncle.*

*Laura was born in New York and she was hit pretty hard by 9-11. In 2001, she and her boyfriend, John, went to ground zero and she came away with an intense desire to have the same sense of pride and strength in herself that she perceived in her grandfather.*

*During her senior year in high school, Laura tried to enlist in air force intelligence, but because her mother was a European refugee it became difficult. Her mother needed to find the judge and the name of the courthouse where she was sworn into American Citizenship, in order for Laura to get top-secret clearance. During that time, many friends and family tried to talk her into going to college instead of enlisting in the military, but she was adamant.*

*John, her boyfriend was already in the air force and was graduating basic training when she was accepted. At her basic training graduation, she told him she had gotten the slot she wanted in air force intelligence. They had been together for three years, but when she went to her basic and he went to an air force technical school they went their separate ways.*

*Laura went to basic at Lackland AFB for six weeks and then on to intelligence training for a year at Goodfellow AFB, Texas. From 2003-2005 in her first duty assignment, Dyess AFB, Texas, she reported daily intelligence activity to the commander and was treated with respect. She was proud of herself and wore the uniform with pride. She enjoyed her job and all that went with it.*

*In 2005, she was transferred to Alaska and in early 2006 received a special classified assignment to Iraq and was contracted out to the Department of Defense (DOD) collecting ground intelligence.*

One day while being transported in a convoy, an Improvised Explosive Device (IED) hit the vehicle I was in and I was thrown about ten to fifteen feet from it. We were riding with a special army unit and lost our gunner, and we had several other injuries. The soldiers in an army humvee picked me up and took me to the Baghdad Hospital along with others who were hurt. The hospital is run by our military but also has some Iraqi doctors.

I was in shock and did not want anyone to touch me. I was beaten, bloody, burnt and had some minor lacerations but nothing was broken. They looked at me and said, "Don't fall asleep." We were all worried about our gunner who we knew took the worst of the hit.

It was a very weird experience for me because I was all beat up, bleeding, had high adrenalin pumping through me but no energy and I was in a fog. I was staring at the wall and none of us could talk.

Even now, I can still see that wall I was staring at and that hard wooden bench and the muddy bloody sand on my hands. Eventually the commander arrived and told us to go take showers and get to work. I called my friend John, because I felt like I was going to die and wanted to tell him that I loved him. He and his parents were on the beach in the Bahamas' at the time, and he went to Iraq shortly afterwards, but we talked weekly. It felt crazy to me to be hit by the IED, thrown from the vehicle, bleeding and bruised pretty severely, lacerated and burned, but told to go take a shower and get back to work. I knew my mind was in shock.

We had mortar attacks three times a day. Usually at nine a.m. there was a car bomb attack or suicide bomber. Black smoke meant it was a car bomb and white smoke was a suicide bomber. Mortars usually came mid-morning. The first month I always felt it was going to hit me and after that I accepted them and adapted.

One month after the IED incident a mortar went off so close the captain and I both looked at each other and knew it was close. He grabbed me and threw me into a wall. The mortar landed a couple of feet beside my left foot and I had shrapnel in my boot and ankle, and my head was split open from the cement wall. We had a really good field medic who took the shrapnel out and cleaned my two wounds, just above my ankle. I am only one of four people in Iraq with my job, so I had to do my job.

About two months after the mortar wounds, one of our detainees killed one of the army lieutenant's in the unit we were supporting. I was standing behind the detainees as they were properly detained, but one of them got up and started to kick and swing in my direction, an army soldier swiftly took his M-4 rifle and with the butt of it hit me in the face accidentally when he missed the detainee. I was between him, the three other detainees, and another army soldier. One detainee took the soldier's M-4 and hit me in the face and the side of my head. I fell into a wooden bench and was knocked out. A riot broke out between the detainees and the army soldiers, which was brought under control and then someone gave me some smelling salts, which brought me back to consciousness.

My reports always went to Washington, D.C., and after the head injuries my reports were not making sense. I had four months left in Iraq and I was stubborn and would not believe anything was wrong. I was not sleeping and was grinding my teeth and I could not read reports anymore so I was getting verbal summaries. I thought I was streamlining the process and was making excuses. The person who was reading my reports went over my head and wrote to DC saying something was wrong with me, "You need to bring her home." Two weeks later a guy came into my office with return orders. I was pissed and told him to "Fuck off; no one else can do this job."

I did go home and the home unit was not expecting me, and they sent me on a training mission to Korea. I was full of pride and would die for the guy next to me. These airmen had no clue, but I thought they did. One night someone put something in my drink and I got violently sick and went back to the hotel. I got to my room and passed out on my bed. A couple of hours later, someone knocked on my door and I was out of it, but opened the door. It was a guy I knew from technical school. He beat my head against the entertainment center and I fell to the floor and was completely paralyzed. He pulled my pants down and raped me and there was blood all over. I passed out again. When I came to, I washed myself off and I couldn't think who he was. I called the base police and was in their office for six hours going over and over the experience. Two days later I was in Alaska and heard that he confessed. During the evidence process for the 'Article 32' hearing, they lost my rape kit. He sent me three death threats and yet was promoted to staff sergeant even though he was under investigation for violent assault and rape and I was denied promotion.

My commander called and I told him I don't want anyone to know about this. The next day the entire squadron knew, he called the whole unit to formally tell everyone my business. I was devastated. 'MySpace' page blew up with nasty messages like, "You're a slut, you deserved it, you whore." I went from 0-1000 messages. Everything changed. I went from knowing I would die for these guys to being suicidal. The rapist and then my commander betrayed me and I hit bottom fast.

My dad flew to Alaska and told my commander, "I am taking Laura to a hospital where she should have gone in the first place and you are not stopping me. Who is your boss? I am not leaving without my daughter!" He took me to a clinic and then I was given a three-month humanitarian assignment to Hurlburt Fields, FL, coincidentally where John was stationed.

*Laura was medically retired in 2008, has had some psychological treatment and has a number of medical conditions related to her injuries in Iraq. In 2009, Laura had a Transient Ischemic Attack (TIA,) and she is still fighting for her claim through the VA. She has battled for years to get a claim for her rape that the VA still denies. The USAF allowed the case to be dropped.*

*\*\*\*Note for reader: I know reading these stories may be painful for you and perhaps it will be difficult to go on reading them. Imagine what it was like for the women living those experiences. If you are not able to read each story, I encourage you to read at least one story from each of the chapters and what is said at the beginning of the chapters. Then please go to the last chapter on Attitude and*

*Accountability to see what you can do about all this.*

*Here is a sampling of what you will find in the last chapter.*

*It is time for action and change. Our military has lost its honor and integrity. It cannot be redeemed but can be transformed. I am calling for full, thorough and unbiased congressional investigations into all the military services including every part of military culture from the bottom up, and top down, including the entire Military Justice System. Sweeping change is required and must take place. I ask everyone moved by the stories of these women to call or visit your Congressional Representatives and Senators at home, or in Washington, D.C., and insist on their support for full unbiased Congressional investigations into all the military services and the Military Justice System to restore the honor and integrity of our military by insisting on positive cultural change. Ask that whoever is part of this congressional process be fully committed to seeking the <u>complete truth</u> and being as courageous as the women who serve in the military, in carrying out the mission to bring positive change to our military culture. Silence equals support for this despicable behavior.*

*Military Sexual Trauma changes everything. The woman who is sexually assaulted will never be the same again. Her body, mind, emotions and her sense of self were violated. She may never feel safe or confident again. Depending on how others respond to her after her assault she may be able to heal and move on. If she is not believed, supported, given the care she needs immediately, treated with dignity, respect, and compassion, she is likely to be left with serious symptoms for the rest of her life. The way our military handles sexual assaults is disrespectful, indignant, cold, harsh, and unjust. Women are shamed, humiliated, denied compassion, medical care, protection, even the kind of investigation that acknowledges the crime and affirms she is believed. Women who are sexually assaulted in the military are denied justice. That must change now!*

# Pregnancy and Discharge

*There was a story given to me in the earliest stages of this book that has been an anchor and inspiration for me. It was this story that touched me deeply and helped me realize how important it was for me to write this book. I felt very connected to the woman on the phone who told me this story and have great admiration and respect for her. I was distraught for several months when she would not respond to my requests to sign a release, so that her story could be included in the book. To this day I do not know why she would not allow me to include her story here and hope to give you a sense of what it would have been if it could be included.*

*She had gone through basic and went to Fort Sam Houston, TX to be an army nurse, but instead was pulled out to be a mail clerk and was ordered to carry the flag in parades. She was meticulous in her work. One day a base postal inspector came and checked everything including using his white gloves and measuring cubbyholes where the mail was kept. She had already delivered all the mail and the inspector was surprised at how clean, neat, organized and superb the mailroom was under her care.*

*After her duty was completed she was outside in her civilian clothes and the inspector, who was obviously waiting for her, told her he forgot something and needed to go back in. It was then that he forcefully raped her, even though she fought well and even found a letter opener to use to help her fight him off. He was able to use that against her and stabbed her in the foot. She reported what happened the next day and was confined to her quarters. Many weeks later, she went to sick call and discovered that the rapist had impregnated her. She was shocked and not sure what to do. The captain told her "Pregnant women were not allowed in the army," and she was told to take off her uniform and was confined her to quarters. He insisted she wear only civilian clothing. She was given a discharge and escorted off the base without any belongings or even money for a phone call.*

*She found work and places to stay until she had her baby at an unwed mother's hospital and gave the baby up for adoption. She told me she was a citizen, a soldier and lost her health, career, her child, and her future, while the rapist got away with no consequences. He had a good life, married, had children, retired from the army and lost nothing. She told me she was proud she served, but "Look what my country did to me!"*

*Her courage after being ejected from the army with a severe foot injury that left her with permanent damage, and being pregnant with no money was, galvanizing and stays with me to this day.*

# Ingrid Larson Alexander – Iraq Era

*Ingrid went to law school at Suffolk University in Boston, Massachusetts and attended ROTC. In her last year she was twenty-four years old and applying for jobs. Ingrid liked the Seattle area, and because she enjoyed her admiralty law class, she began to apply for jobs in admiralty, immigration, and international law, in Seattle, Oregon and Alaska. Ingrid was denied each of the jobs she applied for due to her lack of experience. She even applied with the coast guard, but they did not have any openings. Next she tried the navy and the air force. After recruiters came to her school, she signed up for the air force, marines, and the navy and researched each of them. Her goal was to enter the JAG Corps (Judge Advocate General, attorneys). When she found out that the marines did not guarantee JAG, she only did interviews with the air force and the navy. Ingrid was accepted into the air force, contingent on her passing their physical fitness test and her bar exam. She told me she enjoyed physical fitness but it was a struggle for her. The air force said she needed to lose some weight and she discovered she was two inches shorter than she had been. Ingrid was lactose intolerant and that was also a problem for her. In January 2002, she went to commissioned officer training along with the medical corps, clergy and other lawyers at Gunter Maxwell Air Force Base (AFB) in Alabama.*

It was tough getting up at 4:30-5:00 a.m., and learning to do push-ups, then eating and going to the gym to practice push-ups, sit ups, and running. I ran eight miles every other day and needed a flashlight and a buddy to run with me. There were only certain places we could run. I also did yoga in my room.

After the training I did the airmen leadership course. There were twelve of us working together and one had to be the leader. One time I had to be upside down on a pole six feet off the ground. I strained my hamstring muscle and was on crutches for a few days. My schedule was pretty exhausting from 4a.m.-10p.m. When that was all over, I had the weekend off and then went to JAG school.

JAG school was at Maxwell AFB and I was there for three months. It was like law school. We did mock trials. At one of them a female JAG instructor pulled me aside to tell me I did a fantastic job and that I was more aggressive and articulate than most women JAG Officers.

April of 2002, I was sent to Fairchild AFB in Spokane, Washington. It was an air-refueling wing and was my first duty station. I was supposed to hear from the JAG on post before going, but did not hear from him. He later apologized to me. I went to the base to look for the JAG office and no one was there. I waited and waited and finally was sent to the staff JAG Officer and was assigned as chief of claims. I had two sergeants and one civilian, who were great to work with. I handled medical claims and accidents on post, in addition to our events. I reviewed claims and determined whether to pay them, deny them, or something in between. I wrote up the information, did research, wrote a claim and sent it to the Washington D.C. Judge Advocate Tort Review. I also dealt with unpaid claims and bills, and dependent claims when the person had left the military. I had one military malpractice case and worked with the Assistant U.S. Attorney's office and settled it. I was chief of medical claims, chief of civil law, and chief of military justice environmental and labor law.

The military justice cases were divided among the JAG officers. I helped prosecute five cases, mostly drug related. There was a drug ring of airmen who were gathering illegal drugs before going to Iraq.

The popular drugs were ecstasy, mushrooms, and LSD. I also prosecuted a woman who was a go between for the drug deals. We had a male judge on that case and I had a former Staff Judge Advocate (SJA) as co-counsel. She told me to wear a skirt to court. After the trial-judge gave me feedback he said, "I saw this poor girl off in the corner and could not give her maximum sentence." He was soft on women in his court and not strong on prosecuting for drugs.

One case near the end of my tour at Fairchild involved an airman I had seen on post. The office of special investigations determines if there is enough evidence to bring a case to the JAG office. I was the legal representative for spousal and child abuse cases, which included doctors, clergy, and child protective agencies. The cases were brought there to determine what resources were needed for each one.

It was April/May and I was assigned a rape victim case. It was a woman airmen who was very timid and shy. She was attending training in Tennessee, hanging out with other airmen and began to feel sick. She asked to go back to the barracks. She was a virgin and one airman started to kiss her. She told him no sex. There were several airmen who had already been accused of rape twice before. The airmen did not accept her "no," and raped her. She was very concerned about her career when she met with the SJA and me, and yet she wanted to move forward with the case. The next thing I know, I am being told by the SJA, a man I highly respected and trusted and who was very ethical, to get a signed statement from the victim that it was consensual sex. I protested and said I think she can stand up in court and do a good job. I told him I don't like this; it is lying. I was already depressed from work on the child abuse cases and this made it worse. This SJA, who had been my model, lost my respect in that moment. I could not look at him after that. He told me the guy was already being prosecuted on a stronger case, and with no witness, it is only an allegation. I had to explain to the victim what SJA had told me and asked if she would be able to write a statement saying the perpetrator did not hear her, and that he, like her, wanted a career in the air force. She did write and sign the consensual sex statement.

*The military culture designed to protect men who rape is evident: in the way investigations are done or not done, the way statements/testimony are changed to reflect their protective interests, and the way JAG Corps insists on a made up story that protects rapists from accountability and the military itself from admitting there is a problem. Women are expected to shoulder the blame, the effects on their health and career and suffer in silence, while the men and the military act as though it never happened. That high level of discounting is what maintains this culture; because if the military denies any sexual assault problem, rape is accepted and there is nothing the military needs to change.*

I was depressed and had tremendous conflict inside while that was going on. I could not deal with it. I had a counselor on base but felt too constrained to say much. I decided to go off base. I had so many hoops to go through to get counseling off base, and then the counselor went on vacation and subsequently transferred, so I did not get any support at that time.

October 2003, I married a civilian pilot and in July 2004, I was sent to Davis-Monthan AFB in Tucson, AZ, where all the old planes were housed. I heard stories of the SJA there not standing behind and supporting their JAG Officers and pitting one against the other. Their SJA was reportedly very hard on JAG Officers and more lenient on sergeants. I was not in a hurry to get there because we worked long hours and when I did get down there the SJA yelled a lot, called us stupid, and treated us like dogs. There was no sense of community in the office. My husband thought he would be able to get a job in Tucson, and I planned to take the Arizona bar exam. I told the SJA I was going to be taking the bar exam and he said I would not get any time off and he was not very positive or enthusiastic about it. My predecessor hated the SJA, left the office in a mess, I was told to clean it up and paint it.

Then I was assigned as advocate for domestic violence victims and as liaison to the community and on base for any victims of abuse or violence. I was also chief of civil law. I began work the first week I was there to create the liaison position, which was brand new and had not existed before. It was difficult to hear the victim's stories because I had grown up with it myself. My dad was an abusive alcoholic my entire childhood. Once my dad tried to push my mom out of the car while it was moving, because he was angry with her. He also punched her, threw her against a wall and hit her with a chair. When I was in junior high school I called 911, and my dad was arrested. Twice he was arrested before I left home. I kept telling my mom to divorce him. He threatened her that if she tried to get a divorce he would steal all the money and leave the country. All of that was why I decided to be a lawyer and study family law. Maybe I should have told the SJA how challenging the job was, but I did not want to appear weak.

July 23-25, 2004, one week before the bar exam, I was going to study and my husband was gone. I learned that weekend was to be a training exercise and we were to rotate six-hour shifts. No one was allowed off. I was assigned to start Friday night and I was getting really stressed, overwhelmed and felt trapped because that meant little study time. I was having suicidal thoughts. I had been trying to get a counselor off post, but I had not finished going through the hoops yet to make it happen. I made a crisis call to the base hospital mental health professional because I was an emotional mess. They suggested I see a psychiatrist and get on some antidepressants. I had previously been diagnosed with chronic depression at Fairchild and I was trying to manage with meditation and yoga. I talked with a psychiatrist, who did start me on antidepressants. Since I was supposed to be at the training, my SJA was notified. I planned to go to work at 8 p.m. as scheduled so did what I could to sleep during the day. I pulled the drapes closed, put in earplugs to try and sleep. I was awakened suddenly and startled when my dog was growling and I saw my boss in my bedroom. Because my door was locked and I had turned off the phone, they thought I had overdosed. Instead I was awoke in a panic and ended up having a full-blown panic attack and going to the emergency room. My SJA had been trying to call to tell me to wear a specific uniform and because he could not get me on the phone he came to my room and I ended up in the hospital all weekend, when I was supposed to be taking the bar exam.

The doctors told me that since I had repeated panic attacks I would need to have a full psychiatric evaluation at the veterans hospital if I wanted to stay in the air force. I did go for the evaluation, but it was noisy and bright in the hospital and I could not sleep and I was not at my best. Because of all that was going on I decided not to stay in the air force. I also began to wonder if I might be pregnant and if that was contributing to what I was experiencing. I did have a pregnancy test and I was, indeed, pregnant. Once I learned that, I knew for sure that I was not going to stay in the air force and understood that was why I was so sensitive. I remember being told when I got to Davis-Monthan that JAG's were being deployed when they had enough experience. I heard many horror stories of sergeants being sent to Iraq without proper information, training, equipment and saw other JAG Officers deploy when they were pregnant. All of those stories had me scared for myself.

I left the VA and sat down with the commander and the SJA. They told me I had to go to a medical board to show I was not qualified and they raised the question of whether I was fit when I came into military service. It took five months to get all of that done and during that time I was having a difficult pregnancy with morning sickness. I missed a lot of work and was given no empathy. I was either sick and throwing up, or I was not on duty. My uniforms did not fit well anymore and I was often late because I was throwing up. I was yelled at constantly and was unable to prosecute my cases because I did not have a uniform that fit.

I was discharged without benefits and told I had a pre-existing condition. Later they said that they misread the dates in my records. I had to go before another medical board to change that. I called all my friends in Washington, D.C., who were JAG Officers, and asked them what words to use and what to say to get through all of it. I do not know how any woman can get through a board like that who is not an attorney or doesn't have someone helping them.

*It is a very difficult, stressful and tedious process. There are some women veterans who act as advocates for other women veterans to file their claims and to go through VA and medical boards for benefits. Colleen Mussolino and Irish were two women veterans who served as advocates but have since died. Susan Avila-Smith and Kathleen Hoffman are doing that work now and are good resources along with local Disabled American Veterans (DAV) service officers.*

I went to a medical board at Lackland AFB and they agreed that all my issues took place in the air force and I was given an honorable medical discharge and with access to my benefits.

I was discharged February 14, 2005, left Arizona and came to Port Angeles, Washington. My husband got his old job back and we bought a house. My son was born five weeks early. I was concerned about the effects of the antidepressants, the panic attacks and my stress on him, but he seems to be healthy and OK. I took time off to be with him and raise him. I stayed up on my legal career and licenses and then in February 2007, I opened my own office.

# Emily Horswill- WWII

*Emily is a delightful strong-minded, feisty, 88 year-old WWII Veteran, who has been an outspoken activist and environmentalist for many years. I met with her in her retirement home. She was four years old when she walked one and one half miles with three other children to the little red schoolhouse. They later went in a horse and buggy. Emily had her first article published at age 13; it was called, "You want to Cut Down Homes Protecting All God's Little Creatures." She graduated high school during the great depression in 1938 and moved to the Pacific Northwest in 1943, for writing and teaching. She took a job at Boeing during the time of Joseph McCarthy and refused to sign his document: a guarantee that she did not believe in socialism.*

The McCarthy document was a diatribe against left wing liberal beliefs, so I lost my job and they took away my right to work card. I only had fifty cents, so I found an old basement to live in with an overrunning toilet. I chopped wood to heat it and eat.

I worked nine hours a day, six days a week until that day I lost my job. Some days, even when foggy, I walked down to the waterfront. My last night, it was snowy and rainy and a man at Boeing was being very pushy and wanted sex. I refused him and jumped out a window fourteen feet above ground. I walked for miles into town in the rain and snow and was soaked. I ended up with pneumonia and could not pay the rent so the apartment managers threw my stuff out. I knew I could clean and started doing that for income. I scrubbed floors and walls in houses. The recruiters were everywhere in those days and they told me if I signed up I could get an education.

I was twenty-three and signed up for the army air force (which no longer exists) and was sent to Des Moines, Iowa for eight weeks of basic training. The women had separate barracks. I was up at four a.m. for exercise and not done until eight p.m. If I needed to go to sick call it was a three-mile walk to the clinic. It was midwinter then and my boots would freeze and stick to my skin. I marched ten to twelve miles a day. The worst of it was having to clean bathtubs without having any soap or scouring bricks. I had KP duty every night in basic and got so tired I forgot to salute. It was a long time standing in line to get a paycheck of $50 a month. I'd even fall asleep in line.

My first duty station was in Washington, D.C. baking bread. There were three of us working in the bakery with no air-conditioning. I got sick. They shipped me to California to Fairfield Air Force Base. I was in the bakery again while big planes came in. Some never returned. On the weekends I went to the USO in San Francisco. I took the bus. Once or twice I stayed at Fairfield. I did not mingle much, although I did go to a few dances because it was a very unpleasant requirement. Once a guy from the navy told me he was taking me to eat. I told him my boyfriend died, and he said, "I'll let you go then, and you don't want to know what I was going to do to you." Emily looked at me then and said, "We were there to service the men you know, it was never spoken, but that was the attitude."

One night I went to meet a guy and I couldn't get the bus back. Another military man offered to give me a ride in the cab. He was on the same base as me. I had to fight him off and finally the cab driver stopped the cab and threw him out. Then something wonderful happened. The captain who ran the bakery saw me being smarter than the others and asked me to come to his office. He said, "Do you know anything about nutrition?" I said yes, and he told me he intended to start a flight kitchen and fix the flyers good food in sacks for their flights. He asked what I would put in them and then he said he wanted me to take over the kitchen. He made me a tech four. There were two other women in the kitchen; one was a corporal and the other a sergeant. He told me the crew would resent me for this and he gave me some books to read. I studied at night.

One night I was in tears, it was about 10:30 p.m. and I was not in bed check; I was still studying. Then I left and went out in the rain and sleet. Someone called my name. It was a guy who played the piano and had a gold cadillac. This guy was seen driving around base a lot. He asked me where the Bachelor Officer Quarters (BOQ) was. I showed him. He was drunk and picked me up and carried me to the furnace room. I couldn't get away and I froze in fear. The next thing I knew I was on the floor in pools of blood and it was about three a.m. I saw a light coming under the door. I did not know what to do. My clothes and coat were covered in blood. I took it to the laundry and went back to the barracks. I was weak, sick and exhausted. I told no one. I was sharing a room with a nurse who had agreed to put pillows in my bed as though I was there, when I studied late at the library. I couldn't go to work that day and for the next few days. I never told anyone until I told you today. *Emily was silent about her rape for over 64 years.*

I would get notes from guys saying to meet them and they would take care of me. I dated one guy later and he said the rapist had taken my bloodstained panties and bragged to the guys that he had me, when no one else could. Later I got sick to my stomach and went to the doctor. He said I was pregnant and said, "If you tell anyone who did this to you, we will all rape you." *A terrifying threat that Emily believed.*

The rapist was the son of a state senator from Oklahoma. They would not let me off the base. I was terrified, grief stricken and pregnant. What could I do? One woman, a lieutenant, talked to me and she offered to give me another test and maybe I could get out at a higher rank. I went back to work for another two months. I was shunned in the dining room, and everyone stared at me. The woman lieutenant asked me who did this to me, and what happened. I did not tell her, because I was terrified they would all rape me. Then I was discharged honorably and was sent out to the Salvation Army Home in Denver, Colorado. I worked in a hamburger shop until I got so big I couldn't.

*Emily actually received better treatment than others who were raped and became pregnant. She at least was given an honorable discharge and sent to a home for unwed mothers. Nonetheless, the military culture of abuse, which protected rapists while punishing the women they raped and impregnated, was evident in the 1940's and continues to this day.*

I couldn't face people. I was alone. My family was in Seattle. They paid my rent, but would not let me come home. I didn't tell them I was raped. When the baby came I was very ill with a kidney infection, and then I got the flu. My baby was very pretty and everyone wanted to adopt her. She was five pounds and ten ounces. I could not work and care for her. A Red Cross woman came to help when I was trying to nurse the baby. I was sick and vomiting because of the kidney infection. I also did not trust the man who managed the apartments and I put the furniture up against the door. There were soldiers walking up and down in front of the apartments. I went to the Salvation Army Home until I was well again.

The Red Cross woman got me a job taking care of a home and baby, for a doctor and his wife. I lived in the basement. I was not doing very well with it and went back to the woman who got me the job. She insisted on calling my dad. He knew nothing of what I was going through. He told my mom, "She is my daughter and is always welcome in my home." He brought me back home. I was in a small plane bouncing around in a storm and a young man on the plane held my daughter most of the way. My dad picked me up when we landed. He was in his 50's and worked as a janitor. When I got home it was my daughter, four brothers, myself and mom and dad. It was my dad who washed the diapers after he returned from work, while I was still very sick with the kidney infection. My brothers were looking for jobs of which there were none. I finally told my father, mother, and brothers about the rape; only my mother treated me badly. She told me to do the housework, and cooking. It was a lot of work and I did what I could, being so sick and having the baby. My mother cried that she couldn't have her friends over. One night she made me hide in the bedroom.

My old high school boyfriend came out to visit and took me out. He held the baby and admired her and confronted my mother for the way she treated me. I remember I had no clothes for the baby or rubber pants. The neighbors were very good to me and helpful. One day they told my mother off and said, "You have a wonderful daughter and a beautiful granddaughter and you are abusing them." My mother told my daughter, Annette, when she was three—"You know your mother has no brains."

I found out I was born with a horseshoe kidney, which did not drain right. When my daughter was eighteen months old I told my mom I was going to work. She said I had to stay home and care for the men. Mother would spoil Annette and destroyed my relationship with her.

I decided to leave my parents' house with Annette and get a job. I was so poor, I could not afford a coat for Annette and it was very cold. I worked for the army on the waterfront. One day I passed out on the street with Annette beside me. I was taken to a doctor and my boyfriend Ernie came to get me. We got married in a church in Seattle, and he became a fine artist and cared for Annette and me. I began writing again in the columns.

Before I came to Seattle, I had a job at the *Minnesota Star newspaper.* I started building a home in Minnesota and saw the forest, and fell in love with the trees.

By the 1980's I was writing 2500 word articles a week when Reagan took office. He didn't like what I was saying. In 1979 to 1981 I was the Outdoor Conservationist Columnist for the *Daily Olympian.* In 1989 I won the Spur Award and one day in 1989 a New York agent ran after me and said, "I want to syndicate your column nationally. Your work is unforgettable." I signed a contract with the *Post Intelligencer* and the New York agent. I was getting well known and helped pass the Wilderness Act, which was unanimously approved by Congress.

By 1988 I had received over twenty awards for writing. I am most proud of the Doctor of Arts of Peace. The recognition of a lifetime devoted to creating a better life for all in this world; a peaceful planet. It is my responsibility to tell the truth to the people, because only in that way can we have a democracy of the people, by the people, and for the people. It is the same for all reporters in print and electronic media.

*Emily went from joy to sadness as she tells me:* Annette is dying; she had surgery for a brain tumor. Annette loved the farm and became an excellent mechanic. She could tear anything apart and put it back together again. She also became a carpenter. Annette is amazing. I have three books I am trying to publish, and if I can, then I can pay for Annette to get help.

## Sandy – Vietnam Era

I was living in Bremerton, WA in 1971, and could not afford college, so I joined the Women's Army Corps. I am part Cherokee and was not quite 20 years old. I went to basic at Fort McClellan, AL, where I trained with only women for eight weeks. The sergeants degraded us and called us names like stupid and dumb. When we had to go into the gas chamber, there was a thick white gas in there. It burned my eyes, and I was coughing and choking because my mask was leaking. A man tried to help me and took me out. I was still choking and coughing but the fresh air felt good. Fortunately, I did not have to go back in. I went to classes, learned to march, and also had KP duty in the kitchen.

From basic I went to Advanced Infantry Training (AIT) to be a clerk typist. For six weeks I learned to do office work. I then became 'permanent party,' as a ward clerk in the outpatient department of Noble Army Hospital at Fort McClellan. One night at the Non Commissioned Officer (NCO) club, a black guy came to me and said, "You better get out of here because there is going to be trouble; use the back door." No way, I told him.

"OK when we come back here, just scream as though I am hurting you, and I won't hurt you, because I want to save your little white ass."

Ten minutes later a group of black males came into the club. They had just turned over a bus and torched it. Then they came to the club with baseball bats, chains, and knives and they started beating people up and throwing furniture around. The NCO, who told me to get out, came over, picked me up and pushed me out shouting, "Get your ass back to the barracks and don't use the roads or the buses!" I was scared then and went through the woods. I got back to the barracks and it was trashed! There were toilet seats pulled out of the bathrooms, mirrors and showers broken, and there was graffiti all over the walls in black spray paint. When I got to my room it was not trashed, but there was a black guy on top of my roommate raping her. I screamed! The black guy, who had warned me, came in at that moment and yelled at the rapist, "You get the fuck off of her and get the hell out of here NOW!"

We were all in lock-down for seventy-two hours as the race riot continued. I was transported back and forth between the base and the mobile home, where the gay guys lived. That was where they said it was safe for the women to stay during the riots. The gay guys protected us. Later I went back to work and the ER was full of those who were hurt in the riot. I triaged all of them and it went on for seventy-two hours. There was mass destruction from the riot, and it all got into the TV news. We were in blackout and could not leave post or have contact with anyone off post.

After the riot there was no debriefing or counseling; it was just business as usual. One day our commander came into the ER, began to talk and then passed out. He had a heart attack, had open-heart surgery, and was back to work in six weeks.

I was promoted to E-4 and sent to Fort Sam to be a medic, and then went on to Fort Belvior, VA. One day I was walking on post when a man in a black mask and gloves grabbed me, took me into the woods and raped me at knifepoint. I blacked out. Later I woke up and realized what happened. The next day I went to the ER and they examined me. They blamed me for being in the wrong place. They did not offer me any counseling or help. About a month later, I went to the clinic for abdominal pain and problems urinating. They apparently did a pregnancy test but did not tell me or offer me any prenatal care or help. They said there was nothing wrong with me. I knew there was something not right, so I went to a civilian doctor who told me I was pregnant. I tried to get out of the army, but was sent to Fort Lewis in Tacoma, WA, until they discharged me in February of 1974. My baby was born the next month. She had spina bifida (incomplete development of the brain, spinal cord, and/or their protective coverings, caused by the failure of the fetus's spine to close properly during the first month of pregnancy). *Depending on what chemicals Sandy was exposed to at Fort McClellan, she could potentially have a claim for the spina bifida in her daughter, which is one of the birth defect conditions for exposure to Agent Orange.*

I was honorably discharged so was able to get health benefits and the GI Bill. I had problems after I got out and ended up being the first woman in the sexual trauma program at the Seattle VA. That was in September 2001. Doctor Wendy Smith was my counselor. I was talking about the rape and what happened and starting to let it go, when two other women vets with MST began to swear at me, called me a liar, and told Dr. Smith to go to hell. I couldn't believe it. She just sat there and didn't do anything to stop it. I left in tears and slammed the door. At my next appointment with Wendy, she asked me to take responsibility for what happened in the group.

In August of 2003, I had a breakdown when Department of Social and Health Services (DSHS) housing evicted my daughter and me. They withdrew my contract to care for my daughter, Marie, and they took her away. They made her a ward of the State and I lost everything I owned and everything I cared about. I was homeless and went to an emergency shelter. It was a crazy place. I left and went to the YWCA, which was safer until I could get to the VA hospital. I spent a week on 7E at the Veterans Administration Medical Center, suicidal, not eating or sleeping. I was in a fetal position and did not want to talk with anyone. There were only two women there and I was one of them. I blacked out when I saw a man sitting in a chair with one leg up and his private parts hanging out. He called me a fat ass bitch. I learned later that I was very violent when I was blacked out and threw chairs and other furniture. After one week they discharged me and I was back out on the street.

I called to try and get back in and talked with the psych on duty. He told me to go through the ER. I did that and got back in. While I was there I demanded they find me safe housing and transportation back to see Dr. Cantor, who was helping me. They got me a place at a boarding home and I was back at the VA four times a week. I had one on one time with Dr. Cantor and I was in a group and in activity groups. That is when I filed my claim for PTSD and MST, which they lost twice.

I got help from Disabled American Veterans (DAV). They found my file and saw that nothing had been done. March 2005, the VA approved my claim on appeal for Post Traumatic Stress Disorder (PTSD) from Military Sexual Trauma (MST). I received 70% service connected MST and 30 % unemployable PTSD. In the letter it said, "We conceded the veteran was reporting the event as it happened."

Then I got on www.Military.com and Vet Wow, and found out I was not alone in my experiences. I also found out that PTSD cannot be cured and I just have to live with it and take meds to function.

Marie is thirty-three now and in an adult family home. They would not give her the care she needed and I am filing charges to get her care returned to me. I am now married to a wonderful man and have my own service dog. He is a golden retriever and we all live in a simple home together.

*The Veterans Administration holds the belief that PTSD cannot be cured; that it is something veterans have to live with. They treat the symptoms only and usually with medications. As a nurse psychotherapist, I have been doing trauma resolution work with veterans and civilians for over 25 years, and can truthfully say that all of them have healed from their PTSD. The therapy work is long and painful at times, yet the outcome is well worth it. To heal they must be willing to remember and feel the feelings that go with the memories. It works best in a supportive group atmosphere. The therapist must be able to stay fully present with the veteran, as they describe their traumatic experiences, and be able to handle the intense feelings that come with those experiences. I will elaborate on all this in my next book, Women Under Fire: PTSD and Healing.*

# Military Sexual Trauma and Punishment

*Military Sexual Trauma is any sexual abuse experienced in the Military from sexual harassment, sexual assault, to rape. It is a personal and sexual boundary violation and affects the victim emotionally, physically and spiritually. The victim (I will now refer to as a woman) experiences extreme vulnerability, helplessness, shame, humiliation, a breach in her sense of self and bodily integrity, and a lowered sense of self-esteem and self-confidence. If a fellow soldier, or worse, a superior of higher rank, perpetrated the violation, the woman experiences betrayal. For those who perceive their military unit or the corps as family, the violation equates to incest. One of their own has violated them.*

*From that moment on she feels unsafe in the military. She has no sense of being protected and safe. She experiences a clear violation and betrayal of the values taught in the military such as honor, respect, accountability, fellowship. She can no longer count on her brother soldiers to 'have her back' in combat. It has been referred to as a grievous psychological injury and is an assault on her as a person, her sense of self and her soul, which leaves her reeling in confusion, shock, shame, dismay, disintegration and dissociation. The woman often becomes numb from the dissociation and has less access to her internal resources, even the ability to speak, ask for help, or tell what happened.*

*MST leads to PTSD—the symptoms begin while the assault is happening; the woman becomes numb and often dissociates. The numbness or dissociation is automatic and unconscious. The woman's sense of self and bodily integrity have been so violated, that she is unable to stay connected fully to her body and the abusive experience, so she unconsciously attempts to cope in the moment by splitting off part of herself, her energy, her personality. This is often what happens in other traumatic experiences such as combat or combat injury. When the psyche is overwhelmed by an extremely stressful experience beyond what is ordinary, the self decides, "I am out of here" and will energetically lift up from the body and observe what is happening to the body. The body is fully experiencing, but the psyche and sense of self, splits off, along with the emotions. This dynamic occurs to preserve the self and later becomes the problem to be solved therapeutically, to reconnect all parts of the person, body and emotions, for full healthy functioning.*

*Forty to sixty percent of women with MST go on to have a full-blown case of PTSD. MST is the number one cause of PTSD in the Military.*[69]

## Symptoms which may arise as a result of MST include:

*Shame and humiliation*
*Anxiety and despair*
*Feeling dirty/unclean*
*Lack of trust in men*
*Health issues*

*Can lead to abuse of alcohol or drugs and poor work performance, sexual dysfunction, problems with intimacy and relationships.*

*From the MST, which is the trauma, often leads to PTSD, which is a survivor reaction to an overwhelming stressor or catastrophe.*

*It is characterized by the following symptoms:*

1. *Emotional numbing: an attempt to wall off your feelings.*

2. *Depression.*

3. *Alienation: split off from feelings, from oneself and others, can't connect.*

4. *Anger and Rage are natural when you feel helpless and powerless.*

-----------------------------------------------------------------

[69]*http://www.casapalmera.com/articles/symptoms-of-post-traumatic-stress-disorder-and-Military- sexual-trauma/Moffeit and Herdy, "Betrayal In the Ranks."*

5. *Guilt—"why didn't I" move faster, get away, see it coming, etc.*

6. *Anxiety and Fears—may be specific to type of traumatic event, i.e., rape, combat.*

7. *Intrusive thoughts:are uninvited, occur anytime, and relate to the trauma.*

8. *Nightmares.*

9. *Flashbacks, a state in which you see, hear, feel, as though you are back in the traumatic event as though it is happening now. The trauma is literally stored in the brain as though it is still happening, which is why it is difficult to "get over it" without therapy.*

10. *Helplessness.*

11. *Hyper-vigilance—constantly searching the environment for danger.*

12. *Hyper-alertness-startle reaction.*

13. *Hypersensitivity to anything that is a reminder of the traumatic event.*

14. *Avoidance of activities that trigger recall of the trauma.*

15. *Isolation—feel distant from others and keep to yourself.*

16. *Mental turmoil – trying to deal with the world outside and your own inner world, while staying safe, blocking feelings, having flashbacks, and intrusive thoughts and trying to understand what is happening to you.*

17. *Attempts at control-this is often seen immediately after a trauma as people are doing some simple repetitive unnecessary action, like taking showers for hours, putting a hubcap on a demolished car, raking leaves by a burned out home, picking up glass fragments after a devastating explosion. This is also an ongoing symptom trying to control everything because inside she feels everything is out of control.*

18. *Emotional labiality— believing that if I get angry I might kill someone, or if I start crying I won't be able to stop. Emotions flood the psyche spontaneously.*

19. *Fear the replay of traumatic event — fear of flashbacks and memories of event.*

20. *Difficulty concentrating.*

21. *Crying spells.*

22. *Suicidal thoughts, feelings, actions*

23. *Loss of Memory – often occurs after the numbing sets in and one may lose memories of the event or parts of it.*

24. *Negative self-image and low self-esteem.*

25. *Problems with intimacy can't trust self or others.*

26. *Elite,no one could possibly understand what happened to me or how I feel since the traumatic event.*

27. *Contaminated—marked for life, never be the same, always be damaged goods.*

28.    *Loss of interest in work and activities.*

29.    *Fatigue from psychic energy used to defend against feelings, intrusive thoughts and memories.*

30.    *Cynicism lack of trust in authorities and systems.*

# Elsa Nethercot – Grenada/Persian Gulf War Era

*Before I heard from Elsa I was feeling sad about all the women whose stories were of sexual abuse in the military. I looked over the stories and saw that it included the army, navy, and air force. Sitting at my computer I said to myself, "At least the coast guard is not involved in this kind of behavior." The very next day I received an email from Elsa telling me she was in the coast guard and had a story of sexual abuse. My body sagged at that point; feeling the weight of knowing how pervasive the culture of abuse was in all the Armed Forces of the United States of America and wondering if writing this would help. Here is Elsa's story.*

When I was six years old in the 1960's, growing up by Puget Sound, I saw a Lassie show and knew I wanted to be in the coast guard or be a forest ranger. In high school I put in an application to go to Spokane Falls Community College to a saddle-making class. My boyfriend had been in the coast guard for a year on reserves and I had just turned eighteen. He went to coast guard school near Petaluma, California and sent me a ticket to come visit him. He knew I was unhappy at home and my dad was an alcoholic. For about six weeks, I lived in the guest housing and liked what I saw and heard of the coast guard, so then decided to sign up.

I went to boot camp January 2, 1982 at Cape May, N. J. for seven weeks. My recruiter sent me out a day late so when I arrived at Philadelphia International Airport no one else was there. I was told that everyone had been there the day before. The local recruiter put me on a bus to Cape May. When I got there, I was cold and scared. All the guys had just gotten their heads shaved, and I had long straight hair down to my waist.

Boot camp was a big "mind fuck." All the women went to Cape May and I was the only one from the West Coast. I felt like a foreigner. Since I was a day late, I missed the first bonding experience and then was somewhat isolated.

There were only seventeen in our company and I was able to make some friends. Boot camp was easy for me and I was selected as company yeoman. There were times I worked in the company commander's office, unsupervised, doing clerical work.

One day near the end of boot camp, I was working by the wall and the company commander came in. He walked up to me and put his arms around me and touched my breast and tried to kiss me. I was able to walk around him, turn and keep walking away and talking as I left the office. I was never comfortable with him again after that, and nothing was ever said between us either.

From boot camp, I went to A-school in Petaluma, California to be a radioman. I was there for six months from March to August of 1982. There were six women and eight to ten men in the class. I got along great with my classmates and the teachers were good. We were learning Morse Code, radio communications and Teletype.

I had met a coast guard corpsman at the hospital when I visited previously, so we became friends easily and then sexual partners.

At one point I had a vaginal infection and went to the clinic. He was there and immediately said, "You didn't get this from me," and he treated me badly and stopped seeing me. He was my only partner and I wondered what he was so scared about. I actually had a yeast infection.

We could drink at age eighteen on base, so there were kids getting trashed on base a lot. I don't really drink that much but when I do, I get drunk, so I stay away from it. I don't want to be an alcoholic like my dad. Towards the last month in school, I was visiting a friend and her husband who lived on eight hundred acres. They were boarding my horse and caring for my kitty. I hung out there instead of the barracks and would ride my horse after class. A shipmate was drinking one night and crashed there because he couldn't drive. In the middle of the night he sexually assaulted me. I froze. I could not speak or move. I felt abject terror. It was different being raped than consenting to sex with someone. I kept saying to myself, "What the hell is wrong with me. Why can't I move?" I wished I had known about the freeze response back then. After that night, I stopped going there and had someone else watch my kitty.

*A freeze response to an attack or trauma is actually the most common response. When someone freezes they no longer have access to their internal resources or abilities to respond in action or words. In another situation she would be able to move or yell but when "frozen" she cannot and the freeze response signals a trauma/assault in progress. This disability, in the face of sexual assault, is what the military needs to learn about because at present, they discount that and attempt to redefine an assault as consensual. When there is coercion, threats, or force used, it is not consensual, and often there is a big difference in rank, power or authority between the perpetrator and the victim. The freeze response also includes the entire assault being frozen within her brain, nervous system, cellular memory, and her energy. The energy flow is disrupted. Anything resembling the trauma can re-trigger a freeze response.*

While I was assigned to a reserve unit in Spokane, WA, I was asleep in a trailer when an E-6, petty officer first class came in and raped me. I froze again. Shortly after that, I went back to active duty.

In October 1985, I was at the Coast Guard Communication System in San Francisco, Point Reyes Station in the middle of nowhere. For two years I was operating a boat and had not used my radio skills, so I was not qualified and had little self-esteem. I was told I was a burden and should not even be a radioman. I already believed what my dad said about me; that I was "stupid, worthless and sick," so I believed the coast guard assessment of me as well.

I met a master chief there, who was nice to me. I was so naïve and hungry for a positive relationship that when he asked me out, I said yes. Late on a weekend night, he took me to his house and his kids were there. I was only six years older than his daughter, who was sixteen. I learned that his wife had committed suicide and that she had been in the coast guard and had many medical problems. He was a really nice guy and I liked him. By Thanksgiving he asked me to marry him and I thought it was great. Our command was not happy and the master chief was reprimanded. I was transferred to group San Francisco and about seven months later we were married.

The unit I transferred to was similar to the unit in Seattle and I really liked it. I was there for two and one half years until October 1988.

I was depressed and had counseling many times, because my relationship to the kids and my husband was not going well. Six months later we divorced.

I put in a request for rate change to boatswain's mate and was sent to boatswain's mate school in Yorktown, Virginia for eight weeks. I was the only woman there. During my training a few of my shipmates didn't believe a woman should be in the coast guard. I became anorexic because I was doing extra time on boats, working hard to excel and skipping meals. I lost about twenty-eight pounds. I was a petty officer, due to my time in service, and my classmates were not very happy because they had more experience on boats but I had higher rank.

I graduated #1 in the class, yet was not given my assigned choice. Instead I was sent to Support Center, Fire Department, Kodiak, Alaska. When I complained, I was sent to the psychologist, who said, "You accept these orders or I sign you off as not fit for duty and discharge you." The job was not in my specialty. They were making me be a firefighter. It made no sense and seemed a waste after all the training to be a boatswain's mate.

*It seems to me that they were discriminating against her because she was female, rather than keep to appropriate standards and give the job to the most qualified person. The abuse here is the coercion to do what they wanted, even though it was not what she was qualified for, trained for, and not what she requested.*

I accepted the assignment at Kodiak and decided to do the best I could. There were two shifts, A and B. I found out that 'A' shift was considered the "squared away" high performers, and that 'B' shift had issues. We worked twenty-four hours on and twenty-four hours off. I was put on B shift, and was moved in to take the job of a male petty officer, who was unhappy. I had to sleep in the same berthing area as the men, but I had a private head and shower. I was there for eighteen months. All the guys were allowed to go to Chanute AFB Fire Fighting Academy and I was not allowed to go, because they did not think I could pass the physical, yet they still expected me to do the same job.

I had 20/400 vision and they would not provide glasses that would fit beneath my self-contained breathing apparatus (SCBA). So for the entire time I was there, if I had to put on my SCBA to go into a fire, I had to go in without being able to see.

*The decision for Elsa not to have glasses going into a fire was extremely dangerous for her and anyone else involved with the fire. It often seems that the military makes decisions like that to try and force a woman out of the service. I am sure there was a way to provide a SCBA with lenses so she could see well.*

There was a lot of bullying going on, especially from the E-3 I had replaced. The bullying was constant and very painful. When the E-3 acted disrespectfully to me, or bullied me, everyone would laugh. My shipmates would say things like, "Baloney nipples, you're only saying that because you're on the rag. You're not going into the fire with us, because you could get us killed."

*I believe it was a command responsibility to stop the inappropriate behavior and uphold the standards of conduct for the coast guard. Here are examples of sexual harassment that were obviously supported by the coast guard since they did nothing to stop it.*

I tried to be one of them, but I did not drink. They made me miserable. Then a new guy came; he was more like me, liked the outdoors and didn't drink. Rumors started because we were friends and he was transferred to the other shift. I was being grabbed, pinched, breasts groped, and they'd hold my arms and legs and act as though they were having sex with me, dry humped. Everyone laughed and I was humiliated and felt powerless.

I continued to work extra to advance and I qualified for E-5. I worked on small boats and visiting cutters. I was the only one who advanced to the next pay grade. I qualified for engines on fire trucks and became the training officer for the Women's Bay Volunteer Fire Department and EMT with the borough of Kodiak.

I was in Kodiak from December 1988, to June of 1990 and requested boatswain at Camp Disappointment in Ilwaco, WA, but instead I was given Aids Navigation Team in Astoria, Wash. I was told that someone else was slotted for Ilwaco, and they never send women there. The commander gave it to a guy with lesser qualifications.

Just before I was due to transfer to Astoria, I was taken to administration and they asked about the abuse. I was asked if it was true. I said, "Yes it was true." I was told if I didn't file charges my orders would be held up. I told them no one would back me and I did not want to file. They continued to insist that if I did not file charges, I could not transfer; so I filed sexual harassment charges. Then they built a partition around my rack, (bunk) and the guys thought it was preferential treatment. The Coast Guard Investigative Team (CGI) got no corroboration from anyone. The guys they talked with said, "She liked it, encouraged it, laughed when we grabbed her, and she wore low cut blouses. Women should not be here they're just a waste and a burden!"

I don't know why they put me through six weeks of hell. I was a high performer and advancing, not getting drunk, and they put me through hell! The outcome was, "Insufficient evidence to press charges," which I expected, and why I did not want to press charges.

*As a therapist who works with children who were sexually abused or incested, I often hear similar comments from the man who committed the incest." Oh, she liked it, she wanted it, she is so cute." Often it was the child's dad or uncle saying that. It is the talk of a perpetrator who is defending his indefensible behavior.*

*Here is another example of harassment by the coast guard toward Elsa, insisting she file charges for sexual harassment against her will, so that she will be miserable and they get to say they investigated. This serves no one, not even the coast guard. They have done everything they could to get her out and she remains committed.*

"Boys will be boys" and, "Be a shipmate and suck it up," was their answer to everything. Any woman who complained was labeled unfit and was processed out or threatened with discharge. To stay in the coast guard, I had to develop coping mechanisms that were terribly unhealthy for me. It wasn't until I started counseling that I was able to change the patterns. Today, when I am around people in uniform I switch off. I realized that I'd spent my whole career in the coast guard not looking at faces, because I was afraid of seeing someone who had abused me.

The coast guard was telling several young coast guard women who had been assaulted that since we come under the Department of Homeland Security (DHS), instead of the Department of Defense, the coast guard does not have to follow the changes recommended by the 2004 Task Force. The DHS has no sexual assault policy, so there is no big brother watching over the coast guard. *This is a pretty blatant demonstration of unwillingness to follow directives and begs for congressional oversight.*

In 2005 I was trained as a Sexual Assault Victim Intervention Volunteer, by the navy for the coast guard. I had to fight with my command at the time to be allowed to go to the training, even though commandant funded it. The command wanted me to take leave and pay for it myself. Their reasoning was that it was not required aboard ship and they used the local group/air station for those services. The amazing thing is that they were telling a shipmate, who had been raped in 2004, and received no assistance from my ship or the group/air station. That made no sense either. This same command tried to prevent me from getting counseling. I was told by the corpsman at the time, "40 year old women don't get raped" and my XO and a woman, told me the "coast guard is not obliged to provide assistance or counseling because you were raped off coast guard property."

I have to say if it weren't for the Clatsop County Woman's Resource Center, I would never have made any changes in my life and I most likely would have stood passively by while the coast guard booted me out for unsuitability, even though I had over eighteen years in. When I walked through their door and got validation instead of blamed and blown off, I cried. I have been a client, volunteer and staff member ever since. I was on the county's Domestic and Sexual Assault Response Team, for one year, but it triggered my PTSD and I had to stop. I have also had several suicidal bouts when I thought about taking my life. While on ship there were times I wouldn't get out of my rack when we were underway, unless I had a watch, because I was so depressed. I felt like I could walk to the fantail and step off. That was my lowest point.

I feel like I can best serve the coast guard now by being able to be a voice that says YOU DO HAVE A PROBLEM! Since I only made it to E-6 many of the junior enlisted folks can relate to me and not be intimidated. It seems that to be heard in the coast guard you have to be a cadet or in a combat situation. Those that serve stateside slip through the cracks.

*When Congress finally acts to authorize investigations and change to the culture of abuse in our military, the coast guard needs to be included in that. Since they now come under Homeland Security, they will still need to comply with rules and guidelines regarding respect, equality and justice for women in our armed forces.*

# Cindy - Vietnam Era

*Cindy attended Kent State University. She wanted to be a journalist in the military and signed up with the air force in 1974. She went to basic training in San Antonio, Texas and her first duty assignment was in Biloxi, Mississippi as an administrative assistant. While there, she got a group together and worked at a children's home with abandoned babies.*

*Her next assignment was to Westover Air Force Base (AFB) in Massachusetts. She was an administrative assistant there until they closed the base and sent her to Hanscom AFB. At Hanscom she switched to the navy and went to their basic at Orlando, Florida.*

*Her first navy duty was as a cryptotech, monitoring Morse Code at the Pensacola Naval Air Station (NAS). From there she went to San Vito NAS at Brindisi, Italy and again she was a crypto-technician. She was happy to go to Italy because she wanted to see some of the world. Cindy felt secure in the military.*

*She was very active on base, played on the navy soccer and softball teams. Cindy describes herself as a number one tomboy; grew up with two older brothers and had many friends. Her story gets intense as she returns with the softball team after playing in Naples. They returned to base tired, sweaty and dirty, yet excited because they won all their games.*

I was still in my uniform and went with the girl across the hall in my barracks to find the other team members who didn't go with us to Naples. They were all going to the NCO club. I just wanted to go to my room, take a long shower and go to sleep. They all persuaded me to go with them to the club where the team was celebrating. The girl (I can't remember her name) across from me in the barracks did not drink beer and neither did I. We drank amaretto. I had two shots of that and I was so tired I started to leave. I said my good byes and headed for the door. When I got to the door of the club, Chief T. was there and offered me a lift back to the barracks. He was our chief petty officer. A group of us had gone to his house many times. We knew his wife and kids, played darts, backgammon, and had barbecues at his house. I felt safe with him. I do remember thinking it was a little strange to ride to the barracks since it was so close, but I was tired and feeling lazy so I said yes.

He was driving a cargo van with two seats in the front and some seats in the back, but empty space between the front and back seats. There were no windows on the side of the van. He pulled up to the other end of the barracks, the side nobody uses. There was a big tree there and he parked under it. My room was at the other end. I was talking about how great the games were and how I played. I was not really paying any attention until he stopped. I started to get out of the van and he grabbed my arm. When I turned to look at him, he kissed me. I pulled away and he said, "I want you and you want me."

I told him no, I only want to leave. The next memory I have is him on top of me and feeling the hard floor under me and hurting me as he was pulling down my pants and lifting my shirt. I was crying then, telling him to stop and leave me alone. I remember saying I was not taking any birth control pills, thinking it would scare him off me. I don't remember anything more then, until I am curled up on the floor of my room sitting in the corner crying and waiting for my friend to come home. I was scared and didn't know what to do or where to go.

I don't know how I ended up speaking with her that night? Maybe she saw my lights on and came over, but I remember her sitting on the floor with me the entire night. We called Lieutenant S. very early the next morning and told her what happened. She met us at the chow hall. It was a weekend morning so the chow hall was pretty empty. We sat in an area where we wouldn't be disturbed and then Chief T. walked in. We all knew that he saw us and knew I was reporting what happened. He walked over to our table and said, "My wife found your ID in my van this morning. I told her you were so drunk you were dropping everything, so I gave you a ride home." Lieutenant S. said, "He just acknowledged he was there." Then he walked away cool as a cucumber. It was at that point I knew my life was going to change. I was no longer a fun person to be around; the volunteer that everyone loved. Instead I was the drunk, unworthy of anything.

Lieutenant S. was going to file a claim the next day and she came to me crying and said, "I am so sorry I can't help you." Within a couple of days Lieutenant S was shipped off to a remote duty station in Turkey. We were left without a female officer. Two weeks later I found out they wrote me up saying I was drunk and disorderly that night. She wrote a statement, which never showed up in my file.

She was never given the opportunity to take statements from any of the others who knew what happened. I was numb, shocked and hysterical. There was a statement in the file saying I showed up at the clinic drunk and disorderly; it was all a lie.

*Here once again is the higher-ranking officer feeling entitled to rape this young woman, lie about it and make up an untrue story about her drunkenness, isolate her and remove all support by sending away Lieutenant S, and removing her statement. This is the culture of abuse in action designed to ruin Cindy's career while saving face for the perpetrator, her chief petty officer, and supporting his career.*

One day when I was on duty, I fell for no apparent reason. When a peer went to report it they were told to tell me I had better be STANDING at my post or they would have me court-martialed for abandoning my post. That fall could have been from the Myasthenia Gravis that I was later diagnosed with. I already had some of the symptoms but did not know it then.

My case never went any further. I was suddenly told that I was being discharged with a personality disorder.

*You have seen this one before. It is one of the ways the military preserves its image and insures that the navy will not be responsible for the effects of the rape on the survivor. Cindy will now be denied medical services. This is a dual trauma, first the rape and lies about her being drunk, then a discharge that effectively insures she cannot get the help she needs to deal with the trauma.*

I wanted it all to be over. I wanted my life back, to be that happy go lucky tomboy girl. I was too embarrassed to tell anyone because I thought everyone would blame me. I just wanted to get out.

I tried to file a disability claim with a female officer at Fort Stewart but they said I had to prove the rape. I have spent twenty-five years questioning why I went to the club that night. I wanted a career in the navy and to have fun. It was all taken from me.

It is bad enough to be raped but then to go tell someone and be mistreated, lied about, and treated like I did something wrong is even worse. It has stayed with me all these years and I always wonder if I will be believed about anything now. I don't understand how they can get away with it? How do they put this on national TV and always make it the woman's fault? There is permission for men to do this to women and there is NO ACCOUNTABILITY for them.

# CAT – Persian Gulf Era

*CAT told me right away that when she was six years old and mad at a boy, she said she would marry a man whose last name began with a T, so she could use the initials CAT. She also told her mother that she would be in the marine corps and she did that as well. She is proud to be one of five bassoonists in the marine corps bands and the only woman in the San Diego Marine Corps band of thirty men.*

I believed I could do anything a man could do. I was going to play my bassoon for the rest of my life, and in the military I could increase in rank. I went to the army to join the band and failed by 1/10th of a point. The testing occurred during Desert Storm, so they raised the standards. I scored enough in my audition to have graduated from the military school of music, but just missed the cut off for the army. A guy from the marine corps called to say he heard I was looking for pointers, for an audition to the marine corps band. It turned out to be a full audition with them and I passed with flying colors. They were the elite, the best. I felt proud. Then my mom reminded me that when I was six, I told her I was going to be in the marines. December 10, 1990 I joined the marines.

I went to boot camp at Paris Island, S.C. for thirteen weeks and there were lots of challenges there. They built me and made me strong. I loved that. There were sixty women in boot camp and not all of them made it. One woman went crazy at graduation. She refused to believe boot camp was over; she thought it was a trick. She never got dressed.

While at boot camp I got orders for the school of music at Little Creek, VA. I had a six-month assignment but was there longer when I failed the audition. The second audition was twice as hard as the first one. I had to play every single scale perfectly plus I had to learn to play cymbals. They required a mandatory twenty hours a week of practice in addition to regular band practices and performances. I also had ear training and physical training. I had to look perfect all the time. Finally they had a graduation ceremony and gave me a diploma.

I had orders for New Orleans but another bassoonist complained because he also had orders for New Orleans. He did not pass his second audition and became a tank mechanic. In the meantime they switched my orders to San Diego. So New Orleans did not have a bassoonist and San Diego had no use for a bassoonist. They did only ceremonies and parades and in all my time there I only played bassoon once.

I was five feet eight inches tall, blue-green eyes, and blonde curly hair. I had a big problem with sexual harassment. Before I got there the guys would walk the halls naked or in their skivvies, if they wanted to. I changed their whole environment when I came.

My roommate was known to be bisexual but I did not know that. I was in my room alone a lot. The marine corps wives told their husbands I was off limits to them and the wives wanted nothing to do with me. The only men who would risk being with me were twenty-five year-old sergeants.

Band officers did not like my presence. This was a marching band. At music school they taught me cymbals in addition to my bassoon. When I got to San Diego the band officer gave me an alto sax to play. I had never played a sax before and he gave me the sax and thirty pieces of music to learn. He told me I had thirty days to learn them and be able to play them while marching. I was forced to learn to play the alto sax. There were three of us in that section of the band.

One day a carpool showed up at my door after a birthday party and one of the guys said, "This is my opportunity to have sex with you. My wife just had a baby and she doesn't know I am here." I talked myself out of that one. I told him, "You can't do this to your wife." He grabbed me and pushed me up against the wall lockers and pressed himself against me, spreading my legs, while I kept saying, "You can't do this to your wife. Think how it will affect her!"

The sergeant who taught me to march with the sax was the overall group leader and played clarinet. I asked where was the middle C and he said, "This is a bad idea" I couldn't swing or play jazz. I was trained classical.

When I came to San Diego and was given my room, I met a sergeant who was short and wore glasses. He checked me up and down. One time he took me to dinner and seemed to love the fact that I was under his control. He never even showed me the band hall.

The next morning I had to find it. He began to pick me up to go for coffee before band and he told me he liked his coffee black and his women blonde.

The next day I arrived for inspection and we all stood in line. We did this every morning. Inside the duty station they had to clear out a room specifically for me. It was one step across to the woman's bathroom so I could change clothes and everything. They put all the men, thirty of them, in one room together. My room was bigger than theirs. It did not seem fair to me.

I had a tank top and men's t-shirt cut at the waist so it did not bunch up in my uniform. I went from the bathroom back to my room wearing that. The band officer chewed me out and told me not to wear those again that I was out of uniform. He told me I had to be fully clothed and not wear anything revealing. He told me when to be up in the morning, what to wear, and where to go. We often stayed up until three a.m. practicing. I love to sleep and nap often and the rumors were that I was out partying or sleeping with my roommate. No one would have anything to do with me except a lance corporal, whose wife was pregnant. He invited me to dinner and I went. I was crying to him, you'll have to pick me up. He came with his wife and she took one look at me and said, "How can you do this to me?" She buried her head in his chest. I said please, I'm not mean, I just want a friend, I don't want your husband! He was a funny looking dufus guy.

I was totally naive going in believing I could make it the marines playing my bassoon, and then retire. One night I went out; it was only the second time. I did not have a car, so I had to be asked. This time my roommate asked me to go and I said yes. The lead alto sax player invited himself that night and offered to drive us to the navy bar. The bouncer at the bar approached me and said,

"I can get you a better drink" and he gave me a drink that had already been prepared. A few minutes later I felt sleepy and groggy.

*She was drugged.*

I had never been drunk and thought that was happening to me. We got back to our room and Lisa my roommate left. The sax player got into bed with me and I could not move my arms or legs. I kept trying to say no and the words would not come out. He touched me and put his penis in me and I was fully conscious but paralyzed. I was devastated. He put his rubber in a coke can. I woke up and was sure I was drunk; I could not function. I showered and cleaned up and threw the can away with the rubber in it. I did not know what to do. I told the tuba player. He said I was raped and had to report it. It was Friday January 18th, 1992. I went to the conductor, who was next in command and reported it. He said, "Are you sure you want to do this?" I said yes. He turned it over to Navy Criminal Investigative Service (NCIS).

I went to the hospital and they documented the rape, but it was three days later, Jan. 21, 1992. They did not find anything. I was told not enough evidence to charge him. I was required to stand and sit next to him in the band. He hated me. Sometimes there were only two of us sent to a function. They told me there was nothing they would do about it. The band officers pretended to care and said if there is anything we can do let us know, but made me sit elbow to elbow with the rapist. The rapist told me, "You're stupid, you have no place here; you don't belong!" When I told the band officer he said, "Maybe the guy is right."

February 20th, 1993 I tried to kill myself with pills and alcohol. I was very upset and crying in my room. A trumpet player walked by and said, "Do you need any help?" I said yes and he took me to the hospital. They treated me well but my records say that I am trying to get attention and not really sad. The record also said that I had a fight with my boyfriend and they were concerned because I had a personality disorder and would take my boyfriend off in the corner and have sex with him.

The band officer told me, "The guy and I could not both be telling the truth, one of you is lying." He told me to go to NCIS and tell them I lied. He told me to say I was not raped because it would look bad on the band and the marine corps. I said, but I am not lying. I lay there comatose, unable to move and Zaden did things to me because he knew what to touch to make my body moist. The band officer said, "You must have wanted it." He also called my mother and told her that it was not a rape because Zaden stimulated me first.

After the rape I was dying inside every time I had to sit beside Zaden. I felt scared and isolated. I accused this guy of something that could end his career and everyone hated me for it. I was trying to get by but had to do everything with him. NCIS was supposed to be investigating him.

There was one other woman there, a gunnery sergeant and repair tech. The band officer suggested I go talk to her. I did and then she betrayed me by telling the band officer what I said to her. After that everyone hated me, and treated me like I had the plague. I was alone. I went to the band officer's commander and she said it would be the same way no matter where I went, I would be treated the same.

In the hospital I kept asking to be transferred and not have to go back to the band. The answer was always no. They did let me go to the office while they made up their minds what to do with me. Finally I was told to get out of the corps and I would have all my benefits, medical, college, etc. They said my choice was to go back to the band or leave the marine corps. They told me they would give me an honorable discharge with a personality disorder if I left. I was put in a room with three male doctors and they drilled me on who I had sex with and never mentioned the rape. The notes say I had a fight with my boyfriend. The diagnosis was borderline personality disorder with focus on getting attention. I grew up feeling ugly and not wanting to be seen, so I knew their statements were not true.

When I got out of the hospital I met twice with a female counselor. Her notes said that I wanted to talk about the alleged rape. When I decided to leave I was out in two days and was four months shy of the complete twenty-four months of service I needed to have benefits. They encouraged me to sign the papers and get out and assured me that I would have all my benefits.

*They are lying to her.*

After meeting with me, one of the commanding officers decided I was not worthy of an honorable discharge, so they gave me a general discharge under honorable conditions. I was raped and attempted suicide, then three days later was given a diagnosis of personality disorder and told to get out of the marine corps. I was denied medical benefits and the GI bill because of the kind of discharge they gave me.

Immediately after leaving the marine corps, I had a review board and they ruled in my favor. That was fifteen years ago but the VA shows I have a general discharge. *The Disabled American Veterans (DAV) are helping her to have another review.*

*CAT's symptoms are hyper-vigilance, terrified when men walk toward her, ready to kill if a man walks toward her, being frozen and unable to move or speak, and unable to keep a job.*

I had a big flashback in the shower and I was in so much anguish and pain I was balled up on the floor remembering the rape. I called the VA and a woman told me, "You're not in the system, we can't help you." I was dripping wet. The woman called the cops, who showed up at the door. My husband went to the door and came to the bedroom to say the cops were there for me to go to the VA. The woman at the VA said I was suicidal, I told her I was having a flashback and needed help. The cops agreed to leave me in my husband's care.

*CAT told me that ten or eleven years ago she had a surgical procedure done and when she was coming out of the anesthesia in the recovery room; she woke up and could not move her arms or legs even when she tried. She was screaming in her head –I can't move! I can't move! I can't move! The nurses were talking and said, "Grab her quick before she falls off the table." The nurse told her, "You've gotta go back to sleep."*

I did go back to sleep and felt God and I became calm. When I woke up again I could move.

I started to get help and for the first time, learned about MST and getting through the VA. Now I am letting the memories come so the big guys don't overpower me again. **It is time for justice. They are going to know I am here and what happened to me!**

*CAT filed a claim for PTSD and inability to work. She plans to go to the charity clinic and get help for her PTSD. A few months ago she picked up a guitar and played music for the first time in fifteen years at a friend's house. Her husband was there.*

It was a small apartment and there were three guys there. My husband stepped out for a minute and I was paralyzed. I couldn't speak or move. The guys said, "Oh look she is nervous" and they laughed. It was not about the music, it was because I was there alone with three guys. I thought I would have to scream and get my husband to come help me.

## Kaylie Ecker– Post Cold War Era

*At age seventeen, Kaylie enlisted in the army and her dad signed for her.*

I was not a very good student. My parents had just divorced and I wanted to get away. I heard that the army was a way to do wonderful things and get paid to have a career. I wanted to make a career in the army.

In August 1994, I went to Fort Jackson, S.C. for eight weeks of basic training. Basic was fun, I liked it, but it was hard to deal with the drill sergeants yelling. I made a lot of good friends and it helped me to grow up.

From basic I went to AIT at Fort Lee, Virginia. AIT was nine weeks long. I was a petroleum supply specialist, a glorified fuel pumper. I learned to test and prepare fuel for helicopters and then pump it in. My drill sergeant was a woman who looked after us girls. The week before the end of AIT— I was sexually assaulted. One day I trained with marines at the marine corps barracks, along with two girlfriends and a guy from our class. The two guys went out to smoke and the guy from my class would not let me leave the room. He locked the door would not let me by him and would not accept my emphatic, "NO!" He pinned me down and raped me. There was another marine trying to get in, who was with the guy who was raping me. He did not get in. I was terrified and could not do anything more than say, "PLEASE STOP!" I was crying and he would not stop. I was afraid he would kill me. He had me pinned down and he was drunk and agitated. When he was done he walked me out of the barracks to the other two girls and I turned and told him YOU RAPED ME! He said, "How do you figure?" I said, "You pinned me down and wouldn't stop even when I yelled no all the time!" I told the two girls and they told our platoon leader. The next day she took me to the drill sergeant and to the hospital, told CID and the MP's and they did a rape kit. The drill sergeant met me at the hospital. There was a woman agent there who was very good and trying to help me. They called in the rapist, the two girls, and their boyfriends. It was a long day for me, sixteen hours. The guy admitted raping me.

We were to graduate the following Wednesday. They let him roam free and graduate and they would not let me leave the company area for anything except to go to the mess hall. I begged and pleaded for them to let me graduate with my class. The company commander insisted on all the isolation, and the women drill sergeant went behind his back and said, "You deserve to graduate, you didn't do anything wrong. You deserve to graduate with your class." The company commander treated me like a prisoner and was not even going to let me go home for Christmas to see my family. My mom called Senator Carl Levin to get me a leave to go home and to Michigan. The company commander called my mom while I was home and said, "She should be over this by now." I was an emotional wreck and felt very alone. My belief in the army taking care of their own was crushed.

*This company commander is punishing Kaylie unnecessarily. There is no reason for her to be isolated or stopped from graduating, except to punish her for reporting the rape. Seeing these stories and the way commanders isolate victims who report and expect them to get over the effects in a day or two begs the question, are they trained to do this? This command behavior certainly repeats itself in many companies as though this is the protocol. Clearly this demonstrates the culture of abuse toward women in the military to make them pay for daring to report being raped by a fellow soldier.*

*A healthier and more just way to handle this would be to provide rape counseling to Kaylie and to give her appropriate support within the company so that instead of being isolated, she is connected to supportive people and friends. Additionally Kaylie deserves to attend and participate in graduation with her classmates and be given holiday and earned leave.*

*Kaylie's belief in the army taking care of its own need not be a mistaken belief. It could be valid. Instead of being betrayed by the army she believes in, that army can become a service corps that does care for its own regardless of gender. The army could demonstrate being honorable in how it addresses rape within its ranks and purposefully making needed changes, transforming from a culture of abuse to a culture of accountability and integrity; making those qualities paramount.*

I went back to Fort Lee as a holdover before going to Germany. That day the company commander said to me, "You know how you can make this go away? You can drop all charges and life will be a lot easier for you then." I said, "No Sir, I can't let this happen to anyone else." I was scared and intimidated, they did not allow me any support and they told me I'd have to go to Quantico by myself and have a marine attorney. I got really scared and agreed to drop the charge.

I went in and signed the paper saying I would not pursue criminal or civil charges against him. I felt like they'd thrown me to the lions and I had no advocate. They made it seem like it was my fault, and I was the criminal.

*The company commander intimidated Kaylie into betraying her own values and her own self-interest.*

I was a wreck, they did not offer me any support or counseling. I had one appointment with a chaplain and that is all. All of my classmates were gone. It was three weeks before I went to Germany. I know that if I had been given support I could have gone through with prosecuting the rapist. He could still be serving in the military and doing this to other women.

*I believe she could have followed through if she had support. Perhaps that is the purpose of not providing support; so women do not prosecute. Bottom line seems to be protecting the image of the military at any price.*

I was sent to the heliport at Katterreach, Germany where I was an aircraft refueler and was augmented out to another unit and almost sent to Bosnia. The platoon sergeant gave me a hard time because I knew my job and did it very well. He said I was a natural leader, yet he gave me a bad time. He was always watching me and making me do extra duty. He was micromanaging me and I saw that he did not do that to everyone.

In Germany I got to see a counselor one time. My platoon sergeant called my counselor to ask why I was having a hard time and she told him. After that I was not allowed to go anymore. He said the mission was more important than my personal problem.

*Kaylie getting counseling support actually aids the mission better than her being distressed, shut down, or not functioning well. When someone is traumatized the sooner they have empathy, support and an opportunity to work through the experience and feelings, the sooner they can heal and return to full functioning.*

I began drinking heavily; one fifth of vodka regularly. I was partying and promiscuous and trying to numb myself out. I never missed a formation or being on the job. I met my husband about then. We were on guard duty together and he walked me back to my barracks about two am. I was terrified and he said, "Something happened to you didn't it?" I told him everything. He was very supportive. He said, "You can keep on drinking or be with me." He gave me a different perspective. When we were moving into base housing, I found my graduation picture and my husband was able to pick out the rapist and the two girls with me without my help.

I did stop drinking, but shut it down. I had nightmares and flashbacks and I thought I was crazy. I was still not allowed to get help. We got married in Denmark and I had my first child while I was in Germany. We were able to stay together and deploy together because we were in the same company. When I got pregnant I was on orders to go to Bosnia. My daughter was six months old and my parents would not accept custody and care for her if something happened, so I was chaptered out, because I did not have an acceptable child-care plan.

I left three months shy of my end of service date. I was given an honorable discharge but it was in Germany, and they did not have the same type of services e.g., army career and alumni program to help me get prepared for civilian life, create a resume' and get a job, or an exit physical. I got out three weeks after my husband came back from Bosnia and then we both went to Fort Rucker, Alabama.

I still have symptoms. In 2006, I went to the Vet Outreach Center for counseling. I was angry, not very outgoing, not upbeat or as full of life and fun as I was before the rape. I was even detached with my kids, and I used to be very affectionate. I refused to go to the VA because they treat me like I don't matter, and all they want to do is give me pills to take.

I asked Kaylie what her ideas were about how to help her and other women. This is what she said:

- Chain of command needs to be trained to be compassionate.

- We can't always suck it up and move on without help.

- Stop treating the victim like a criminal.

- Stop punishing the victim.

- Rape has been and is accepted protocol; WHERE IS THE OUTRAGE!

- I'm expected to put my life on the line for our country, yet I am treated like the scum of the earth. That is not right.

# Sharon Kufelt – Vietnam Era

*Sharon was twenty-one, blonde, slim and living in Denver, CO in 1969. She had been trying to put herself through college as a fine arts major, but was having a hard time. A friend of her family, a retired air force officer, recruited her. He told her the air force was an excellent career and that she would get paid while she finished college. He went on to say, "You could become an officer and there are many fields open to you. Women have equality in the air force and travel the world while serving. You wouldn't have to be in danger because women would not go to war and you could even retire after twenty years."*

*Her extended family had made a career in the military or had served during wartime, so it was an easy decision for Sharon. She joined in February 1969, and went to basic training at Lackland AFB, in San Antonio, TX.*

The women were segregated from the men and basic did not seem hard. I was held over there for seven weeks until I received orders for computer school at Shepherd AFB, also in San Antonio. One day, while in tech school, I came back to my all-woman dorm and saw a woman on the floor who had slashed herself and there was blood all over. Many of the women were screaming. I covered the bleeding woman with a blanket and told someone to call security and an ambulance. The medics came and took her away and we cleaned up the blood. No one came to talk with us or do any counseling. We never heard what happened. I think we were all shell-shocked for a couple of weeks. To this day, I still see the images, hear the sounds and smell the blood. It seemed strange that we never heard anything more after something that traumatic.

I graduated at the top of my class at tech school and was stationed at headquarters Pacific Air Forces (PACAF), Hickam AFB, Pearl Harbor. I was twenty-one and ready to go and they stopped me. I was told I would be on curfew for six months. It made no sense because there were eighteen/nineteen-year old guys running around free. I was also told there were places I could not go because they were not safe. I asked "Why are women not safe?" They said there were areas where women were being raped. So their solution was to lock up the women. We were literally locked up at bed check and had to be inside by 10 p.m. I served under the women's commander and the first sergeant where I lived, and had another set of superiors where I worked.

I loved my work, I loved wearing the uniform and I loved being of service to my country. Then I started hearing stories of Vietnam. I heard about the drugs and black market and the problems with the Viet Cong. I began to wonder about that war and why we were there.

One day I went to see the eye doctor and he turned off the lights to examine my eyes and instead sat in my lap and began to massage my breasts. I was stunned, shocked, terrified and could not make sense of it. I did not know what to say or do. I felt so intimidated by him and being so new with low rank I did not report it. I was more terrified to report it than not.

In the barracks I was one of the oldest at twenty-two, and I had nothing in common with the nineteen-year old women there. I did have one other woman I talked with, who told me she had a similar experience with a doctor. We compared notes about walking on base, getting catcalls and snide remarks from both officers and enlisted men. It was impossible to stop that.

One day I was walking on the backside of the beach when a guy came out of the bushes and assaulted and raped me. He was not vicious or violent but definitely forceful. I did go to the women's squadron and told the first sergeant what happened. She said, "Well you weren't hurt, so shut up." The commander said, "We're trying to bring more women in so we are not going to say anything."

I learned to obey officers and I did what they said. I was not given any support or counseling. Luckily, I was on birth control pills and did not get pregnant. I took antibiotics to prevent any sexually transmitted diseases but I was not very happy with the military after that.

Then I met an airman on base who was a staff sergeant who was soon to be discharged. We married in 1971, but he had no benefits. I could not draw housing because he was my dependent, and he was non-military. I was a sergeant and the lower ranking men I worked alongside, their wives and children, all had full benefits, medical, PX, commissary. All they had to do was show their ID card. Because I was a woman and I was the active military spouse, my husband had no such benefits. It was discrimination. I did not like how I was treated and felt betrayed by the air force, the military, and the recruiters who lied to me. I felt I was not valued by the air force and felt betrayed by them for not keeping me safe on their base. We had army, navy, air force and coast guard. The women in those services were all experiencing the same things, it was very prevalent. Women are not treated as equals in the military and there are extreme levels of misogyny in all branches.

I know many other women who were sexually assaulted and raped back then and even now. I went to a conference and luncheon honoring women veterans in Oakland, CA and fifty percent of the women there admitted to being sexually assaulted and some were even homeless. I have a friend whose mother was an army nurse in World War II who was gang-raped in Europe and had no treatment or help.

*Sharon went on to receive her Bachelor's degree in social anthropology and holistic and alternative health in 1979. She divorced in 1983, and still struggles with the effects of her rape/assault. She has chronic depression and is in and out of homelessness.*

*Her story demonstrates the culture of abuse prevalent in the air force and the inequality in the system in relation to women. It also shows us this abusive culture was present in World War II and illustrates the power of rank and the protocol to do what those of higher rank say, even if it is wrong or inappropriate.*

****Note to Reader:** *There are only three more stories in this chapter and a smaller chapter with three stories before you reach the focus on accountability and my call to action. Thank you for your courage to read this book and your willingness to stand up for our women under fire and demand action, positive change in our military culture, and justice for these women and the many others who, until now, have been denied that.*

# T. G. – Grenada Era

When I graduated from high school, I was living in Baltimore, Maryland with my daughter. I worked at McDonald's and was receiving social services. This was not the life I wanted and I saw no future or better life for my daughter. I was not receiving any child support from my daughter's father.

When I turned twenty-one I decided to join the military. My dad had retired from the army and was working for the government. I talked with him about what I was thinking and he said it would help me create a better life for my daughter and me.

March 17, 1979 at age twenty-two, I signed over custody of my daughter to my mother, so I could join the army. I went to basic training at Fort McClellan, AL in the Women's Army Corps (WAC's). Basic training was for eight weeks and my bunk buddy Barbara, was caucasian and like a sister to me. She was quiet, had big hips and didn't make it through. I was sad that she couldn't make the runs. After two weeks of basic they retired the Women's Army Corps (ended it), and had a ceremony. In basic, the younger women would cry out to me for help, especially to help them pass inspections. I did well in everything and did try to help others.

I hated the gas chamber. They made me go through twice and I don't know why. It was disgusting and burned my skin, eyes and inside my nostrils. It was awful and made me nauseated. I just wanted to be out of there to clear my lungs outside. It took me over twenty minutes to clear my lungs.

*It was required, as part of the program, to go into a room with nerve gas, mustard gas, and tear gas, walk around then take off the gas mask and state name, rank and serial number. Many women experienced symptoms, illnesses, and loss of function from those experiences and the army has not been accountable.*

After basic, I was sent to Fort Sam Houston, San Antonio, TX for Advanced Individual Training (AIT) School as a 76 Juliet, which is a medical supply specialist clerk. The training was for eight weeks. I scored 883 out of a possible 1000 points. I loved AIT because I felt respected there. I had a thirty-day leave after AIT and went home.

My dad was in Germany as a civil service worker getting an upgrade before his retirement so I missed him but did get to see my mother, daughter, sister and brothers. I was considerably smaller than when I left for basic, because I lost weight.

My first duty station was the 31st Medical Detachment in Kitzingen, Germany. I was assigned to the clinic there. I went through Frankfurt overnight and thankfully was able to change clothes and shower. The next day I had to travel alone. That was scary for me, to be in a foreign country alone. I was glad to be done with it. I ended up at a place called Bad Kissingen. The post commander told me that I was sent to the wrong place. I was scared again and feeling panicky. I stayed there for the next two days and on the third day two black guys came to pick me up. I did not want to go in the car with them. I was scared and conflicted. I wanted to succeed in the army for my daughter, but I was afraid to get into the car with the two black men who were strangers to me. I fought with myself, but I did get in. I sat in the back and the two guys were in the front. They took me to the clinic. When I got to the clinic all I wanted was to be where I was comfortable. I wanted to take a shower and change my clothes.

They told me, "You are the first single female to come to our facility and we do not have any billets for you."

They put me where they could and I had to move five times in two months. I had no money and did not get paid. No one asked me how I was, or if I needed help. I had no place to go or anyone to talk to. Most of the people at the 31st Medical Detachment were married. I wanted to find and contact my dad, but I had no money. I had to get to a phone and call my mom, collect, then found out where my dad was. After a month I finally got paid and contacted my dad.

It helped to talk to him. I was finally starting to feel safe.

One of the black guys who picked me up was the Non Commissioned Officer in Charge (NCOIC) of the clinic and the other guy was the section sergeant NCOIC and was always around. After one month the section sergeant left and I was to run the supply room. It was a complete mess. The guy that was there before me did not have the correct Military Occupational Specialty (MOS). As a private in charge of a section I had all of the demands but none of the respect. No one asked me how I was doing, or if I needed help. I had no support and no one to talk to. No one cared. I was able to pass two IG (Inspector General) inspections in two years and I still hated it. It was terrifying for me because I did not know I was going to face IG inspections. It was very hard to follow someone who did not do his work and there was a big backlog to deal with.

I had to set up all the proper procedures and rules, but then no one honored them. No one listened to me, and what I was dealing with. I was responsible to supply the clinic, the doctors, issue supplies, create records, deal with tents, vehicles, equipment and on top of all that I did not have a home, a place to rest, recover and feel safe. I had to keep moving. All of that went on for two years.

I felt very vulnerable and ended up sleeping with my NCOIC. After he seduced me into believing he would keep me safe, I found out he was married and had children. I told him I could not be with him if he was married and had children. He said, "It doesn't matter. I can fuck you whenever I want! You are going to sleep with me regardless of what you say."

He made it very hard for me by trying to keep me in the basement all day where it was moldy, full of mildew, and there were no windows. He only let me out for lunch. He wrote me up for every little thing, including if I talked with anyone in the supply room. He tried to give me an 'Article 15' (disciplinary action), and tried to say I was AWOL. The NCOIC did that from the day my dad came to visit and had lunch with me. After that my dad started to come regularly and support me.

*Once again you can see the attitude of entitlement that men have and the level of control they can have over women in the military. T.G. was kept much like a prisoner, rather than a competent soldier doing her job. This NCOIC was also badgering her by using his authority and military protocol to write her up for a variety of infractions. He was trying to make a case against her because she knew of his inappropriate behavior.*

*Each branch of the military needs a true advocate that has the authority to challenge inappropriate behavior and a council/board she can go to that has both the power and authority to demand change from the military. Change in the military must take place at every level from the squad, platoon, company, battalion, brigade, division, and corps leadership. Every level of command must demonstrate appropriate attitude, behavior, communication, demeanor, expectation, and respectful follow-through in all interactions with military women. There must not be a double standard for women; instead there may be specific differing requirements that are appropriate for the specific differences between men and women's bodies.*

My dad was very hurt and angry. He could not believe what they were trying to do to me. He acted as my lawyer and we won. By that time I was ready to leave, but I still had some time to go.

The captain made me scrub the entire basement with a toothbrush. I did it one whole day and then I couldn't do it anymore. I did not want to go AWOL, so I went to the MP station. I put my ID card on the desk at the MP station and put myself in one of their cells and locked myself in. My dad told me to go back to work and that it would be OK.

One night I was asleep in my bed and some guy came to see my bunkmate. I asked the CQ (Charge of Quarters) to give me a five a.m. wake-up call. In the night I woke up to this guy with his hand up my vagina. I threw beer steins at him and then knives. My roommate was trying to help me. The next day I went to work and let the doctor know what was done to me. I also went with my roommate to the MP station and we both reported it. I just wanted to be out of the army and away from all this.

After I locked myself in the cell, I was sent to the army hospital at Wurzburg, to the psych ward. My parents came and brought my daughter and my sister. I got to go with them for a few days and was put on meds. They allowed me to go home with my parents. I was devastated. I just knew my military life was done and over.

I got an inner theater transfer after two years and went to Nuremberg, to a dental clinic. I had a great commander and it was a much better experience. I was his driver.

Then I was transferred to a warehouse. My section sergeant was an alcoholic and would come in and embarrass me. He often had black eyes. He was an embarrassment to others as well. Other sergeants criticized him. When he came to the cafeteria they ignored him and my friends made fun of me. I did not sign up for that and no one in the command seemed to care. I toughed it out until my time was up, but I was very unhappy. I had planned to re-enlist for my career, but I was not given a chance. They would not let the enlistment sergeant talk with me. I processed out at Fort Dix in a line with many others and no one would talk to me. Then I came home.

I think these are people with no morals or conscience. If it doesn't affect their homes or children, they don't care! I had an honorable discharge with a good conduct medal ordered, but it never came. That was 1983.

I went to college, but I had to stop when my job with the state of Maryland came through. I was given a job in a warehouse with pre-release inmates for the Department of Corrections. I had to take an accredited course to get the job and I was one of their distinguished graduates. I was rated 6684 with the state of Maryland.

I am still not receiving any compensation for PTSD or for MST. I never got my educational benefits either. I don't trust any man or anyone in the Veterans Administration.

My daughter is now thirty-six and my son is twenty. Both are troubled.

In 2000, I met my husband on a ward at the Veterans Hospital in Baltimore, MD. We were both seeing the same doctor. We were married and then I found out he gave me HIV. I was forty-three by then. I had an accident and was in the emergency room. I saw a computer screen that said my husband was HIV positive. I asked the doctor why they did not tell me that. They told me they could not because of "confidentiality." That is not right! I believe they are responsible for me getting HIV from him. He was a disabled Vet and died from his HIV. They found some loophole and took the money from what I was supposed to be getting from the State and Federal Government. They take $50 out of my Social Security disability check, because I am not paying for my medications. Right now I am struggling to have enough money to buy food for my kids and me. If I don't find another place to stay I will be homeless by February. I have been working with the State Department of Vocational Rehabilitation to get re-employed. I don't trust anyone and don't have any support.

May of 2007, I was denied compensation and I am appealing through Vietnam Veterans of America (VVA).

# Ellen Haynes – Iraq

*Ellen grew up in Missouri and at age eighteen worked as a medical receptionist. She was bored and her work was not holding her attention so she decided to join the army. As a child she had always wanted to join the military, because her dad was a marine.*

I went to basic training at Fort Leonard Wood for nine weeks in November of 2003. I found it extremely challenging, because if one person messed up, we all paid for it. Many men did not believe women should be in the military, and it was reflected in their attitudes towards women soldiers. The women drill sergeants told us not to pay attention to them and were harder on us than the male drill sergeants were. They knew what we needed to do to survive in the military. I kept to myself a lot.

Directly following basic training, I had sixteen weeks of training to be a combat medic at Fort Sam Houston, Texas. There were more women than men in that training, and the men still had a negative attitude towards women in the military. We were trained as equals, so I don't see where that attitude comes from. They trained us to be medics working in a war zone, in military hospitals, or just about anywhere. There was a lot of competition in basic, but the medic training was more cooperative and we were more supportive of one another.

From Fort Sam Houston, I was sent to Fort Campbell, Kentucky. This location was ideal because I was only four hours from home and I had family nearby. I served as a 91-W combat medic for the 101st Airborne Division, and worked in brigade support as a battalion ambulance driver. I found out that I was assigned to do range detail, which meant I worked on the mechanics of the ambulance and did nothing medical. I felt my training had been a waste of time and the army was not using my new skills the way I expected.

In October 2004, I learned that I was pregnant. The father was a guy I had been casually dating. He and I were married shortly after I found out. They gave me office clerical duty from December 2004, until June of 2005. I delivered my son, Marshall, at Fort Campbell and then I had six weeks of convalescent leave and stayed on post the whole time. In August, I went back to my original unit and found out we were to deploy to Iraq in November. My husband's unit was also scheduled to deploy. He did not want our extended families to raise our son, so my husband decided to leave the military. He did not want to risk both of us being killed and having someone else raise Marshall.

From August to November we were packing, and I was training and spending time with my husband and my son, as my unit prepared to deploy. We left November 18, 2005.

My unit flew out of Fort Campbell on a commercial airplane to Ireland and we were not allowed out of the terminal when we stopped. We flew to Kuwait on the same plane. After our arrival in Kuwait we took a bus to a camp outside Kuwait City where I spent one month training and doing nothing. This seemed like a waste of time and energy to me.

December 19, 2005 we flew to Iraq, arrived in Baghdad at 4:30 a.m. and did not get to Camp Rustymiah until 1:30 a.m. the next day. We were located in a suburb southeast of Baghdad. It was a very smelly place surrounded by a garbage landfill, a sulfur factory, and a sewage facility; and every night there was an orange film over the sky, probably from the sulfur factory, which smelled like rotten eggs.

We had a main dining facility with one part for troops and one for local nationals who worked on the Forward Operating Base. In the area for the local nationals, food was prepared with curry, or cayenne pepper. KBR contractors ran the dining facility; some were locals and others came from surrounding countries. The military cooks were put on guard duty or went on convoys. Fridays we had steak, lobster and also crab legs grilled outside. Sundays we had roast beef or turkey and Monday through Thursday we had a regular menu that included stir-fries. They also had a place to get corn dogs, hot dogs, salad bar, sub bar for sandwiches, and dessert bar. Their sodas were very bad with little carbonation and a higher syrup to water ratio than ours do in America.

I worked and stayed at the old Iraqi hospital that my unit took over. It was the size of one of our emergency rooms back home. On the first level there were three small rooms and four to eight litters on tables or stands. This is where we took trauma victims and put them on one of the steel tables. We had cabinets filled with supplies that we used all the time. All this was in a huge open room. About six feet from our cabinets were litters on stands for our walk-in health clinic. Two feet outside our windows were huge cement barricades six feet tall to protect the windows. We also had a pharmacy, lab, x-ray, mental health facility, physical therapy and dental clinic. We were called a level two facility.

On the first floor we had an Iraqi shop that sold DVDs, tobacco, jewelry, electronics and snacks. There was also a little Iraqi restaurant, a barbershop and a gym. There were two other gyms on the camp as well, which were safe for us to use.

Our unit slept on the second floor. The contractors slept on the third floor. In the basement there was a phone center, internet lounge, movie shop and some big rooms used as a barracks. There was an outside patio with a courtyard in the center. We also had a PX nearby.

Our camp had a boxing ring and five or six shops like a PX, run by Iraqis. We could buy one to five seasons of a TV show for $25. They had some really nice silver and some granite or marble necklaces and bracelets. Once every three months an Iraqi traveling flea market came and brought their cultural items like burkas, scarves, pictures, jewelry, and thick king size blankets for $25 made of imitation mink.

When I first arrived at the hospital, around Christmas, I watched how they were doing sick call, stocking supplies, and treating incoming trauma patients for the first week. Then they watched us do it for one week and gave us feedback and some training. We took over on Christmas Day and it was a horrible. We had two casualties in two hours. A soldier on the guard tower, six feet above the ground, was wounded when a worker put an IED by the gate and detonated it. The guy on the tower was blasted. We cleaned his wounds on the front of this body and bandaged him then when we rolled him over we saw that his whole bottom was gone and he was bleeding out. We tried to stop the bleeding to get him stabilized so we could send him to a bigger hospital. When I was getting his personal stuff together he reached around his neck, took off his dog tags and said to be sure his wife got it. There was a little tiny baby shoe charm on it. I told him he would be OK and could give it to her himself. After we cleaned up there were six more casualties hit by an IED, including the brigade commander and the sergeant major. The gunner on top of the Humvee was also hit; it was a woman who was killed instantly. The driver only had minor cuts and bruises. When we worked on the sergeant major we found tourniquets on his legs and most of his left leg was gone below the knee. We did what we could and sent him off in a helicopter to another hospital. The sergeant major had a lot of military experience, yet still got blasted. It made me wonder, "We had no experience, what would happen to us?" This thought ran through our minds because most of us were nineteen and very green. Right out of high school into the military with no time under our belt in the sandbox, we were trying to live so we could save lives.

It was our first day on the job and the sergeant major's first day on the road. We had four doctors and forty-two medics at our unit. Everyone was running around trying to do something to help but we were all in a panic and unprepared. After all that, we had evening sick call. About 8 p.m., we were cleaning up and got a call that the soldier from the tower did not make it; he died. At 9 p.m. we had a debriefing about his death. We felt guilty and some medics were crying. Most of us were eighteen or nineteen years old. Our first day and first experience in Iraq, our first casualty dying and the realization that our sergeant major lost his leg, brought the whole horror right to us. I was stunned, angry, and upset when I found out he died. I thought if we had rolled him over sooner we would have seen the bleeding and maybe we could have saved him. I went through the woulda, coulda, shoulda and finally realized it was God's decision. I had a lot of turmoil and questions. Everyone has a time and if it's our time to go, that is how it is. We had to learn to do what we could and leave the rest to God. Some medics could not do it and asked for administrative jobs within the unit.

*In Vietnam we did triage' and would examine each casualty thoroughly to determine what was most needed immediately to preserve life. Often the exit wounds were the most serious. In my basic training as an army nurse they included several weeks of specific hands on practice with triage'*

As a medic I could do stitches, give shots and medications. The new philosophy with metal fragments and pellets is to take out only what is on the surface, and leave the rest to work itself out in time. (*In Vietnam we took out all the metal we could.*) We had an RN, a family nurse practitioner and an MD who did general surgery, put in chest tubes, and intubated (placing a tube down the throat to insure proper breathing). We also had a reserve unit with three specialists in a mental health clinic. They rotated around to different camps if they had no aid units.

We were a level two hospital, like an aid unit. There was a level three Combat Area Surgical Hospital (CASH) in Balad, thirty miles north of Baghdad and fifteen clicks (kilometers) from us. There was also an Evacuation Hospital in Kuwait and an intermediate stop for casualties was Landstuhl, Germany.

It was crazy the whole month with mortars coming in every night. During Ramadan, the Iraqis had a curfew and it was quiet.

After that first month it got quieter. When mortars came in we ran for the bunkers and usually did not wear our bulletproof vests except at night. We always did a roll call after a mortar attack. When the all clear sounded we took off our Kevlar vests, put our weapons away and waited to receive casualties. Many times there were no casualties and sometimes we had incidental casualties from sprained ankles running to a bunker or other injuries like a guy whose uniform sleeve caught on a door handle.

For three months there was only sick call and it was very quiet. Then in the spring we got very busy again with mortars. Once we had twenty-two patients and shrapnel hit only one of those. Mostly they were injuries from running to safety. The first part of April we had two IED attacks and then on my last day we had a sixteen year-old boy caught in the crossfire between Americans and the Taliban. He was shot three times. I am not sure why we saw him because we usually did not treat Iraqis. The boy was screaming. His heart rate was good but he had lost a lot of blood. The bullets missed his vital organs, but hit his trachea, which closed off, so we could not intubate him (put a tube through his mouth to trachea). We put in two chest tubes and tried to do a tracheostomy (making a cut between the collar bones and putting in a metal tube so he could breathe). His veins collapsed and his blood pressure dropped and the IVs stopped. With the helicopter crew waiting, we lost him. His mother was there the whole time and when we lost him, she let out an anguished scream. That was really, really hard for all of us. It is one thing to lose a soldier, but another to lose an innocent kid. That was the worst for me, my hardest case.

We had every age range on our base camp, eighteen to thirty-eight year-olds, some having adult relations, married or not. I kept to myself and did not get involved with sex and all the soap opera stuff.

I was married and had no interest in any of that. We all could support each other and give each other a hug if we needed one. My room was large, about ten by five feet with partitions. There was plywood over the door. I found an old Iraqi bathroom with three stalls but no toilets. The drains all filled in with concrete. In my room it was very quiet; I did not hear any noises outside. There was a bench by X-Ray where I would sit sometimes and play video games, read, or draw. It was right outside the clinic, so I could stop anytime and go in if they needed me.

One day, I was sitting on the bench playing a video game and an NCO E-6 walked by. He was a physical therapy specialist. He stopped to talk to me about the bible and religion. He said he was having a hard time. I tried to be positive and tell him not to be discouraged. We went to church together and he would sing in the choir. About a week later, he asked me for a hug and I hugged him in his office. He took my arm and twisted it behind my back. I told him to "Stop! That is not funny." He told me to walk to his room, two doors down. It was now 9 p.m. and no one was down there and I was not going. He forced me down to his room with my arm twisted behind my back. I was trying to figure out how this was happening and what he was talking about. He pushed me into his room and onto a couch. I got up and said, "I am leaving!"

I told him "Just leave me alone."

He said, "No, you will enjoy this."

"Please don't hurt me, please don't hurt me!" I repeated several times.

"Don't scream. You can't do anything to me because I outrank you. You will lose your family, your job, everything, because you are married and I am not! It will be consensual." He had already locked the door.

I said, "Look I don't want anything to do with you or what you are thinking, just let me out of here!"

He said:"I want a kiss."

I told him he was crazy and, "No way. I am married!" The next thing I remember I was beside his bed, which was against the wall and had an air mattress on top of it. I saw my PT (Physical Training) shorts were off, my socks were off and I don't remember how all that happened. He was on top of me and I was screaming, "NO! Please don't do this to me, please don't hurt me!"

He did not use any protection. When I tried to get up he said: "I'm not done yet," and pushed me back down and then he performed forceful sodomy. Then he threw my clothes at me and said: "Get out of here!"

I did not know what to do. I went to my room to try to figure out what happened. I felt totally lost. I searched myself to figure out what I might have done to bring this on. I couldn't think of anything. I knew about MST and did not want to tell anyone. I did not want to be another statistic. I decided to just keep my mouth shut and deal with this on my own.

*If there was not a culture of abuse in the military and the army had advocates of the type I previously described, Ellen would have felt safe to go there and have a complete exam, get emotional support and a full report taken in confidence. That report, including the results of the exam, would have provided the evidence needed to support her case.*

About ten days went by and I stayed clear of him. Then one day a doctor asked me to take some paperwork to him at the clinic. I took the paperwork and told him what the doctor had said and before I could turn to get out, he locked the door and did it again. It was in the clinic this time after the clinic was closed. I was angry. I could deal with once but this was too much. I still did not want to jeopardize my career, but I did not want him to keep raping me. I did not know what to do. I agonized for days.

I had been seeing a mental health guy to deal with all my issues from Iraq and my life and asked him a hypothetical question. I asked him, "What would you tell a person to do about a sexual assault?" He said he would tell her to report it because no matter what she thinks will happen, it won't happen the way she thinks it will.

*He is so completely wrong in telling her this and he is not even aware of that. He set her up for a very traumatic experience that will affect her health, her career and her life.*

The E-6 rapist threatened me right after that. He said, "I will tell them you are an adulteress having an affair with me and that you came on to me, and you will go to jail."

*He is confident in this, because he is part of the culture of abuse and knows he will be protected and supported in continuing his heinous behavior.*

I begged him to let me go! I can't lose my job, my career or my family over this. He did this to me about eleven times from February 2 and April 9, and then I snapped. He went home on leave and I told my husband what was going on. I was crying and having a panic attack suddenly afraid of losing him and my son, but it was 3:30 a.m. in Iraq. I knew I couldn't see my mental health counselor but they called for him anyway. I told the counselor what was happening to me and he was upset that I didn't tell him sooner. He told me that he couldn't tell my command because of privacy rules.

I found out my husband had sent emails to both my brigade and division command. They sent me home on leave and would not send me back to Iraq until the rape report was resolved, because they did not want it made public. I was angry because I wanted to go back to my job and be normal and I was angry with my husband for doing this to me. I could not think straight, I was a mess, crying, anxious, and not thinking clearly.

*This is a typical response of a caring and angry spouse wanting to do something and the expected rejoinder by a traumatized wife who is desperately trying to hold onto a reality of normalcy that no longer exists for her. That is not to say she cannot heal and move on, but she is now forever changed. Note that she was sent home on leave, because the army did not want this made public. That is another aspect of the culture of abuse, the cover up; hide truth from the public. You, who are the public, need to know so that you can respond and demand appropriate action, accountability and positive change. Making this public is the purpose of this book.*

My rear detachment commander, Lt. R said: "Get over it." That is when I started to have panic attacks and be very stressed on duty. I was at Fort Campbell on trash duty, picking it up all over post. I was not getting any responses or messages about what was happening with my case. A woman lieutenant was treating me like I was trash and gave me the worst jobs. It felt like I was being punished and felt worse from the retribution, than from the sexual assaults. They said that I would hear something by the end of May.

Finally they told me there was no evidence of sexual assault and the case was dismissed. I was furious! Then I was told to go get checked out by my mental health counselor. They asked me if I wanted to get out of the army. I said, "No." My counselor said: "They are requesting you be separated for psychological reasons."

I said, "I was told to come here to get a paper saying I am fit to return to my regular duty in Iraq." He showed me the separation paperwork, which led to me crying and being very angry. I did not know where this had come from and it seemed so unfair. The NCO who brought me there knew nothing about the separation either. He was told to get a paper saying I was fit to deploy. I showed him the form where it showed they wanted a Chapter 517 (not fit for service) evaluation done, and I was getting more upset and angry the more I reviewed it.

Up until this situation I had great reports and exemplary service. I was given the Good Conduct Medal, Army Commendation Medal, and a Certificate of Achievement. There was not a single negative report.

From that point on, the commander insisted I have an escort wherever I went. They watched everything, even when I had a doctor's appointment for me or my son. They cancelled my leave and pulled me in many different directions, e.g., when they gave me a job sitting in a fake helicopter with two black soldiers and weapons. For three weeks different units came to do mock drills. My job was to run through the woods screaming and then get shot and fall to the ground.

CID told me I could not deploy because the perpetrator was still there, and they were trying to figure out where to send me. It was the middle of June by this time and the investigations were still ongoing. They found four other victims and one had witnesses who saw the E-6 perpetrator grab a woman and he rubbed her genitals and was all over her in public. This happened in Kuwait before going to Iraq and the chain of command was notified. The only outcome of that was the E-6 perpetrator was not to speak to the victim. I was told I would have to return to Iraq to attend his hearing.

In July, the doctor said I could do my job and go back to Iraq when the perpetrator was moved. I took the doctor's paper back to my unit and it was quiet for a day. The next day they escorted me back to another doctor about the chapter 517 paperwork. He asked me, "Do you want out of the army?"

I said, "No! This was retribution for reporting the rapes. None of this happened until I filed the report. They had no problem with my mental health until I came forward to report the military sexual trauma."

He looked at the paperwork and said, "They are saying you are not capable of making that accusation."

I was furious! Any woman would be furious to hear that.

He asked me again if I wanted out of the army.

I told him, "No, this is my job and my career. I plan to retire in twenty years."

He said, "Well this is the third time your unit submitted this paperwork and they are going to keep doing it until somebody finally says you need to be gone. So I am going to agree with them and kick you out."

*Each officer she sees during this process has the option to stand up for her, to seek and speak the truth. Doctors like this last one are colluding with the culture of abuse and punishing the victim.*

I was distraught and in tears. It all went up the chain of command and they told me I was going to be chaptered out. I went to JAG and told them what was going on and that this was retribution for reporting MST. They agreed with me. JAG said I was supposed to be given time to recover from the trauma and instead I had six weeks of hell. I was also supposed to have shown behavior warranting separation, and they had none. JAG said there was insufficient evidence for this and it was cruel retribution for filing a report of MST. I stopped crying and took some breaths and left confident they could not kick me out.

*Ellen was relieved and rightly so. However, without an advocate she did not understand that JAG needed to act on her behalf, or the culture of abuse would have its way with her. She had their opinion but not their legal action or support for her.*

Then it was August and it was quiet. The investigation was closed. They had the 'Article 15' hearing for the perpetrator and he was found guilty of sexual harassment, maltreatment, indecent exposure, and abuse of power. They did not find him guilty of rape even though that was the worst of his behavior and all they gave him for punishment was to demote him to E-5 and took two month's pay. It was not even a slap on the wrist. He was not charged for anything he did to me, they said there was no confirmation that it took place. He had raped two E-4's, a captain, and an E-3, in addition to me. (E-3, E-4 etc., are different ranks for enlisted soldiers)

*There is no confirmation because that system is not in place.*

*For every unit, there needs to be a safe place to go, staffed with a nurse, doctor, and advocate for the victim. In this safe place she would be listened to with compassion, supported in giving a full detailed report, a complete physical exam performed including a rape kit and pictures taken, if necessary. I believe it is important for the advocate to be a <u>civilian</u> empowered to do the reporting and advising, and to insist on following protocols designed to protect the victim and NOT the perpetrator and military corps. The civilian advocate would not be under the command and control of the military, so is less likely to be threatened or sucked into the sick system. Once the exams and reports are done, the victim would be assigned to a counselor who does not work for the military and who will help her through the processes of investigation, hearings, and dealing with the effects of the rape. This counselor along with the doctor would write orders, which the command must follow to protect the victim and her career. In addition she would be escorted to the JAG office and given someone there to advocate for her and who also would advise her as the case proceeds. One of the first orders would be to have the perpetrator removed from his position and placed in custody while the investigation is ongoing. Ellen, or another, on the other hand would be allowed to return to duty when the counselor believed she could. Right now the system is backwards and rigged to protect the perpetrator and the military so the perpetrator roams free and the victim is isolated, watched and punished.*

The end of August I was told I would be going back to Iraq and to get all my stuff ready. I had nothing to take, because it was all there so I packed my bags and got ready to go. My husband was angry that I was going back and threatened to bust our computer over my head. I went to the MPs to report his threat and left with my son after I filed the report. In the meantime, my husband had told Lieutenant R in my rear command, that I had just lost it psychologically and kidnapped my son and that I was on my way with him to Missouri.

He shut off my cell phone so I could not get messages or phone calls. The MPs told me to stay away from the house for seventy-two hours and my son was not allowed to stay in the barracks, so I stayed with my sister-in-law. In those seventy-two hours my husband gave some graphic drawings to my chain of command. One was a vehicle on fire, which was a symbol for the commander because of her last name and one was a picture of a woman with a bullet hole in her head. He told them I had done those drawings. I do draw and when I found out about the pictures I asked to see them, to be able to tell them if I had drawn them. I told them I was a pretty good artist and I would tell them if they were mine. They would not let me see them.

Monday the lieutenant went to a mental health counselor who was down range in my unit and by law couldn't be my provider. He had never seen me but the captain in the mental health squad wrote a large report saying: specialist Haynes is not fit for duty, she is borderline schizophrenic with severe PTSD and has a personality disorder with mixed mood and anxiety; all of which existed before joining the military. It is in her best interest to discharge her immediately.

*Sad to say this mental health counselor has sold his soul to the army, and is using his authority to hurt women rather than help them heal. Only a culture of abuse would allow him to write such a report without examining Ellen. If the system is not changed this type of abuse will continue and get worse. This kind of behavior dishonors all that the military stands for. Unless there are checks and balances built in, the culture of abuse will run rampant and destroy our military from the inside out.*

I was told I would be returning to Iraq on September 2. Then they said the flight was delayed. Then I was told I was being chaptered out of the army. I went to the sexual assault coordinator and showed her that I had asked for a unit transfer and had paperwork from the sergeant major at the hospital saying he would put me under his command in his unit. My commander, who was now a captain, put me on her punishment detail where I had to sit for twelve hours. I was to call her when I went to meals or to the bathroom and when I returned. I did it the first day and the second day the sergeant major said: "Why are you here?" I showed him the paper from the captain and he said, "Get out of here, this is not a daycare!"

So I went to the battalion office and showed them the paper from the captain and told them what the sergeant major had said and asked them, "What do you want me to do? "The captain said, "I will discuss this with her."

I was really close to breaking, but I had the weekend off.

Monday, I had a morning appointment with the captain and I took an NCO with me. Captain T looked at me and said, "Here are your separation orders. Your chapter paperwork is done and you have until September 22nd, to clear off post and be out of the army."

I said, "What are you talking about? JAG overturned this. It was not even legitimate."

He said, "We have new evidence."

I went back to JAG and they went to brigade legal and asked how did this go through? The JAG Officer was shown the picture of the lieutenant burning in hell and words "Die Bitch Die," and told me that is why they are separating you. I asked, "Can I see it?"

It was not my drawing or my handwriting. I asked them where they got them and I told him they weren't mine. The JAG said, "You seriously didn't draw these?"

I said, "No."

I was really upset. Three days before that, I learned I had possible cervical cancer. Now if they kicked me out, I couldn't even get medical care. I was told I couldn't leave until I had some tests done, then when the tests were done I learned I had cancer of the cervix, stage 4 cervical dysplasia.

JAG told my command not to do this, it would likely end in a long trial and most likely this soldier would win. This is clearly retribution and it shows neglect by the army to discharge this soldier with a diagnosed medical condition that needs treatment. It was never cleared by JAG. They did it anyway.

I contacted the Miles Foundation and they contacted the Secretary of the Army. I talked with the Secretary of the Army who said, "I will take care of this, you can tear up your papers." The Secretary of the Army told the commander not to do this, because it would cause a huge legal battle and that I had three doctors say I was OK to return to duty and only one who never saw me, that said I was not. They had a closed meeting and then they told me everything was dropped. I went to work on Monday morning and they asked, "Why are you here?"

I told them what the Secretary of the Army had said and they responded back that they had their own closed meeting with the company commander, brigade and division commanders and they said, "You're gone!" I was devastated. They escorted me all over post and made me process out and leave. Since that happened, I have contacted my congressman but was given no help. The attorneys wanted $20,000 for a review board, so I could not do that.

*I was in touch with Ellen in March of 2013. She did lose her husband and told me her son was doing well. Ellen is in school working on a social work degree and did get to a review board in August 2010. She said it was the hardest thing she had ever done. It was emotionally draining and they denied her request. She also told me she sought mental health care at the Veterans Administration, but was bounced from provider to provider for medications, with no one to talk to, or get help from. In a recent August 2011 email Ellen told me, according to regulations they cannot separate her from the army with a PTSD diagnosis since 2005. What they need to do instead is refer her to a medical board. They also cannot do that after her discharge and instead must do a medical retirement. She filed a claim with the board of corrections to reverse the denial and wants them to admit their actions were wrong so she can move on.*

"But the 'good ole boy' system won't allow that. They turned my whole life upside down and I lost everything I had, all because I did the right thing."

# Layla Mansberger – Iraq

*Layla was seventeen and still in high school when she decided to join the army like her grandfathers had. Everyone in her family was going on to school and she wanted to be different. Because of her age, her parents had to sign for her. Two weeks after her graduation from high school she went to basic training at Fort Jackson, South Carolina. That was in 2003. She went through her eight weeks, pushed herself to the max and had a great experience.*

It was like being part of a family and I maxed out everything in PT (Physical Training) and even surpassed some of the guys. From there I went to AIT (Advanced Infantry Training) for nine weeks in my MOS (Military Occupational Specialty) food service. I liked the training and had the experience of cooking for 4000 people.

We trained with the marine corps. I don't know why, but the army and marines trained together. I was the most experienced person and was made the class leader and shift leader. The marines were upset that a female was in charge. There were only two women in our unit total. The marines threatened me and said if they saw me outside of the class, "We'll show you a real woman's place."

One night, I went with classmates to a dance club for students. When I was ready to leave the others were not and I did not have anyone to walk back with me. I went outside and the marines were there and started harassing me. I was looking around for someone to walk back to the barracks with me and then some of my friends from basic saw what was happening, came and got me and took me back home. Then I got in trouble with my drill sergeant for going back with people not in my class; he would not listen to me. He denied me passes for two weeks and then finally listened to what happened and I got my passes back. In the process, the marines were taken care of. They did not harass me anymore and were no longer in my class.

After AIT, I went home and was in the reserves for several years. I was respected in my unit and was in charge of the kitchen. Then in 2006, I was activated and put in a unit where I did not know anyone. My unit was not activated, only me.

We went to Fort Dix, New Jersey every month for two years. We did training to prepare us to go to Iraq. It took me awhile to get used to the new unit and the people. They did not know me, or what I was capable of and it took a while for them to develop respect for me. I never had the same level of respect as in my home unit. I always felt like I was an outsider and then the day we were to deploy I fell and hurt my ankle and could not deploy with them. From that point on, I felt like an outcast.

I deployed to Iraq in November of 2008, was put in with strangers in the Dining Facility Administration Center (DFAC) and was not with my unit anymore. They showed me to my room, which was in a trailer and at first I did not have a roommate. I worked nights from 4 p.m. until 7 a.m. and then slept. I did that seven days a week and had a day off here and there.

When the guys came through the food line, every third guy made rude comments about sex, wanting to sleep with me and harassed me. They were soldiers, officers and contractors. It was like they turned wild dogs loose over there to be mean to women. One civilian contractor was really bad and told me he could get into my room whenever he wanted to. I was very naïve and did not believe him. I told him, 'You're a liar, leave me alone or I will report you." The next day he found out where I was and opened my door while I was sleeping. I told him to leave or I'd get him in trouble. I went to my platoon sergeant and told him what happened. The contractor lied and told him he had a work order for my door and the platoon sergeant accepted that.

It seemed like I was just supposed to deal with all that and there was no one to talk to. The guys who came through the food line were harassing me all the time. The only respect I received was from those I worked with. Since I was the only woman on my shift, I got it all. Very rarely another soldier would put someone in his or her place. Even the officers were hitting on me and they weren't even supposed to be talking to me.

The people I worked with knew I was in a lesbian relationship with someone back home and they treated me better, but the guys coming through the line did not know.

January of 2009, a rocket hit across the road from me and I had a concussion and was dazed from the blast. I told my command but they never had me checked out. It happened again in March.

Also in March, after being there almost five months, a soldier I worked with and who knew about me would get upset when I was joking with other guys in the line. He had a girlfriend back home and one day he told me he was having trouble with her and that he wanted to talk to me. At that time I was working 4 a.m. to 4 p.m. and always walked to and from work with some of the guys. So when he came by to walk with me it was no big deal.

He was knocking on my door at 0330. I told him he would have to wait until I got ready. When I was sitting on my bed putting on my boots he was at the door and locked it. I said, "What are you doing? This will not end well for you." I was his senior and letting him know the trouble he would be in if he did something wrong. He kept moving toward me and in a flash he was on top of me and trying to get my pants off me, getting pissed off and then ripped them off. Then I was begging him to stop and reminded him of his girlfriend back home and his career. He kept at it and I kept fighting as hard as I could. He finally got enraged and slammed my head into my wall and was raping me and saying, "See what you are missing." Then he flipped me over and anally raped me. After he smashed my head into the wall I was not able to fight anymore and was dazed. When he was done he hit me over the head one more time and thanked me for a good time. I was in shock and was totally silent and could not move for a while. I got up when I could and took a long shower to try and get his smell off me. It was now 0415 and I had to be at work at 0430. It felt like everything was in slow motion. I was trying to get myself together and cover up the marks and bruises on me so no one would know. I did go to my NCO who was newly in country. I told him what happened and he said, "How do I know you didn't want it? You women are all the same, ask for it and after it happens, claim rape. You are all sluts and whores." I could not tell him I was a lesbian because he was homophobic and I would have been kicked out.

I felt totally alone and did not think I could trust anyone. I was trying to get by and do my job, but it was very painful for me every day. I was working eighteen-hour days, not sleeping and something in me snapped. I was reaching out to friends on instant messaging and it was not going well, then a good male friend came by and saw me with my M-4 rifle and took it away from me. He took the magazine out and kept that and the bolt and sent me to combat stress. I did not tell them about the rape or trying to kill myself, only that I could not sleep. They gave me some strong sleeping pills, which helped me sleep but I could not take them all the time because they made me very groggy. If it wasn't for my friend I would be dead now.

August 2009, a soldier who had let me borrow his DVD's came to my room because he wanted them back. He said something to me about rumors that I slept with other guys. I told him there was no truth at all to those rumors, but he made a move for me and threw me on the bed, turned me over and raped me anally. He even tried to put his whole hand inside me. It hurt so much I was screaming to stop him. He stopped and got up and went out. I was hurting so much and could not believe it happened to me again. The next day I went to the Sexual Assault Resource Coordinator (SARC), who took me to the emergency room. My platoon sergeant was calling me and I told them I was at the doctor. He kept calling and said I would be written up if I was not there in fifteen minutes. Finally the SARC took the phone and told him to leave me alone. The next day they put me on quarters for a couple of days, so I did not have to be around everyone and field questions. They pretty much made my life miserable until I went back home.

In September, I went to Fort Dix, New Jersey and had a post deployment checkup. I told them about the rapes, explosions, suicide attempt, and how I was treated and they sent me to Behavioral Health. They believed me and validated me. That was a big relief. Then they put me in the wounded warrior unit to figure out what was wrong with me physically. I left Iraq with pain all over. It took them almost two years to figure out what was wrong with me. I had Lyme Disease, Fibromyalgia, and Traumatic Brain Injury (TBI). I was getting counseling all that time and it really helped, but my unit did not treat me well, because they could not see anything wrong with me.

I could not eat, because I was nauseated and had just gotten over Swine Flu and they said I would eat or be taken to the hospital. I told them to take me to the hospital. At the hospital they did a full body search and saw I had been cutting myself on my hips. They urged me to go inpatient. I had not been on any meds so when my anxiety went up I cut myself to make the anxiety go away. I agreed to go to inpatient and they sent me to a civilian hospital and I was so grateful. I was treated very well and was there for two weeks where I had medications and really good therapy. After I got out it was

December and I went home for the holidays, but it did not go well. I argued with my girlfriend and we split up.

January 2010 I went back to the wounded warrior unit and had intensive outpatient group therapy three times a week. It was going very well and I was starting to feel better when they switched me to Fort Meade, Maryland. I lost my group therapy, and all my support for no reason.

When I arrived at Fort Meade, they called me a troublemaker and they harassed me daily. I was not functioning well, couldn't get up in the morning, or get to appointments on time. I knew no one, had two new doctors and no one cared about me. They made me be at the front desk where everyone would see me and I hated it. I had not slept in three weeks because they changed all my meds and was on Percocet for my pain. Then they said I was 'high' on drugs and made me do a drug test and put me in a substance abuse program. It didn't matter what I did; they saw me as trouble.

*Layla was medically discharged in October 2012. She is healing from her traumatic experiences and still has a great deal of physical pain.*

*Another story, from the earliest days of interviewing women veterans, was very important and inspiring to me and could not be included. I always felt this story was important for other MST survivors to know and hope to tell at least a part of it here. So many women felt they could have done something to prevent the rape, yet could not. In many cases they were drugged or numb and in shock. In this case, the woman was very fit and strong, yet was still overpowered and there was nothing she could have done to prevent being raped.*

*This woman was in military police training and volunteered for airborne when no men in her class raised their hands. She was not sure she could do it, but nonetheless tried out. She ran two miles twice a day in combat boots, did pull-ups, push-ups and passed the pretest. For four weeks they jumped off a fifty-foot tower into a concrete pit filled with sawdust. The instructors seemed to hate the women and were mean to them, believing women would denigrate their silver wings and macho image.*

*After that, they had to jump from a 250- foot tower with chutes that would open up. They were supposed to drop them feet first, but they purposefully dropped the women up high, so they came down on their butts and the pain radiated to their feet. Next they jumped out of a C-141 and told her to jump first, so the men would not chicken out.*

*Later in her career she was an assistant adjutant for an MP headquarters, where a major who was her direct superior and boss, overpowered and raped her during a required trip. He told her, "If you report this, you will never work again in this man's army, and you know they will take my word over yours."*

*Sad, but true, that they would indeed take his word over hers. It often seemed that any male's word, however false it was, would be taken over a woman's, however accurate and truthful her's was. Men are seen as more valuable and more powerful than women. This is part of the culture of abuse in our military.*

*She never reported the rape because she did not want more pain and trouble and she felt ashamed that it could happen to her. She told me, as a woman you are safer if you keep your mouth shut about rape and sexual assault. That is the culture in the military and their way of saying, "This is no place for a woman."*

*This woman veteran also told me,* "Women were treated much better when we had the Women's Army Corps (WAC). The men would catch hell if they messed with the women. When the WAC disbanded, the men had no accountability. Women felt safer coming back to their barracks with other women there. When women were assigned to other units with men, there was no support and there were double standards for men and women."

*Notice the distinction. When there was a Woman's Army Corps with their own leaders, it held all of the military to a higher standard of accountability. Without the presence of a Woman's Corps and support from women, male leadership does not maintain accountability. Perhaps women trained as military leaders are more able than men to uphold strong values and hold leaders and soldiers accountable for their actions.*

# Spousal Abuse and Betrayal

*"In the Armed Forces of America, the rate of domestic violence is more than double that of the civilian population. Each week someone dies at the hands of a relative in uniform. Why is there almost nothing in place to stop the rise of the war going on in military homes?"* [1]

*A 2001 a Task Force Report on Domestic Violence in the military stated that the services to prevent escalation were insufficient and they recommended investigation of all reports of domestic violence. Why has the military not acted on those recommendations? Why are more and more soldiers returning from combat and murdering their wives? Success in soldiering, fighting, gives them their identity. Within twenty-four hours of returning from the battlefield, they are home with no debriefing or transition assistance. Is it any wonder that they cannot turn it off?*

------------------------------------------------------------

[1]Stephanie Mines."Domestic Violence in the Military." *Massage and Bodywork Magazine,* September 2003.

*"The military often fails to readjust soldiers back into home life by failing to offer adequate counseling to re-socialize them into a nonviolent lifestyle. In 2002, a string of domestic homicides illustrated the grave need for post-deployment counseling.*

- *On the evening of June 11th, Sergeant Rigoberto Nieves shot and killed his wife, Nancy, and then killed himself. Sergeant Nieves had been serving in Afghanistan.*

- *On June 29th, Master Sergeant William Wright allegedly strangled his wife, Jennifer, after being back from Afghanistan for about a month.*

- *On July 9th, Cedric Ramon allegedly stabbed his estranged wife, Marilyn, at least fifty times before setting her house on fire.*

- *On July 19th, Sergeant Brandon Floyd shot and killed his wife before killing himself in the home they shared. Sergeant Floyd had returned home from Afghanistan just months before the murder.*

*These homicides were all committed on the same military base, Fort Bragg, and all of the soldiers had recently returned home from battle. As the string of domestic violence homicides at Fort Bragg so dramatically illustrates, domestic violence is a pervasive and endemic problem in the military."*[2]

-----------------------------------------------------------

[2]Patricia Horner. "Domestic Violence in the Military: Addressing the need for Policy Reform."*The Law and Society Journal IV.2004/2005.*

*It is easy to see the larger problem yet still the military denies it. There is more - "Back in January of this year, a young mother named Shalamar, was stabbed to death in broad daylight, by her army husband. For two years, Shalamar said she was physically and mentally abused at the hands of her soldier husband, and she said more than once he threatened to kill her. In May 2001, Shalamar went to court and reported her husband Damien had slapped and choked her. A month later, he pleaded guilty to assault and was sentenced to twelve months' probation and ordered to enroll in a counseling program. Shalamar continued to be abused and again reported it to police. Her mother was so worried; she says she called officials at Ft. Bragg herself. In December of 2001, Damien allegedly kidnapped Shalamar. He tied and taped her to a chair. She reportedly told friends he choked her, raped her, and beat her in front of her son. He made her kiss the toddler goodbye, saying she would never see him again. Shalamar managed to escape and Damien went to jail.*

*Within a month, charged with nine felonies, including first-degree kidnapping and rape, he was out on bail and, by his own request, was discharged from the army. Three days after his release, on January 13th of 2002, Shalamar had plans to meet Damien's brother for lunch and to talk. When she arrived, his brother wasn't there, but Damien was. Outside the restaurant, in broad daylight, Damien allegedly sliced Shalamar across her neck and stabbed her multiple times in her chest and abdomen. At twenty-four, Shalamar Franceschi was dead."[3] A friend and co-worker of Shalamar's, said that Damien raped, sodomized and held Shalamar's mother hostage at gunpoint on Fort Bragg and that the army should have done something. Damien was instead put in civilian jail and was out in three days to murder his wife. The command on Fort Bragg knew about Damien, his active criminal behavior/domestic violence, but did nothing.*

------------------------------------------------------------------
[3]Transcript, 25 September 2002, *Oprah Winfrey Show.*(NBC)

*Soldiers are taught to be hyper-masculine, aggressive, to assert their masculinity to dominate, and they do. They do it very well and are rewarded for that in the military. That ideology and behavior is expected, yet at home it creates risk. Wives are expected to relinquish power to their husbands and be subordinate to them, yet when their soldier husbands are deployed; it is the wife/mother who does everything: including child-care, home care, cooking and finances. The more deployments, the more independent the women become. The more independent they become, the more they begin to resent and resist returning to being subordinate. Their husbands, on returning from battle, must then reassert their will, power and control. It is in doing that, when they click on and resort to violent behavior. The problem is not new. The military has been avoiding facing this issue for many years.[4]*

*A "60 Minutes" documentary entitled, "Bringing the War Home," analyzed Pentagon records from 1992-1996, showing domestic violence five times higher than in the civilian population. It was also shown that the military, "Routinely failed to punish service members for it."[5] In the Domestic Violence Report April/May 2001, a study was cited at Presidio, where 53.3% of the engineers were very violent and 23% of them used weapons.[6] January 29, 2009, Katie Couric did a news report called "The Hidden Casualties of War," in which she said more than 25,000 spouses and domestic partners were attacked over the past decade and nearly ninety spouses died.*

-----------------------------------------------------------------

[4]Christine Hansen. "A Considerable Service: An Advocate's Introduction to Domestic Violence and the Military." *Domestic Violence Report.* April/May 2001.
[5]"Bringing the War Home." 29 January 2009. *CBS News.*
[6]Christine Hansen. "A Considerable Service: An Advocate's Introduction to Domestic Violence and the Military. *"Domestic Violence Report"* April/May 2001.

*Couric spoke with Lynn McCollum, Army Director of Family Affairs and said, "The army usually rallies around the soldiers and leaves the victim to fend for herself. And then when she finally does get help, the complaint is—the system is entirely stacked against her." McCollum gave only neutral responses. Couric said, "It's not only the victims that aren't getting help, it is also the soldiers." Couric confronted McCollum with a post deployment health questionnaire in which a soldier expressed concern that he might lose control during conflict and hurt a family member; then one year later did kill his wife. Couric pressed McCollum, who finally admitted that a mistake was made when the military did nothing with the concern of the soldier. [7] Every reporter needs to be relentless with military leaders and hold them accountable for their passivity about domestic violence.*

*Dr. Mic Hunter in his book, Honor Betrayed, describes military women being punched, kicked, and beaten up with twenty-two percent surviving life threatening violence such as, being shot or stabbed. He reports almost twenty-two percent active duty military women being physically and sexually abused by their partners. Twenty percent of their doctors on hearing of the abuse, did nothing and gave these reasons: domestic violence is a private matter between the partners, it takes too much time, the women are responsible for what happens to them and they feared for their own safety if they angered the perpetrator. [8]*

*When the fact of domestic violence is kept hidden, there is a cover-up and tacit support for it to continue—and it does. When reports of domestic violence are made and protection orders followed, the behavior is identified as abusive, illegal, immoral, and inappropriate.*

-------------------------------------------------------------

[7]"Bringing the War Home." 29 January 2009. *CBS News.*

[8]Mic Hunter, *Betrayal of Honor: Sexual Abuse in America's Military* (Barricade Books, 2007) 73-83.

*The violence is acknowledged and not condoned. The perpetrator and their behavior is brought into the open and both are condemned and held accountable. The military services need to be leaders in insisting on accountability for this ongoing behavior and act honorably on behalf of the soldier perpetrators and their victim wives and children.*

*Perpetrators of domestic violence are focused on controlling their victims, keeping the abuse secret and isolating their victim to protect themselves as abuser. The military supports them by turning a blind eye to the abuse and not holding them accountable for their violent behavior at home. Since the military trained them to be aggressive and violent, they see that behavior as OK. Without any higher authority to tell these abusive soldiers that domestic violence is wrong, they feel supported in acting out their violence on their wives and partners. The perpetrator has no reason or motivation to stop and their control extends to preventing their wife/partner access to counseling assistance.*

*Because the primary rule in the military culture is to never do anything to embarrass the armed forces, they must protect their image at all costs, even if that cost is the life of a wife/partner who is considered a liability by the military. "The women who are their victims find little protection or justice from the military."* [9]

*Combat values in the culture of the military described by Dr. Mic Hunter are: violence is the norm and accepted, see others as objects, limit empathy, and protect the larger unit/military even at the expense of any individual. These values encourage and contribute to domestic violence.* [10]

---

[9] Amy Herdy and Miles Moffeit,"Off Duty Violence."*Amnesty International Magazine,* (Spring 2004)

[10] Mic Hunter, *Betrayal of Honor: Sexual Abuse in America's Military* (Barricade Books, 2007) 79.

*Domestic violence in our military is a problem that must be addressed and condemned. Perpetrators must be held accountable for all their abusive actions, and treatment provided to both the perpetrator and victim. If the military is not going to address it, and they have demonstrated repeatedly that they cannot be trusted on their own to deal with it, then Congress must insist. It is essential that the culture of violence in military families be stopped. Soldiers must be trained and taught where their violence is OK and where it is not. This begs some questions, can a soldier who is trained to kill, learn what is and is not an appropriate target for their aggression? Can a military train men to be killers during war, wartime games and be gentle at home with their loved ones? Is domestic violence among military families a problem in other countries?*

## Maria – Peacetime Era

*Maria grew up in Lancaster, Pennsylvania and from age twelve was enamored with the navy women in uniform who would walk down the main street of her town. When she was sixteen, Maria went to the recruiter's offices to find the navy recruiter. She stopped at the first one to ask where to find the navy guy and the army recruiter enticed her to join the army. She went into the delayed entry program because she was too young at the time.*

I went on active duty in October of 1977 and went first to basic training at Fort Jackson, SC and then to AIT until February of 1978. My mother was not happy for me to be in the military. No one in my family had been in the military.

I grew up around boys and men, so it was not different for me to be in a co-ed unit in basic training. One day a Vietnam Veteran backed me into a corner and I pushed him away and reported it to my drill sergeant, who talked with the guy and it never happened again.

In AIT there was a man who was changing his MOS who harassed me regularly and insisted I marry him. He began to stalk me and continued to stalk me when I went to Fort Hood and found he was also assigned there. I told him if he came near me again I'd report him. He called me a bunch of names and left me alone after that.

February of 1978, I was assigned to the 15th AG Company at Fort Hood, TX as a records clerk. I was part of the First Calvary doing in-processing and liked it. They chose me because I spoke both English and Spanish; I was Puerto Rican.

One night a guy came into my room in the barracks when I was sleeping and he was on top of me. I woke up and started to beat on him and chased him off. I went to the CQ (Charge of Quarters) and raised hell about that guy getting into my room. I also went to the first sergeant to report it. The soldier who came into my room was not in our unit.

I had a boyfriend during that time and became pregnant, so had to move out of the barracks. My boyfriend, Melito, and I were going to get married before he went to Germany and I was supposed to transfer with him. Instead I became an unwed mother. My roommate introduced me to Cammron, who was a real charmer and I began to date him. My NCOIC (Non Commissioned Officer In Charge) brought me information on Melito and showed me that he had signed for a paternity test. I was conflicted because Cammron wanted to marry me and now Melito, my baby's father, was agreeing to be responsible for our baby.

January 1979, I had the baby and on February 14th, Cammron and I went in uniform to the courthouse and got married. I had known him only four months and never lived with him. My NCOIC had a talk with me and said he didn't think it was a good idea to marry Cammron. He was giving me fatherly advice but I did not listen. The first weekend after I married him, Cammron began to drink heavily and hit me. I fought back but he hit my stomach, pulled my hair and hit my arms and legs. I kept fighting but he was much stronger than me. I weighed about 125 pounds. I had sent my baby to Puerto Rico so my mother could care for him while I was on active duty, and now I was in shock wondering what I had gotten myself into. I did not say anything to anyone except my parents and friend back home and tried to do my work and not draw attention to me, so no one would ask me any questions. I was now isolated from the people I knew before. Cammron drank every weekend and got drunk and was beating me up all the time.

In April, I was beaten down from being hit every day and sexually assaulted by him repeatedly. I was anxious, depressed and crawling around on the floor crying. Whenever he was around I was expecting to be hit or sexually assaulted and so was very jumpy. I went to the clinic for the anxiety, depression and headaches. All they did was give me pills for the headache. Then I was even more devastated, so I put myself on orders to go anywhere away from there, but they disapproved it.

I continued to be traumatized. One day my husband pulled my hair when I was writing, and he pulled the table over and was going to bang my face into the floor. I became enraged and it gave me strength, so I grabbed the pen and stabbed him with it and told him if he ever touched me again I would kill him. He stopped then and after that he would tell me what he wanted to do in detail, instead of doing it.

In the meantime Melito was paying child support and around May, my mother got sick and could no longer care for my son. I went to Puerto Rico, got my baby and put in for a hardship discharge. I was discharged in June of 1979, and eventually went back to Puerto Rico with my son. I divorced Cammron in February of 1980, and when Melito returned from Germany, he came over to Puerto Rico to see us and we rekindled our relationship. We married in August of 1981, moved to Indiana and had another baby later that year. Melito went back into the army to make it a career and we went on to have twin boys after that.

## Susan Smith – Bosnia Era

*Susan knew four languages and had traveled around the world in 1987/1988, visiting thirty-one countries in eighteen months. She had just returned from a job in South Africa, when the wall came down in Germany. At thirty-four, she was thinking it would be great to learn Russian and work for a company in the Soviet Union.*

*However, in December 1991, she married a Korean language specialist and by February 1992, she had started basic training in the army. The command started her as an E-4 because of her college degrees. She had the highest rank in the company and was older than all three of the drill sergeants. They resented her rank because it was given to her, and they had to earn theirs in the army. They had no concept of the amount of work she had put in to earn her degrees. Her basic training was at Fort Jackson, South Carolina. There she was made platoon sergeant and was doing the paper work for her unit, in addition to her own basic training. Most of the women were eighteen years old while she was thirty-four. They called her grandma.*

*After basic, Susan went to the Defense Language Institute
(DLI) in Monterey, CA, where she was in class with all branches of
the military, the CIA and the FBI. She tested too high to learn Russian
and was given Chinese to learn instead. Summer 1992, she completed
the training and from there went to AIT, Military Intelligence Training
at Goodfellow AFB, San Angelo, TX, for eight weeks.*

It was nicer than the army; the instructors were not as rigid
about the rules. They even told dirty jokes there. I had a great drill
sergeant, but the commander did not like me, because I bought myself
an old Porsche and he was envious. I was always watching my back
with him.

In basic, I had yellow mucous coming out of my nose and was
coughing. I went to the clinic, they took x-rays and told me there was
nothing wrong and gave me antibiotics. Later in DLI, I had bronchitis
and sinusitis. I was trying to keep up and having a hard time. After
two weeks they gave me a different antibiotic. Every time I went to
sick call, they gave me a pregnancy test. That seemed odd.

When I went to the AFB, I had pain in my jaw and went to
a dentist there. They treated me more aggressively and told me that
the infection was now in my jaw. They wanted to do surgery on me
and did. I had a turbinate reduction and they went inside my sinuses
to allow them to drain. The surgery was at Darwell Hospital, Fort
Hood, TX. I had to drive five hours by myself after the surgery. The
surgeon was kind enough to let me stay the night and drive back
the next day. While they were doing the surgery I was just falling
asleep, when I heard the doctor telling one of the dirtiest jokes I'd
ever heard. I looked around and noticed that there were no females in
the operating room. There was one surgeon and one anesthesiologist,
plus two corpsmen. I was concerned when I saw that, but before the
joke ended I was unconscious.

I went to the recovery room and had pain from a catheter. In the hospital room I told the male nurse that I was hurting from the catheter. I told him I thought I was sexually assaulted while I was in surgery. My vagina felt like I had had sex and I felt inflamed where the catheter was. I wanted to report the sexual assault and the male nurse said, "You've just had sinus surgery." The next morning I had to pack and leave to drive back. I got pulled over on the drive back and was crying. Blood clots were coming out of my nose. Later when I went to pay the ticket, the same cop that pulled me over said, give me back that ticket and let this be a lesson to you.

When I returned home, I learned that my husband had stolen my car keys and abused my car. Then he made me move by myself and harassed me so much, I had to move again. I only lived with him for three months and filed for divorce. I found out that my husband had been lying to the army. He told the army he was in school when he had actually been AWOL, driving around in my car. My drill sergeant convinced me not to report my husband and I didn't. I had no close friends there, because my husband managed to cut me off from my family and friends. I was feeling pretty alone.

In December of 1992, I was assigned to a field station at Kuna, Hawaii, next to Schofield Barracks. There was an underground tunnel there for intelligence work and it was in a secured facility. My husband was unfortunately sent over at the same time and we shared a hotel room for a week until I got housing. My dad called to say he had not received payment for the loan, and he was holding me responsible for a loan I knew nothing about.

While I was in Hawaii, my husband stole my papers, ran up large bills and did not give me incoming messages. I think he was waiting until I got my $5000 bonus and was planning to use that to pay off all the bills. He was promising me to stop doing the things that were unacceptable to me. I believed him then. We got a nice house on the island and we were put on opposite shifts, which worked better for me. He was in the field in a support unit and I was strategic, meaning not deployable, on a 24-7 rotating shift, but no equipment. I had a desk and chairs. None of the admin people had a top-secret clearance to see what was going on. Only my company was there. I was up at 6 a.m. for PT and had nothing to do because I had no equipment to do voice intercept. All we could do was sit, read or study for a few months until they got some equipment. We did have old tapes we could listen to for practice. I had no work and no supervisor.

After three or four months, I learned that I was pregnant, but I did not want to tell my husband for fear he would hurt me. He had been holding me down all the time and telling me I was screwed up. The pregnancy test went right to command. They gave me seventy-two hours to decide what to do. I asked for three weeks and for them not to tell him. I did tell him when I had to, and he was happy. Later he insisted that I write him a check for $5000. I refused and he began to jump up and down on my stomach. I weighed 130 pounds and he was 230 pounds. I was ambivalent about the baby, but I was fighting back, kicking, screaming, and biting him. He left and went to my commander and told him that I had attacked him, that I was crazy and out to get him, and he was afraid.

I left and went to the Pearl Harbor women's shelter. The next morning they told me I was ordered out of there and could not stay. I left and went to work and tried to talk to my commander. I was told if I tried to talk with anyone about this, I would be court-martialed and kicked out of the army.

*First her drill sergeant used his power and influence to get her not to report her husband's theft, violence, abuse, and lying to the army, and then her commander threatened her with court martial if she told the truth, because he was taken in by her husband's manipulation and deceit. This is how women in these type of circumstances become even more vulnerable, trapped, and alone. What needed to happen was that her drill sergeant would encourage her to report what was going on in her marriage to a counselor. From there a report could have been filed and some clear structure and support given to her. Her husband would have been required to have his own appropriate counseling that would include a full assessment. In addition, part of the structure given would include no contact between them and orders to support that. The no contact order would require that they not live or work together and he be reassigned. He would need ongoing group therapy in which he is held accountable for his behavior and given structure and skills to change his behavior. At some point they would also need to have couples counseling to teach them more appropriate and healthy ways to relate to one another before it would be safe for them to live as a couple.*

The next day I worked in the command office. I wanted to go to the hospital, but they would not let me. That day I received a bouquet of flowers, which my husband had charged to my credit card. There was never a time that I was able to tell what happened to me, because of the threat of being court-martialed.

A couple of months later, my house was robbed and I called the insurance company to report it. They said, "Oh we already got a call telling us you'd be calling with a false claim, so we're on to you." I felt very trapped. I also found out that my husband had the key to my car and had cancelled my car insurance without my knowledge. He also had my phone number charged monthly, and told the phone company that I was in another state.

The army forced me to go to anger management classes with my husband. I filled out a form with my stress levels and experiences My husband grabbed it and started reading it out loud. I complained and got couples counseling. I went to the bank and found that my husband had taken $8,000 out of my personal account. I stayed at the bank until they gave me my money. Then I went to another bank and deposited the money with specific instructions it was my single account and only I could access it.

I got a restraining order against my husband and no one would acknowledge it, or help me. I was working at the administrative office and living in the barracks. There was one nineteen year old gal there having sex with the guys. My husband was stalking me and everyone denied it. One day I asked for help; for someone to walk me to my car and at first they would not, then I said: go look at the guy behind the dumpster and tell me if it is my husband.

The command sergeant major did check, saw my husband and agreed to help me. Then others began to see my husband stalking me, because he was not very good at it. Gradually people began to realize I was not crazy and all these things were really happening to me. Then people were more supportive. My command sergeant quit and got me a new E-7. I started to tell him he's taking on a problem and I told him about the order for me not to talk. He said it was an illegal order and he'd get it changed. I told him I don't lie and will do whatever I need to do to resolve this.

I filed a complaint with the city of Honolulu and a police report. I also filed divorce papers. The police could not find him to give him papers for assault, felony, and divorce. They finally found him about six weeks before I left Hawaii.

At my obstetrical appointment the doctor saw no movement and said nothing except to come back in five days. The doctor expected me to have a spontaneous abortion but that did not happen. They did a dilatation and evacuation in June. *(Her baby had died in her womb and the surgery was to clean it out.)* No one talked with me about the experience, my feelings or my loss. I had two jobs, working at the bakery and catering for the command. I was paying all the bills my husband had run up and no one would help me.

I was still trying to see the brigade commander and they would not let me. Before that, I tried to talk to a chaplain and he listened, but then told me his sexual fantasies and that certainly was no help. I finally went to my commander and told him everything. I also tried another chaplain who said, "You're going to die anyway, and you don't want to die with the sin of divorce on you, so you should stay with your husband." I left.

Thanks giving 1993, I was ordered to go to the sergeant's home for Thanksgiving. He could not believe the drama that the command had made of all this and how hard they were trying to cover it up. I was called into command and they grilled me about my relationship with sergeant J, and told me they had witnesses that the sergeant and I were having an affair. I learned to have copies of all paper work and files, so when they asked me about something I could show them. They called me back six weeks later and asked if I was scared. My attitude was that I am not going to let them take me down. They were pissed that they had nothing on me and kept trying. They were trying to pin a charge of adultery on me. One of the guys in the CID unit told me, "That is what they try to do with MST victims; if they are married and raped; they try to charge them with adultery." I was in Hawaii doing intelligence work from December 1992, until April 1995.

The sergeant major was finally willing to acknowledge my protection order. There was a criminal trial against my husband for kidnapping, assault and other charges. They told me if they did the trial I would have to fly back to Hawaii on my own money. By the time they arranged for the trial, I was gone from Hawaii. Because I was in so much debt I could not do it and so negotiated. The charges were dropped to a misdemeanor, which was basically a slap on the wrist.

He was sent to Fort Lewis when he heard I was sent to Seattle. I did not know anyone. I was out of the military then. I took all my documents and protection order to his command at Fort Lewis. I told them of his criminal acts and to let me know when he is on leave. His wages were garnished and he filed for bankruptcy.

When I was transitioning out of the military, a guy told me to file a claim with the VA for PTSD. I was diagnosed with PTSD and in May of 1995, I went to the Seattle VA. I was in the program there for two years doing one on one cognitive behavioral therapy. I have been in and out of treatment for 12 years.

While I was in the support group, I found they all had trouble with paperwork and claims. We all helped each other. A nurse helped them and they all got their claims through. After a couple of years I started to advertise giving help to women vets with claims and getting through the system. I have continued to do that at the Seattle VA and at American Lake VA.

Then I was given an active duty case, a Sergeant Wood of the Stryker Brigade in Kuwait. I had to deal with a general at Fort Lewis and with the Pentagon. I got her a full medical board with x-rays in one day and got her out of the military. The story was on *CNN and*

*Good Morning America* and then I got many more clients after that. I also did wellness fairs for women who served and got more women with MST. (See article in appendix, "Vet Becomes Crusader for Victims of Soldier Rape")

# Jessica 1985-1990

*Jessica had always been patriotic and loved to watch Mash on TV, so at age 18, even though she was married, her husband supported her joining the army to be a medic and make that her career. Her basic training was at Fort Dix, New Jersey and from there she went to Fort Sam Houston, Texas for AIT. She enjoyed her experiences and felt respected.*

*Her first duty assignment was to Dwight David Eisenhower Army Medical Center at Fort Gordon, GA. Her dream to be a medic was unfulfilled and she was instead placed in administration.*

I lived in the barracks on base and did extra duty because I loved what I was doing and wanted to make a good impression. I began to notice things that did not seem right to me, such as, different kinds of malpractice. You know military doctors cannot be sued. In one case, the wrong breast was removed and in another, the lab tech micro-waved fresh blood and the patient died. To his credit, he put a radiation sticker on it, but no one paid attention to it and gave it to the patient anyway. The lab tech was being court-martialed and hung himself. When I found out about the malpractice stuff, I decided to blow the whistle, went to the inspector general and testified about what I learned that was malpractice.

I was being harassed for being a whistleblower, and I felt I had nowhere to go. When you work in a hospital, the people there are family, and the patients are not necessarily the ones on your side. I went against family and not just the chain of command, but some co-workers as well. Many times I ate alone, but would have people come to me in private and say how brave I was. I never felt brave. Towards the end I felt like a total idiot, because nothing I did in the end made much difference.

My husband did not like it in Georgia, left and found someone else, so we were divorced in 1987. Then the following year I met a medic that I liked, we started a relationship, eventually married in 1988 and had our daughter. He used to drink heavily and went to rehab, but did not complete the program and was kicked out of the army as a rehab failure with an honorable discharge.

His Abuse started out small. First it was verbal belittling then he began to slap me around, and tell me I provoked him; then he would beg for my forgiveness and say how much he loved me and how passionate he was about me. I don't know how long he was doing drugs. He had been slapping me and choking me sometimes when he was drinking but then stopped. I was friends with an active duty woman whose husband was beating her. She was given an 'Article 15' and demoted when she was beaten so badly that she could not report for duty, but he was only given two weeks of extra duty and did not lose pay or rank. At that point, I was getting abused so much that I couldn't see how much of it was his fault.

After my husband got out, he was drinking more and slapping me more. It would only happen about every two months but then became more frequent. I went to my chain of command the first sergeant, and my female captain company commander asking for couples counseling or anger management or something; they would not help me because he was now my dependent. Then I went to drug and alcohol rehab program to ask for their help and they basically slammed the door on my face.

One time I was five minutes late for duty and they gave me an 'Article 15' and demoted me. Another time, I did not salute an officer fast enough and they gave me another 'Article 15,' even though they don't usually do that for such minor offenses, they did it to me. I am sure it is because I blew the whistle on the malpractice in the hospital.

Our son was born on Christmas Day in 1989. He had a genetic illness that affected his muscles and he was essentially born dying. That was when things got really bad and my husband started using crack cocaine and insisted I do it too. I was so distraught I went along with him. It did help me get through the six months until our son died, but I also took more abuse from my husband.

My son died in June of 1990. A few weeks later my husband choked me until I passed out. He later hit me over the head and tied me to the bed. Then he had a bunch of other soldiers come in and rape me, all because I refused the drugs. I finally got free and went to the military police, but they said they could not do anything because it did not happen on base. It did not matter to them that some of the men who raped me were active duty soldiers from their base.

I moved back into the barracks and to the drug and alcohol center and turned myself in, but they would not treat me, because I did not have high enough rank and I did not have enough time left in service. I became suicidal and overwhelmed with emotions because of my son's death, the gang rape and not being able to get any help with drug rehab. I was on the psych ward at the hospital because I was suicidal. I begged them to keep me an inpatient until I got kicked out, but they wouldn't do that. I begged them to give me leave and let me get into the civilian rehab and they wouldn't even have to pay. That was after they said they would not give me inpatient rehab themselves because it would "cost too much and I wasn't worth it since my rank was so low and I had so little time left in service." Those were pretty much their exact words.

The worst part was that my husband told me I deserved it all because I was smoking crack, so I must be a whore, because all women who smoked ended up as whores. That is why he treated me like one, and sold me out to the guys who raped me. I saw one of them two years later at the store, and he told me he thought it was all a game, that I was just kinky and was really willing. He did not think of what he did as rape because, to him, there was no way that a husband would do that to his wife.

They kicked me out of the army in September, because I was unable to report for duty after my husband slapped and choked me so badly I could not function. They gave me a general discharge under honorable conditions for unsatisfactory performance, all because of what my husband did to me, so I went back to him after I got kicked out. I came really close to death at least a few times when he choked me until I passed out and wished he would kill me. I was staying with him so he would kill me. I was there for a few weeks until Cannon Hall (Civilian Rehab Center) had a place for me. October of 1990 I got into a rehab program.

It took me many years to get to the point in my life where I am now, finally learning to be okay with myself and to accept myself for who I am. I had some really fucked up shit happen to me, and I dwelled in it for far too long, but today I am working on just getting better. Sometimes just breathing, and that doesn't come easy, is the hardest thing I do. Each and every single day I take it easy on myself, and that takes nonstop work, it's a conscious and constant effort, but it's worth it; I am worth it.

I knew I had a problem. I had turned myself in to get help when I was still in the army, so I didn't need denial to be broken down. The counselors spent most of their time convincing me that I couldn't go back to my husband no matter what and that I was co-dependent and it would kill me. They even had me say, "I'm Jessica, an addict and co-dependent," to get it through my head; and it worked. The day I graduated, my husband came to my graduation, I told him I wasn't going back to him, and didn't get in his car. One of the counselors gave me a ride downtown to a shelter where I stayed for a few days until I got a room at a YWCA. It was a group shelter for women.

I still think that if I only had the help earlier, if only all those doors weren't slammed in my face, I could have stayed in the army. I hope that it's easier for women in the military today to get the help they need if they are victims of domestic abuse and/or rape. I stayed with my husband for a few weeks after the gang rape and he spent those weeks telling me what an awful person I was and how I deserved everything that happened to me. I never had anyone tell me any different, so I learned to tell myself different. Today I feel that, as a human being I have value and worth, but it took me a LONG time to get there. I did leave him when I went into treatment and never went back to him after that.

I want to say that a Victims Unit, or Sex Crimes Unit, or Domestic Crimes Unit needs to be on every single military base, and that those units need to be kept entirely out of the chain of command, or more women will continue to go through what I and others have gone through.

The army was supposed to help us when my son died and they did nothing. That was because I blew the whistle. The commander only received a slap on the wrist for not helping me, a reprimand for not doing what was protocol to help me with my son's death.

So much has happened in my life since then. I have made many mistakes, some of the wreckage of which I am still dealing with, but today I have learned that the most important thing I need to do each and every moment is to be easy on myself. That is the hardest and most worthwhile thing I have ever done, and it is a constant and ongoing challenge, but thankfully, I can look myself in the mirror and remind myself that I am worth something.

*There was one more story I will summarize here, since I cannot tell you the whole story. It was a young WAC who married a man that was a mental health counselor. He tested high in most everything, was highly valued in his unit and was an athlete. She described him as very sensitive and intelligent, but immediately after marrying her, he became violent and abusive to her. He had two children who told her he always did that before. He was violent and abusive with the children, as well as her, but managed to keep it hidden from those in command. He went through the typical cycle; first the honeymoon, then guilt and apology, then he told her it was a mistake and he will do better, please forgive him. She felt embarrassed and did not know what to do. He was careful to be sure her bruises were not visible to others. She felt intimidated by him and sought counseling outside the military. She always believed with all his good qualities that she could fix the situation, especially because he was a mental health specialist. That part never made sense to her, nor did the fact that he was getting away with his domestic violence.*

They were deployed together and after three months he gave her a black eye. She was working in drug rehab at the time and had to meet with her supervisor, who was aware of what was happening to her. She went to an outside group for help and her husband was in total denial of his behavior. One day, she caught his elbow before he connected with her face and his elbow hit her teeth and drew blood. He yelped and made a scene and told her he was going to call the military police. His young daughter got out of bed and told him, "Someone needs to call the MP's on you, dad. You're the one who hurts us." The WAC talked with her first sergeant, chaplain and commander. Her husband made an official statement. He was given a job with the first sergeant and she was <u>taken from her job and put in the basement mailroom and isolated without emotional support from anyone.</u>

She was an expert at her job, was an expert shot, and felt the army tried to make her the loser instead of her husband the abuser. She left the military after an excellent career of almost ten years, because of the army's mishandling of the domestic violence.

It is important for the military to support military families and that includes not discounting soldiers who abuse their wives and/ or children. It is all too common when men are trained to be killers and to be in control, that they become violent in their homes. The military needs to be accountable for the results of training soldiers to be killers. That means instead of turning a blind eye to it when one of their best soldiers is identified as an abusive husband/father, they need to let the soldier know that they know, tell them it is not OK, and insist on full disclosure from all family members and therapy.

I believe it is important when spousal abuse occurs, that the military takes clear firm action: gets all the details from all family *members, provide each of them with protection and then determine the best course of action, which may include living separately and no contact, while the perpetrator is in therapy. All perpetrators need to be in therapy both individual and group. Individual therapy makes it too easy for them to look and sound better than they are. In the group they will likely be triggered and the abusive behavior will surface so that it can be dealt with. It is also important for the victim to have individual therapy to feel safe and rebuild her sense of self, her confidence and the ability to express herself clearly, and especially to learn to set firm limits and hold them.*

# Attitude and Accountability

These are the themes that came through the women's stories. First, there was more pressure on women to be professional, know their job and perform at higher standards than were required of male soldiers. Second, their skills and proficiency had to surpass all expectations of men, to be simply accepted and treated with any semblance of respect. Third, they felt a sense of urgency to show leadership and management abilities whether acknowledged or recognized for it.

Male attitudes toward women were harsh, dismissive, arrogant, demeaning, disrespectful, and demoralizing. Those attitudes made it clear that women were not wanted in the military. Men tended to see women as government property for them to do with as they pleased.

That attitude was very widespread from the lowest to highest ranks. If the leadership in any or all branches of the military truly taught respect for women and <u>meant</u> zero tolerance for sexual harassment or assault, then women would not be perceived and treated in such disgusting ways. I remind the reader that not all men in the military hold these attitudes or behave in these ways, yet it is very pervasive and must be acknowledged and stopped.

One of the women said, "The army is the best place for a rapist," because there is an unspoken rule that rape is tolerated, in spite of the so-called zero tolerance policy. She told me, "If you come forward and report you will pay the price and they will hurt and harass you. The army policy is stated as zero tolerance but they all look the other way." Sexual assault is the most underreported crime in the military and yet the numbers of reported cases is higher than ever and less than eighty percent of cases are actually reported.

Over and over in these stories, it has been shown that if a woman reports sexual assault or someone else reports it on her behalf, she is punished severely and the perpetrator is protected, promoted, and permitted to continue inappropriate abusive language and behavior. This retaliation is definitely a problem in relation to leadership attitudes, execution, and training. Women who report their assault later, are required to come up with someone to corroborate their story, yet sexual assaults are usually done out of sight. There lies the catch twenty-two.

One of the tricks the Veterans Administration uses to deny benefits to women, is to ask if they need to drink alcohol to get to sleep. If she says yes, then they track it back to her service and deny the claim based on alcohol intoxication. Both men and women with PTSD symptoms use alcohol to self-medicate and it is not used against men. Why is it used against women veterans?

Irish, a women veteran who helped other women veterans file claims, and who this book is dedicated to, told me that it is very difficult for women to be successful with a PTSD claim and to get help. She said there are very few women's programs, and women who have MST will not attend mixed therapy groups. She also said that women don't believe they will get what they need from the Veterans Administration and that they are more likely to be hurt than helped.

There are also many women who believe the risk to them being unfairly labeled in the system is too great to bear. This is true of women who have been sexually assaulted and those who are lesbians. Perhaps in the case of lesbians, the repeal of Don't Ask, Don't Tell, will result in those women being treated with the dignity and respect they deserve.

Other noteworthy themes are the threats and intimidation tactics used to coerce women into sex with those of higher rank, and not reporting the rape or sexual assault. Women are told, among other things, that if she reports the assault, she and her family will be persecuted or killed, that it will reflect negatively on the corps, and will permanently mark her file and ruin her career.

It has been shown that women who are assaulted, whether by their own spouse or another soldier or higher ranking officer, are usually isolated from all support, ostracized, and further victimized after coming forward. When a rapist confesses, the military ignores that confession and instead charges the woman with making false statements, puts her through yet another violation of her rights, and makes her life a living hell.

Men are also being raped in the military services and they too are being doubly victimized. Much of what is described here regarding women applies to them also. Perhaps if men and women who were sexually assaulted in the military by military personnel, joined forces they could have more influence in changing the system. The problem is that women with MST do not trust men, project their anger onto them, and cannot tolerate the feelings the men have.

Because women are so demeaned and diminished by the military and are considered government property, there is no justice for them. The U. S. Armed Forces seems to be giving a strong repetitive message that justice in the military is only for those they value, which all too often are the perpetrators. The Military Justice System at every level and all the way up to the Supreme Court, gives immunity to rapists in the military. All of this must stop! It is time for accountability to prevail.

On February 15th of 2011, Attorney Susan Burke filed a class action lawsuit in the Eastern Virginia Federal Court on behalf of seventeen military men and women who claimed that the DOD and Pentagon did not prevent, investigate or prosecute their perpetrators from violently and sexually assaulting them, nor did they implement congressionally mandated reforms to stop rape and other sexual assaults. The plaintiffs in the case were from each branch of the armed forces. Eleanor Smeal, President of the Feminist Majority Foundation, speaking at a press conference said, that ninety-five percent of the rapes and assaults to military personnel are from repeat offenders and serial rapists, that the military response has been inadequate, and has engendered more crime. She went on to say that the pattern of promoting, rather than punishing rapists in the military, must be changed and all previous responses to commissions and task force recommendations have been woefully inadequate.[1] Over the past

------------------------------------------------------------------

[1]Newsbrief, *MsMagazine*. 15 February 2011

sixteen years there have been eighteen different panel or commission reports.

Keith Rohman, the lead investigator in the case, cites the immunity that the military has from sexual harassment and assault in the workplace, due to the 1950 Feres Doctrine. Rohman acknowledges the military has not had to be accountable.[2] Why should they be above the law?

"There's no investigatory training. They don't tell you to look for evidence," says Greg Jacob, who spent ten years in the marines and rose to the rank of captain. Instead, they hand over a manual for court martial, which explains, among other things, that the investigating officer should consider, first and foremost, "The character and military service of the accused." Jacob says that essentially means weighing each soldier's past and future value to the unit." "It's an HR approach to criminal conduct," he says. "Military justice imbued me with the ability to be judge and jury. Honestly, I had no idea what to do."[3]

Rebecca Havrilla told Jesse Ellison of The Daily Beast, "Someone who is a misogynistic asshole isn't going to change their minds, because of some PowerPoint presentation. If you have a leadership that doesn't give a shit, nothing's going to change. It has to start from the top down." [4]

---

[2]Jesse Ellison, "Gates, Rumsfeld Sued Over U.S. Military's Rape Epidemic." *The Daily Beast.* 15 February 2011.
URL: http://www.thedailybeast.com/blogs-and-stories/2011-02-15/robert-gatTes-sued-over-us- Militarys-rape-epidemic/p/
[3]Ibid
[4]Ibid

At a press conference at the National Press Club, Anuradha K. Bhagwati, Executive Director of Service Women's Action Network (SWAN), made the following remarks:

"Rape, sexual assault, and sexual harassment are a plague upon the United States Military. A pervasive climate of sexual violence and intimidation threatens our national security by undermining operational readiness, draining morale, harming retention, and destroying lives."

"As a marine commander, I witnessed my own senior officers violate sexual harassment and sexual assault policies, shirk their responsibilities to their own troops and lie to families by ignoring reports of abuse, transfer sexual predators out of their units instead of prosecuting them, promote sexual predators during ongoing investigations, and accuse highly decorated enlisted service members of lying about their abuse, simply because they were women. Any attempt to hold these officers accountable was met with threats and retaliation. I saw some of the nation's finest service members leave the military after their abuse and betrayal, while their perpetrators and the officers who willingly protected them, to this day remain in uniform."

"Today, as the head of an organization devoted to eliminating sexual violence from our military, I see that little if anything has changed. The government has studied this issue for decades, over multiple administrations, and yet, assaults on our troops continue year after year, with no end in sight."

"We have reached a crisis point with this issue. In FY 2009, 3,230 service members reported rape or sexual assault throughout the military. The Department of Defense itself acknowledges that 80% of sexual assault survivors do not report the crime. If we do the math, in 2009, approximately 16,150 service members were sexually assaulted."

"Reporting sexual assault and sexual harassment in the military is brutally intimidating at best, and a death sentence at worst. Perpetrators often guarantee a victim's silence by threat of retaliation. Also, unsympathetic commanders who fail to protect survivors are all too common. Often times it is commanders who are complicit in cover-ups of these cases."

"In this context, encouraging victims to report is irresponsible at best. And yet, the Department of Defense is relentlessly focused on getting more women and men to report, without doing anything to put perpetrators behind bars, without guaranteeing survivors' personal safety, anonymity and confidentiality, privileged communication with victim advocates, or access to a lawyer. The work of the Department of Defense's tiny Sexual Assault Prevention and Response Office (SAPRO) largely consists of poster campaigns, data collection, and provision of training and education materials to the armed services. It should not be a surprise that the military cannot stem the tide of sexual assault in the ranks because SAPRO has no teeth, and it has no teeth, because the Department of Defense has deliberately not vested it with any judicial or law enforcement authority. SAPRO's notorious poster campaigns to 'prevent' rape are rife with victim blaming and rape mythology, including a shocking poster that encourages servicemen to 'wait until she's sober.'"

"Rape, sexual assault, and sexual harassment are often career-enders for victims. Unlike in the civilian world, a military rape survivor cannot quit her or his job, or re-locate to a different community. They are often forced to live with, work with, or work under the supervision of their perpetrators."

"Unlike in the civilian world, survivors have no access to redress when their chain of command fails to protect them or fails to punish the perpetrator. Unlike in the civilian world, survivors have no legal right to sue their perpetrators, their supervisors, or their branch of service for damages."

"It is time to finally acknowledge that the Military Judicial System is broken when it comes to cases of rape, sexual assault and sexual harassment, and that an alternative system must be created to guarantee accountability and justice for these crimes. American youth should not sacrifice their right to bodily integrity when they step forward to serve our nation. They bravely and honorably volunteer to wear the uniform with the understanding that they may make the ultimate sacrifice. That is enough to ask of them. But we must not continue to subject them to sexual violence, torture, and betrayal by their fellow personnel. Your daughters and sons, your sisters and brothers, your mothers and fathers, our American heroes, deserve better." [5]

"Carri Goodwin enlisted in the marine corps in August, 2007 at the age of eighteen. While at Pendleton Marine Base, California, Carri was raped by a marine in her unit. She was bullied by her command for reporting a rape and the marines forced her out with a personality disorder diagnosis. She did not tell her family she had been raped and had received no support or assistance from her command. She did not tell them she was taking Zoloft, a drug for anxiety. Mr. Noling, (Carri's father) said that he noticed Carri was drinking heavily when she returned from the marine corps. Five days after she returned home to Alliance,

-----------------------------------------------------------------------

[5]Anuradha K. Bhagwati, Executive Director Servicewomen's Action Network remarks, *National Press Club,* 15 February 2011.

Ohio, under age at twenty, after two years in the marine corps, Carri went drinking with her older sister. The drug Zoloft reportedly interacted with the alcohol and she ended up dead that night with a blood alcohol content of .46, six times the legal limit. Later in going through her possessions, her family found journals that described the rape and how the marine corps treated her after she reported it."[6]

Gary Noling shared all this while attending the National Press Club press conference on 15 February, 2011. "According to Mr. Noling, Carri's rapist was accused of another rape at Camp Pendleton in 2006. The rapist received non-judicial punishment for raping Carri. He is still in the marine corps."[7]

Panayiota Bertzikis, a plaintiff in the lawsuit, "Says she was raped by a Coast Guard shipmate while out on a social hike with him in Burlington, Vt. Bertzikis complained to her commanding officer, but she said authorities did not take substantial steps to investigate the matter. Instead, she said, they forced her to live on the same floor as the man she had accused and tolerated others calling her a 'liar' and 'whore'."[8]

Veteran Kori Cioca, twenty-five, of Wilmington, Ohio, tells how she was raped, and her jaw broken, while serving in the U.S. Coast Guard. In 2005 she was hit in the face by a supervisor who broke and dislocated her jaw and raped her, reported Kimberly Hefling of the *Associated Press*. Even though the man confessed to having

-------------------------------------------------------------

[6] Ann Wright, "Military Fails to Protect Service Members from Rape— Class Action Lawsuit filed against the Pentagon," 24 March, 2011.

[7] Ibid.

[8] Kimberly Hefling, "Veterans Say Rape Cases Mishandled." *The Washington Post-AP NewsBreak* 15 February, 2011.

sex with her, Cioca said in the lawsuit she was told if she pressed forward with reporting the sex as a rape, she would be court-martialed for lying. Command did not keep the rape confidential and allowed other military personnel to harass Cioca and spit on her. Her command also directed her to sign a paper saying she had an inappropriate relationship with her rapist, but she objected to signing a false statement and they countered by stating it was an order to sign it. The rapist pleaded guilty only to hitting her and his punishment was a minor loss of pay and being forced to stay on the base for thirty days. Her punishment was to be sent to a duty station without a surgeon after her coast guard physician told her command she needed surgery on her jaw, and then she was assigned to an all-male barracks. She was discharged from the military for a 'history of inappropriate relationships.' "You think of a coast guardsman, you think of somebody in the military holding themselves at a certain level," Cioca said. When somebody walks up to you and shakes your hand and says, "Thank you for your service." Little do they know they're shaking the hand of a man who rapes and beats women in the military."[9] The article said Kori still has numbness in her jaw and nightmares.

"My body hurts every day. My face hurts. I get the most horrible headaches. My body has been trespassed. The honor that I had was stripped from me. I'm no longer proud of myself. People tell me thank you for your service, but my service wasn't what it was supposed to be," she said. [10]

Technical Sergeant Rebekah Havrilla, one of the women in the lawsuit, served in the army from January 2004 until September 2009. She was commanded to attend classes about the prevention of

-----------------------------------------------------------

[9]Kimberly Hefling, "Veterans Say Rape Cases Mishandled." *The Washington Post-AP NewsBreak* 15 February, 2011.

[10]Ibid.

sexual assault and harassment; they made a mockery of it by prohibiting certain behavior then allowing participants to engage in that same behavior during class break. One soldier in her class stripped naked and was 'punished' by being made instructor for the next sexual assault and harassment training.

Sergeant Havrilla was deployed to Afghanistan in 2006, and was not only harassed by her supervisor repeatedly, but was raped by a soldier from the canine unit she was assigned to. This rapist photographed the rape. In 2009 she saw the rapist at Fort Leonard Wood and went into shock. She went to the chaplain for help and was told, "It must have been God's will for her to be raped." [11] Michael Isakoff reported on the *Nightly News,* that on her last day in Afghanistan a fellow sergeant trapped her in his room and would not let her leave until he got what he wanted. He pushed her down on the bed and used his body weight to keep her down so he could rape her. During the rape he took photos which he then posted on a porn website. Rebecca felt completely and utterly exposed. Except in this culture of abuse, how could anyone say those heinous actions were God's Will?

Sara Albertson served in the marine corps from 2003-2008, and was raped by a fellow marine of higher rank. A senior officer climbed into her bed while she was sleeping and forced himself on her. When she told her command about the rape, they told her she and the rapist would be charged with 'Inappropriate Barracks Conduct' and that she could not discuss this with anyone, but was required to report it, and she must follow her rapists orders because he outranked her. It was strongly advised by Corporal Albertson's counselor that

------------------------------------------------------------

[11] *Cioca et al v.Rumsfield and Gates, C.A. 11 cv 151*

she not have to interact with her rapist and her command forced her to do just that repeatedly for two full years, in spite of her panic attacks and request to leave to deal with the effects of the rape. Her appeal to have different housing than her rapist, were also denied and he was promoted to lead the program she was assigned to.[12]

Two shipmates raped Petty Officer DeRoche in a hotel room, while on port of call in Thailand. One held her down while the other raped her and this was repeated several times. When they were done they put her in the shower, washed her and put her out on the street. She found her way back to the hotel and told a female friend what happened. The friend took her to the military police, who brought her to the sexual assault coordinator and from there, to a medical exam. She was bruised and injured to such a degree that the physician stopped the exam and began to cry, he was so distraught about the extent of her injuries. After she reported the rapes, she was imprisoned on the medical ward and denied food. She was forced to be on call for twenty-four hours a day and could not leave the ship.[13]

Panayiota Bertzikis another plaintiff, served in the coast guard from 2005-2007, and in May of 2006 was thrown to the ground, punched in the face and raped while on a hike. When she reported the rape she was told to stop talking about it, or she would be charged with a crime equivalent to slander. Bertzikis obtained copies of photos and the rapist admission of guilt through the Freedom of Information Act, but her command did not even investigate the charges and forced her to live on the same floor in the barracks as her rapist and work with him. They told her if they worked together they could "work out their differences." *This command is completely ignorant of the*

---

[12]*Cioca et al v.Rumsfield and Gates, C.A. 11 cv 151.*
[13]Ibid.

*difference between a violent crime and a disagreement.*

When Bertzikis was transferred to Boston, Massachusetts she was harassed incessantly with names like, "liar and whore" and a group of other coast guard personnel cornered her and tried to rip off her uniform saying she would "pay for snitching" on their friend and they threatened to rape her again. Perhaps worst of all, when she went to the "victim advocate" for help, she was advised not to report this assault and harassment because she would be seen as "difficult," would not get any assistance and further, her assigned attorney said to her, "If [her rapist] did not have a history of sexual assault, why would he assault anyone now?" [14]

From this example it is clear how ineffective the current victim advocate training and functioning are, when they seem to serve the same culture of abuse that led to the rape. In addition, how ignorant the Military Justice System is that it does not take into account the power of the overall attitudes and homage paid to the existing abuse culture exhibited by the military.

Katelyn Boatman was on active duty in the air force in 2010. After graduating from the Survival, Evasion, Resistance, and Escape (SERE) School, was assigned to Tinker AFB in Oklahoma. While there as an aviator, she was subjected to severe harassment by her command, e.g., her commander asking her in front of other aviators if she "liked it in the ass." When she refused to respond he called her a "prude cunt."

-----------------------------------------------------------

[14]*Cioca et al v.Rumsfield and Gates, C.A. 11 cv 151.*

In order to continue her duties while dealing with the constant and pervasive sexual harassment, she stayed in her living quarters when not on duty and avoided social events. Her command labeled her an "attitude problem" and ordered her to socialize or risk being demoted. She then attended a holiday party in December 2010 where two work colleagues drugged and raped her. She reported the rape, an investigation was begun and then her command intervened and closed it down.[15]

Nicole Curdt, a plaintiff in the lawsuit, was in the navy from 2000-2003 as a Damage Control Firearm Apprentice (DCFA). While assigned to a ship and on watch, a member of her command cornered her in an isolated passageway by the noisy engine room where he sexually assaulted her after telling her he heard she was a "good piece of ass." Soon after that, Nicole sought out the new chaplain brought on ship and asked for confidentiality, which he granted. Then without her permission the chaplain made an anonymous report to command. The next day her rapist told her that, "Everyone on ship was looking for her," because the command had ordered the chaplain to produce the source of the complaint. She was interviewed by command and she was directed to cooperate with CID. While she was cooperating, she refused to sign her statement because it was full of omissions and inaccuracies. She was told if she did not sign the document she would be court-martialed, so she did sign it. She was then punished by being demoted to E-2, fined one month's pay and restricted to her quarters for sixty days and then given an "Other than Honorable Discharge for "Serious Misconduct."[16] If the military followed the structure given by this author throughout the stories, then Nicole would have a legal advocate to advise her, who would not have allowed the manipulation and coercion by the navy to prevail. Forcing any service woman

-----------------------------------------------------------

[15]*Cioca et al v.Rumsfield and Gates, C.A. 11 cv 151.*
[16]Ibid.

to sign in inaccurate statement is illegal and immoral.

Jessica Kenyon, another plaintiff, was in the army from 2005-2006 and while in AIT was harassed by her teacher, a sergeant. She did not report this because the commander was openly misogynistic saying, "This unit never had any problems until females came into it." While home on leave for the holidays, an army national guard soldier raped Private Kenyon. At that point she went to the sexual assault response coordinator and was told to put the rape "on the back burner" and focus on the sexual harassment. Her command told her the rape would be used against her if she reported it. She did report it and paid the price. She was ostracized and retaliated against, both at her assignment and her next duty station in Korea. Upon arrival she was told they were warned about her and the sergeant made a unit-wide announcement to caution everyone. Then in the spring of 2006, a squad leader sexually assaulted her and she did report it.[17]

Plaintiff Andrea Neutzling, served in the army from 2000-2004, and in the reserves until 2010. In 2002, while in Korea she was sexually assaulted by an intoxicated soldier and reported it to her command. Her assailant was restricted for five days and that was the end of it. In 2005, while deployed to Iraq, another soldier in her military police unit sexually assaulted her. This time she did not report it. Later in 2005 on another deployment of only two weeks, two drunken soldiers from the unit that she was replacing raped specialist Neutzling. The rapists threatened to beat her if she struggled and she ended up with bruises on her elbows and shoulders from being held down. At first she did not report the rape knowing it would not do

-----------------------------------------

[17]Cioca et al v.Rumsfield and Gates, C.A. 11 cv 151.

any good and would only hurt her, but then she discovered the rapists had made a video recording, which was being passed around. She then reported the rape and her command said they did not believe she was raped because she 'did not struggle enough'. The commanders from both units agreed not to disclose the rape to investigative services, because they did not want to delay the departing unit and they downgraded the report to sexual harassment.[18]

Plaintiff Kristen Reuss served in the Ohio National Guard, 135th Military Police Company from July 1998-July 2004. In July 2001, her commander sexually assaulted Ms. Reuss on three occasions. The third assault occurred on an annual training in Alpena, Michigan where Kristen Reuss confided in a female lieutenant. Even though Ms. Reuss did not disclose the name of her attacker the lieutenant indicated she knew who it was and that he had assaulted other female soldiers in the past. Within hours investigators were questioning Reuss and others who stepped forward saying they too were assaulted. The local police jailed the commander after he failed a lie detector test. After returning to Ohio, Reuss learned that the charges had been dropped and the commander was forced to resign from the guard. Two years later in 2003, while deployed to Baghdad, Kristen Reuss discovered that her assailant is now a major in the army reserves and that he had previously been charged with domestic violence and theft. [19]

Jessica Nicole Hinves, yet another plaintiff, served in the air force from 2007 to April 2011. In January 2009 A1C Hinves was raped at Nellis AFB when her assailant broke into her room through the bathroom at about 3 a.m. Jessica reported the rape and went to

-----------------------------------------------------------

[18]*Cioca et al v.Rumsfield and Gates, C.A. 11 cv 151.*
[19]Ibid.

the hospital for medical care. Friends of the rapist began to harass Jessica and she persisted in following through with the military judicial process. Then days before the scheduled court martial trial, the new commander of four days ordered the trial stopped. The rapist was then given an award for "Airman of the Quarter" and Jessica Hinves was transferred to another base.[20]

Private Stephanie B. Schroeder, a plaintiff in the class action suit against the Pentagon, served in the marine corps from 2001-2003. While going to the bathroom, a fellow marine raped Schroeder in 2002. He shoved her down, punched and hit her until he forced her onto her back then ripped her pants down and raped her ejaculating on her inner left thigh and then berated and spit on her. She reported the rape to her command and was laughed at and told, "Don't come bitching to me because you had sex and changed your mind." The command asked the rapist if he had raped her and when he said no, they accused Private Schroeder of lying and put her on restriction telling her, "Shitbags like you are not allowed to have liberty." She was told to stay in her room and was not permitted to seek medical or counseling help. Later when she shared her experience with another marine, the command issued a non-judicial punishment to her so that she could not be promoted, forfeited her pay and allowance, and was restricted again for two weeks. There was no investigation or punishment for her rapist and she was forced to work with him. When she was transferred to a new duty station she came with the label "troublemaker." Within two weeks her new superior attempted to sleep with her and when she refused, he began to humiliate her at work and allowed others in the unit to laugh and mock her. Private Schroeder reported the sexual harassment and within weeks the same superior entered her room without her consent while she was sleeping and assaulted her. The next morning she was disciplined for having

----------------------------------------------------------------

[20]*Cioca et al v.Rumsfield and Gates, C.A. 11 cv 151.*

a male in her room and given extra duties all night and regular duties during the day. She then decided to move off base and a week later her command attempted to discipline her again for having a male in her room and when she argued she lived off base, they reprimanded her for moving off base without permission.[21]

How long will our Congress and the public be complicit in allowing this all-pervasive culture of abuse toward women in the military to prevail? What will it take to change the overriding misogynistic culture of abuse in our armed forces? When will we hear a public and congressional outrage toward this abusive military culture? If not now, then when?

The DOD has proven they cannot change the military culture of abuse even though they have had decades to lead that action. To date they have not done more than give lip service to the issue of sexual assault in their ranks. The DOD and the military have demonstrated repeatedly that not only is there a systemic failure to protect women in the military there is an overarching protocol, which punishes women while promoting rapists. The DOD and the military are not dealing effectively with their systemic failure and are instead clinging to their culture of abuse. It is time to fully investigate this abuse culture, clean house and begin anew with appropriate policies and actions that restore honor, integrity and accountability to our military and bring justice to women serving.

Kase Wickman wrote a scathing indictment of the DOD in her Raw Story article on June 29, 2011. She identified the Government

------------------------------------------------------------

[21]*Cioca et al v.Rumsfield and Gates, C.A. 11 cv 151*

Accountability Office report, which stated that the Pentagon failed to properly investigate the 2594 MST cases reported in 2010, and that none of the cases were sent to the Inspector General's Office for oversight as required. In her article, Kase Wickman also noted that the army was given <u>4.4 million dollars</u> specifically to redesign sexual assault policies and programs in fiscal year 2009 and failed to do so. "Given that sexual assault crimes undermine the core values of the military services and degrade mission readiness, the effective and efficient administration of military justice for addressing these offenses is essential to the maintenance of good order and discipline in the armed forces, and consequently contributes to the national security of the United States."[22]

The culture of sexual violence against women that is allowed to exist in both the U.S. Military and private contractors needs to come to an end. When almost a third of all women serving are raped, and over two thirds sexually assaulted, this problem is rampant and systemic. (Press TV, Jan 28, 2011) "19,000 Soldiers each year are raped in the military, both women and men, and what is Congress doing about it?" Demands Representative Jackie Speier of California, on the House Floor, on October 25, 2011. She went on to say that our soldiers cannot expect to have a successful military career if they report rape. Reporting sexual assault is a career ender. Representative Speier said that thirteen percent of rapes are actually reported and of those, ninety percent are involuntarily discharged from the military.[23]

------------------------------------------------------------

[22]Kase Wickman, "Pentagon Fails to Probe Thousands of Sexual Assaults: GAO." *Raw Story,* 29June 2011

[23]http://www.youtube.com/utser/ JackieSpeierCA12?feature=mhee#p%2Fa%2Fu %2F0%2Fch8EQosXVco&mid=510

Marciela Guzman, a navy veteran from 1998-2002, said that sexual violence is a systemic problem prevalent in our military and that the boys club culture is strong. A fellow soldier raped April Fitzsimmons, an intelligence analyst in the air force from1985-1989. She reported the rape and the perpetrator and then was removed from the base. Fitzsimmons held that the military represses all attempts to change it.

"Few problems have been more persistent or produced more bad news for the military than the issue of rape within its own ranks,"[24] yet nothing has been done. The Department of Defense's (DOD) token attempt to address the epidemic by creating the very limited and still underfunded Sexual Assault Prevention and Response Office (SAPRO), which distributes posters, collects data, but has no enforcement or investigative authority, has been a constant reminder of how the military thumbs its nose at any attempt to implement genuine reform. In fact, the director of SAPRO from 2008 to 2011, Dr. Kaye Whitley has absolutely no experience or training dealing with sexual violence, said Greg Jacob, the policy director of Service Women's Action Network (SWAN). The DOD has ignored this growing epidemic for years and no one has been held accountable. Donald Rumsfeld has not been held to answer for his knowing refusal to implement reform measures mandated by Congress. And on Rumsfeld's recent book tour, not once during his numerous interviews did any journalist ask a single question about this issue.[25]

The military has become an entrenched system that all too easily blames victims and retaliates against those victims with systematic harassment and intimidation. Victims are subjected to ridicule and

---

[24]"Army Rape Accuser Speaks Out," *60 Minutes,* CBS, 20 February 2005.

[25]Antoinette Bonsignore, "The Military's Rape and Sexual Assault Epidemic."*Truthout,* 3April 2011.

they all too often become convinced that the shame will be too much to bear. Investigations into military sexual assault seem designed to further victimize the survivor and make her so miserable she will withdraw the charges.

There is and has been a failure of leadership in our military and it must be rectified. Victim blaming is protocol with the full support of military leadership. The women who are sexually assaulted are blamed rather than focus on the perpetrators and accountability for them. Why are we not following the paraphrased suggestions of Jackson Katz, who in his Ted Talk February 2013, suggested we ask why do men rape and why do we keep hearing about scandals in our military; how does our military keep supporting rape and domestic violence? He said we need more men with courage to stand with women and break their silence and collusion with the institutions that hide violence against women. He is clear that it is a leadership issue; leaders in decision-making positions need to change their thinking, attitudes and behavior or the problems will persist as they have for decades.

Lucinda Marshall's Op-Ed in the LA Times, January 30, 2008, details how the, "U.S. Military trivializes rape and sexual assault by its own soldiers on its own soldiers, and she ends by highlighting how convicted rapists are buried with military honors even though rape and sexual violence are considered war crimes. This is merely one more example of the misogyny implicit in military culture. The military's continuing disregard and disrespect for the safety of women's lives even within their own ranks, and in disregard of international law, should give us pause to wonder just whose freedom we are protecting."[26]

------------------------------------------------------------

[26]Lucinda Marshall, "Rape in the U.S. Military." *Latimes.com,* 30 January 2008.

I agree with Jackie Speier, "It is time for the Pentagon to stop treating legal directives as mere suggestions. And it is time for Congress to abandon its role as a bystander. Division and strife within the ranks hurts our ability to defeat the enemy. In addition, military service is one of our nation's highest callings. We cannot, as a country, allow violent criminals to besmirch the honor of the armed forces, and we certainly cannot condone a system that is designed to protect the perpetrators and punish the survivors."[27]

Carri Jones (pseudonym) a gifted musician now 59, served in the First Calvary in 1974 when she was twenty-one. She told Kasey Cordell of the *Portland Monthly*, that she endured horrendous abuse at Fort Hood, Texas. Not only did her buddy soldiers drill holes in the bathroom walls to watch her shower, but her commanding officer locked her in his quarters and forced her to watch pornography with him then drove her to a remote area of the base during the day and raped her. If that was not bad enough, a group of pilots in training gang raped her and strung her up by her hands, stripped off her clothes and had a pillowcase put over her head under the guise of Prisoner of War (POW) training. She was left hanging so long it caused permanent damage to her wrist tendon resulting in her never being able to play her clarinet again. She refers to all this as an epidemic hidden plague within the military.[28] Epidemics and plagues need to be addressed before they destroy our military.

The recommendation in the 1997 report by the Secretary of the Army, was—active leadership was required to create an environment of dignity and respect and that passive leadership condoned the opposite. Even though that was sixteen years ago, passive

----------------------------------------------------------------

[27]Jackie Speier, "Rape of Military Women 'a national disgrace.' *San Francisco Chronicle.*17 April 2011.

[28]Kasey Cordell. "The Hidden War." *Portland Monthly.* August 2011.

leadership is still allowing a culture of abuse to persist. Although that was specifically about the army, it is also true of each branch of the military. It will take a higher authority to cause the military to actively change. The only higher authority is our President/Commander in Chief or the Congress. It is clear that the military will not change without being forced to do so. They may be able to coerce young women to sign away their rights, teach values of honor and integrity that they <u>do not</u> uphold, and expect their enlisted soldiers and officers to follow orders, but they, <u>the highest authorities in our armed forces, do not themselves follow directives given to them.</u> They are poor models for those they train. To change a culture requires all the leaders to not only teach 'how to,' but to model it.

Clifford Stanley, the Undersecretary of Defense for Personnel and Readiness wrote in a *USA Today* Op-Ed on March 2, 2011 that "Preventing sexual assault within our military is a leadership responsibility, and we must all be held accountable for eliminating it from our ranks. The American public should rightfully expect that when their sons and daughters raise their right hand to serve our great nation, they do so in a culture and environment where dignity, respect and protection prevail." I agree, and the question to Mr. Stanley is, "When will they be held accountable and who will do it? When will that kind of environment be created and by whom?"

Why is it a requirement for women who enter the military academies or the military itself, to accept that they are government property and have no say in what happens to their body? Military men need to be seen as strong and competent and expect women to be seen as less. If a woman is viewed as a threat to a man, he may cause her pain to bring her down to a lesser position in his eyes.

Many men seem to say, this is <u>our military</u> and we are going to do everything we can to insure that women are miserable and don't stay.

Erin Solaro writing an opinion in the *Seattle P-I* April 4, 2004 said, "A military that would never tolerate its troops raping even one Iraqi woman should not tolerate the rape and attempted rape of one servicewoman, much less five percent of the force. Both sexual assault and sexual harassment, as well as, domestic violence, should be removed from command discretion to prosecute. Once the facts of the case have been established, prosecution should be automatic." She goes on to say, "Military women must bear witness by pressing charges. They are not the victims. They are casualties who have suffered honorable wounds in the service of their country. It is their assailant and their collaborators who have dishonored themselves, their service and their country."[29] Solaro believes many rapists are repeat offenders and says, "Commanders who tolerate such criminals and their actions and passive accomplices, should be prosecuted. In extreme cases, the flags of the units with such history should be retired. Battle honors earned against a valiant enemy should not be sullied by cowards who prey upon comrades." Solaro goes even further by proclaiming, "To deprive a woman of legal recognition for her contribution is to do more than demean and deny that contribution. It is to brand her as second-class, less worthy of respect and legal protection. It is also to encourage predators. When an institution lacks integrity, honorable individuals cannot redeem it, even if they are in the majority."[30]

-------------------------------------------------------

[29]Erin Solaro." P-I Focus: Prosecution should be automatic in cases of sexual assault, harassment in the Military." *Seattle P-I.*4 April 2004.
[30]Ibid.

Those in the military who have raped and sexually assaulted their sister soldiers have dishonored the military." An institution that tolerates such conduct dishonors and damages America," said Solaro.[31]

Lauren Hersh blogged that the "Festering crisis of sexual assault within the U. S. Military…claimed more than 50 victims of sexual assault a day in the last year of Defense Department data." She asserts that widespread attention and media coverage indicates that now is the time to address this shameful legacy. The UK, Israel, New Zealand and Australia are way ahead of the U.S. in reforming their system to have greater accountability for perpetrators and justice for victims.

The U.S. is up for review by the United Nations Human Rights Committee this year and with the military sexual assault scandals and stories now known worldwide it behooves our military to address this issue with appropriate action.[32]

Not only are there seriously unresolved injustices to women sexually assaulted in the military, the report of the Government Accountability Office showed that nurses, doctors and other military health care personnel are untrained and inconsistent in handling victim's injuries and reports of sexual assault. Some healthcare professionals are unfamiliar with how to treat injuries from sexual assaults and how to protect the confidentiality of the victims. The GAO report found the office of the Assistant Secretary of Defense for Health Affairs has failed to communicate appropriate information to their healthcare professionals and paraprofessionals.

-------------------------------------------------------

[31]Erin Solaro." P-I Focus: Prosecution should be automatic in cases of sexual assault, harassment in the Military." *Seattle P-I.*4 April 2004.
[32]Lauren Hersh." Military Sexual Assault: The Time to Address This Shameful Legacy is Now." *The Blog-Huff Post.* 31 March 2013.

The auditors noted that service members lack confidence in the program and do not seek the care or treatment they need. Sexual violence requires a specialized level of care including the collecting of forensic evidence. Consistent training and preparation has largely been absent. The recommendation to develop department level guidance on the provision of care to victims of sexual assault was <u>disapproved</u> by the DOD.[33]

"The GAO report indicates that military leadership has failed for over 25 years to fundamentally address this crisis of sexual assault in our military, half measures regularly put forward by Congress and DOD are not answers," said Nancy Parrish, President of Protect our Defenders in an email statement to *Raw Story*." Every aspect, from prevention and victim care to investigation, prosecution, and adjudication is fundamentally dysfunctional and there has been no coherent effort to fix the deficiencies." She is right on point with that comprehensive statement.

"The DOD is responsible for failing to effectively govern its personnel. The problems are so long standing and pervasive that, at minimum, they constitute gross negligence on the part of leadership and actually reflect, albeit informal countenancing of the violation of the rights of women in the service and of victims of assault, men and women."[34]

The Lackland Air Force Base sexual assault scandal reared its head in 2012. General Mark Welsh, Air Force Chief of Staff, told

-------------------------------------------------------------------

[33]Lisa Rein. "GAO: Military Sexual –Assault Care Flawed." *Washington Post.*30 January 2013

[34]Kay Steiger. "Military Provides Inadequate Care for Injuries Suffered During Sexual Assaults." *The Raw Story.*30 January 2013.

the House Armed Services Committee in January 2013, that there were 796 reports of groping to rape in 2012, an increase of nearly thirty percent from the 2011 count of 614. Admittedly eighty to ninety percent are never reported so we know the numbers are actually much higher.

The air force investigating the sex scandal has so far found that 32 of their basic training instructors were alleged to have had coercive sexual relationships with 59 recruits and airmen and six instructors have been convicted in court martial of rape and unprofessional relationships. Nine more await court martial.

Sig Christenson, *Express-News San Antonio,* reporting on the Lackland AFB scandal for a year said that all the cases are women and it was more about power than sex.[35]

Not a single survivor of the Lackland sex scandal was interviewed during their investigations. How is that possible? How can the air force conduct an effective investigation into the scandal without talking with victims who experienced it? Representative Jackie Speier said she wrote a letter in November 2012 requesting air force survivors' voices be heard and her letter was ignored. Even though survivors were present and willing to testify during the House Armed Services Committee Hearing in January 2013, all of the military leaders present and many congressional leaders left and did not hear them.[36]

-----------------------------------------------------------

[35]Richard Lardner. "Air Force Calls Number of Sex Assaults 'Appalling'" *Associated Press.*23 January 2013

[36]Holly Kearl. "In Air Force Report, Where Were the Survivors?" *AAUW Dialogue Blog.* 24 January 2013.

Virginia Messick was 19 in her fifth week of basic training at Lackland AFB when her instructor raped her, by ordering her to deliver towels to an empty floor in the trainee dorm, did his dastardly deed then threw her clothes at her and ordered her to take a shower when he was done. Messick completed her training, following orders given to her, and staying silent about the rape because her rapist was the person she was to report it to. She was the first recruit to speak out publicly about her rape by Staff Sgt. Luis Walker who was sentenced to twenty years for assaulting ten women from his position as basic training instructor.

None of these episodes at Lackland would be known today if not for a female trainee— **not** a victim, who reported what she knew—the fear of retaliation to victims was so great.[37]

As women in the military grapple with: the problem of military sexual assault, the pain of retaliation that follows reporting, and the lack of accountability and prosecutions, an air force general overturned an actual military jury verdict and sentence on one of his own. Lt. General Craig Franklin, Third Air Force Commander dismissed the case against Lt. Col. James Wilkerson after he was found guilty of aggravated sexual assault, sentenced to one year in jail, forfeiture of all pay and discharged from service at his court martial on Aviano Air Base in Italy. Franklin, an F-16 pilot and former commander of the 31st Fighter Wing where Wilkerson served, was the convening authority in the case and did not have to give a reason for overturning the verdict and sentence and re-instating the perpetrator, Lt. Col. Wilkerson, to full active duty status. General Franklin is accountable to no one.

-----------------------------------------------------------

[37]James Risen. "Attacked at 19 by an Air Force Trainer and Speaking Out." *The New York Times.* 26 February 2013

The victim was a 49 year-old physician's assistant, who was awakened when she felt Wilkerson groping her breasts and digitally penetrating her. She sought medical care the next day, reported the assault, endured public humiliation and the case went forward when Wilkerson failed a polygraph. This case was somewhat of a positive model to start with, because the assault was reported when that occurs in less than 13% of cases, it went to court martial when that happens only 20% of the time and the prosecution won the conviction when that happens only 7% of the time.

The overruling of the guilty verdict and sentencing was a shock to the victim and many in Congress were outraged. The action by General Franklin accentuated the good old boys culture of abuse toward women in the military and self-preservation at all costs.[38]

Senators called the action of Lt. Gen. Franklin a travesty of justice. Senator Claire McCaskill of MO said, "I don't think one general should be able to overturn a jury. I have a high degree of frustration." Senators Barbara Boxer and Jeanne Shaheen said that decision is unacceptable and it "raises serious concerns about the Military Justice System as a whole."[39]

McCaskill, a former Jackson County, MO prosecutor, was laser focused on a military culture that fails to bring justice to women even as the doors to leadership in combat open to them. McCaskill, Boxer,

-------------------------------------------------------

[38]Nancy Montgomery. "Case Dismissed Against Aviano IG Convicted of Sexual Assault." *Stars and Stripes.* 27 February 2013.

[39]Frank Oliveri. "Senators Blast Military After General Overturns Sexual Assault Verdict." *Roll Call.* 5 March 2013

and Shaheen, all three women on the Senate Armed Services Committee are holding the military's feet to the fire even as military leadership discounts their failures to hold perpetrator's accountable.[40]

The pattern of violence and injustice in our military is undeniable and military retribution toward reporting victims has been relentless and widespread, while congressional inaction has been infuriating. Kudos to Senator Kirsten Gillibrand of New York, the new chair of the Senate Armed Services Subcommittee on Personnel for calling the first hearing on military sexual assault in 16 years.

Cynthia Dill the 2012 democratic senate nominee from Maine wrote in the *Huffington Post*, "We are here, then, to bear witness to their plight. We are lawyers who speak for these injured veterans who tragically have nowhere else to go."

"Some of these veterans call us from homeless shelters; others phone from cars that have become their homes. Some send us handwritten notes, because they don't have access to a computer. Others are driven to endless research, day and night, searching the global internet for support and validation. Each individual story is gut wrenching. This is wrong. This is immoral. This is unjust."

"This is not the way America should treat its warriors. This is not how America should honor those who put themselves in harm's way, in service to our great nation and in preservation of our freedoms."

"When we ignore their pleas, when we turn our backs on their tragedies, we debase the integrity of our military. In our scandalous

------------------------------------------------------------

[40]Editorial. "McCaskill Leads Fight on Sexual Abuse in Military." *Kansas City Star Op-Ed.* 6 March 2013.

silence, we allow a subset of predatory, power-crazed men to manipulate the system and to get away with sexual violence, and in our silence, we nurture that cruel system and allow it to destroy the lives of our military men and women."

"What these Veterans seek, and what we intend to bring them, is acknowledgement, justice and reforms. We must develop a strategy to redress the wrongs that have been done to these survivors who have endured endless bureaucratic battles and cultural abuse from the very government they served."

"The damage is real. Their benefits are denied, evidence is lost, and the excruciating delays, perhaps done purposefully, in processing these claims allow additional crimes to be committed, with impunity."

"We urge Secretary Hagel, Senator Gillibrand and the Congress to do a few simple things, urgently."

"First, issue a public apology to those who have been harmed. Second, make an appropriation to allow some redress of the financial hardships that have been shouldered. Third, establish a claims process without delay for eligible veterans who have been raped, sexually assaulted and subjected to other forms of violence."[41]

Senator Lindsey Graham, himself a veteran of the U.S. Air Force, in an impassioned opening statement before testimony at the Senate Armed Services Committee Hearing on military sexual assault 3/13/13 said: "Clearly the message we're sending to female members of the military is that we're way too indifferent, and that your complaints are falling on deaf ears, and to all of our commanders: how in the world can

---

[41]Cynthia Dill. "Justice for Veterans Sexually Assaulted in the Military." *The Blog Huffington Post* 11 March 2013.

you lead your unit in a responsible manner if the people in the unit feel like the system doesn't care about them?...I will do everything I can within reason to make sure that stops."[42]

From that same Senate Hearing: "Commanders were never held accountable for choosing to do nothing. What we need is a military with a fair and impartial criminal justice system, one that is run by professional and legal experts, not unit commanders," said Rebekah Havrilla, a former army sergeant, during her testimony.

Senator Richard Blumenthal of Connecticut said, "The problem is the equivalent of having an IED in every unit."[43] That is quite an apt description.

Jennifer Steinhauer wrote in *The New York Times,* that Senator Susan Collins of Maine, a member of the Senate Armed Services Committee in 2004, remarked that, "One reason it has been so difficult to move forward against sexual assault in spite of the commitment in the Senate is because we've not put a human face on this. The victims make the violence very real and compel you to act." *The New York Times* article also reported that committee members want to see all military sex offenders discharged from service and to take the prosecution of offenders out of the chain of command.[44]

Now survivors are coming forward and telling their stories and finally this contemptible ongoing crime in our military is getting notice and attention. The problem even extends to our military

------------------------------------------------------------

[42]Erin Delmore. "This is My Story: Senate Hearing on Military Sexual Assault." *Andrea Mitchell Reports.* 13 March 2013.

[43]Bill Briggs. "Rape on Duty: Senate Panel Members Suggest Overhaul of Military Justice System." *U.S. News on NBC.com.* 13 March 2013.

[44]Jennifer Steinhauer. "Veterans Testify on Rapes and Scant Hope of Justice." *The New York Times.* 13 March 2013.

academies. The Air Force Academy reported a 50% increase in sexual assaults in the 2011-2012 academic years and nominated Maj. Gen. Michelle Johnson to lead the academy. Gen. Johnson graduated from that academy in 1981 as the first female cadet wing commander and went on to become a standout athlete and the academy's first female Rhodes Scholar. Let's hope, under her scrutiny, there will be more accountable leadership at the Air Force Academy and female cadets can be safe with their brother cadets.

On March 18, 2013 a guilty verdict was handed down in a civilian court in Steubenville, Ohio against two football players who raped a sixteen-year old girl. Because of the dynamics in this case, coming on the heels of the airing of this important issue in the media, it needs to be included here. These boys chose to commit the rape of the sixteen-year old, their victim. It is appropriate and just that they be found guilty and sentenced. The media reacted with empathy for the boys and not the victim. What is wrong with that picture? How can our media be so empathetic toward violent criminals who believed their coach would protect them while they assaulted a young girl, and not seem to have any legitimate concern or empathy for the victim, who will suffer the long term consequences of being raped and all that it will do to her for the rest of her life?

These two boys were proud of what they did and believed they would not be held accountable because they were protected and above any accountability. Where did that belief come from? That is the same belief men in the military have. Their commanders will have their back and will protect them from any accountability (that has been true). The higher in rank an officer achieves, the fewer there are who could identify abuse of power and call it out. They protect one another. Even the groups that select officers at the highest levels for promotion are small. They have their own supporters and their own club.

The other side of that is that the victim in these cases is blamed for what happened and the victim is expected to be the responsible one and even prevent the rape. This belief perpetuates the problem in society at large and in the military. Let's get real here and look at who commits these crimes and just what kind of crime it is. Remember it is about power; power over someone. It is about demeaning, demoralizing and humiliating the victim. It is a hideous violent crime against another human being because of what is inside and driving the rapist. It is the rapist that is responsible not the victim. It is the rapist who needs to be held fully accountable, not the victim. I would go so far as to say, it is those leaders who condone and cover up these heinous crimes and the behavior patterns of the perpetrators, who are equally responsible. It is important to teach boys in society and men in the military to respect women and that must be consistently modeled and demonstrated through behavior in our homes, communities, and in our military. What boys see and hear modeled toward women in their lives and what men see and hear modeled toward women in service, is what they believe is appropriate and how they will treat women.

Another epidemic in our armed forces is domestic violence, and our military is just as inadequate in handling that issue as the sexual harassment and sexual assault of women. The only real difference is the relationship between the abuser and the woman. Does it matter to her if her assailant is a husband, boyfriend, another soldier she knows, or a commander? Either way, it is incredibly painful and a betrayal of her trust.

Chuck Fager, an independent Quaker journalist covering a Fayetteville, N.C. community meeting in August of 2002, highlighted the attempts at damage control by the military and phony optimism promoted by Deborah Tucker, the co-chair of the Task Force on Domestic Violence. He points out the systematic denial and cover-up of rampant family abuse in the military brought to light by the recent murders at Fort Bragg. Chuck watched, "A uniformed officer shrugs and tells a TV reporter that there was nothing special about the recent killings: "They were just an anomaly." [45]

Fager notes that while the *Fayetteville Observer* colluded with the military in writing the story, they were thwarted by the wives incessant intense phone calls. Dozens of military wives were "Spilling out gruesome tales, not only about beatings and abuse, but of a military culture that, despite PR protestations, remains deeply and systematically indifferent to their plight. The recent killings, these witnesses made plain, were just the bloody, impossible-to-ignore tip of a very large and otherwise submerged iceberg." Fager asks in his article, "What accounts for this institutional tolerance of domestic violence?"[46]

In a follow up to his article, Fager described an army medical team report and an article in *Vanity Fair* by Maureen Orth regarding the murders at Fort Bragg." Both reports painstakingly documented in their different ways the destructive impact of much of the army environment on families and marriages."[47]

------------------------------------------------------------------------

[45]Chuck Fager. "Reflection: Domestic Murders at Fort Bragg." *Quaker House* 19August 2002.

[46]Ibid

[47]Chuck Fager." Ft. Bragg Domestic Murders: An Update." *Quaker House*. January 2003.

"Four soldiers recently confused their wives for the enemy and killed them. Marilyn Griffin was stabbed seventy times and her trailer set on fire, Teresa Nieves and Andrea Floyd were shot in the head, and Jennifer Wright was strangled. All four couples had children, several now orphaned because two of the men shot themselves after killing their wives.

The murders garnered wide attention because three of the soldiers served in Special Operations units that fought in Afghanistan, and because they clustered over a five-week period in June and July. The killings have raised a host of questions about the effect of war on the people who wage it, the spillover on civilians from training military personnel to kill, the role of military institutional values and even the possible psychiatric side-effects of an anti-malarial drug the army gives its soldiers. On the epidemic of violence against women throughout civilian domestic violence, however, there has been a deafening silence."[48]

"Of the 1,213 reported domestic violence incidents known to military police and judged to merit disciplinary action in 2000, the military could report only twenty-nine, where the perpetrator was court-martialed or sent to a civilian court for prosecution. The military claims to have no data on the disciplinary outcome of the 12,068 cases reported to family services in that year. They also have no record of the outcome of eighty-one percent of the police cases. This poor record-keeping and apparent reluctance to prosecute offenders can be explained by the military's institutional interests in burying the problem of domestic violence."[49]

-----------------------------------------------------------

[48]Catherine Lutz and Jon Elliston."Domestic Terror." *The Nation.* 14 October 2002.
[49]Ibid.

Lutz and Elliston describe a sign in a special forces training area that says: "Rule #1; there are no rules. Rule #2; follow Rule #1." Such a macho, above-the-law culture provides not a small part of the recipe for domestic violence. Combine this with a double standard of sexuality, one in which, as many soldiers and their wives told us, some couples expect infidelity to take place on special forces deployments—where the men operate with unusual autonomy and are often surrounded by desperately poor women—whereas the infidelity of wives, reactive or not, real or imagined, can be punished with violence."[50]

In their article on domestic terror, Lutz and Elliston reported on meeting a special forces soldier who told them Memorial Day ceremonies left him <u>miffed that he could get medals for killing people in battle but was arrested for trying to kill his wife.</u> It is up to the leadership of the military to make it exceedingly clear, where aggression and violence are warranted and where it is not. These young men are taught to view women and life in certain ways in order to be killers yet no one tells them how to turn it off or clarify the differences between behavior on duty and behavior at home with their families. Soldiers are trained to be killers and use lethal weapons; under the right circumstances they will do that regardless of who they are with or where they are. During the Bush administration we all were taught directly and indirectly that we are to worship our military and soldiers, yet when they are home with their families they are not worshipped. When their wives and girlfriends do not treat them as royalty, these soldiers may explode into intense violence against their intimate partners. This is especially true if the men feel they have lost control over their family. Patricia Horner reported, "The masculine culture of the military socializes men to expect certain kinds of behavior from their wives. In this culture, violence often occurs as a result of a man's

---

[50]Catherine Lutz and Jon Elliston."Domestic Terror."*The Nation.*14 October 2002.

perceived status being challenged by his "subordinate" wife. As long as subordination of women is overlooked in the military, policies which protect women from their abusive soldier husbands will have little effect." A 1979 report by the U.S. Inspector General stated, "Military service is probably more conducive to violence at home than at any other operation because of the military's authoritarianism, its use of physical force in training, and stress."[51]

"Violence against women in the military is essentially disregarded, proof of which resides with [the] fact[s]; much of the violence is ignored by military officials. The military's own criminal justice system has been systematically tolerating the behavior of military men accused of sexual assault for years. Military wives realize that even if they do muster up the courage to report a domestic assault, little action will be taken in response. In addition to fearing a lack of action, military wives may fear potential consequences of speaking out. In a recent study on the fears of military wives, the vast majority of victims said they feared what would happen to their own wellbeing if their husbands were disciplined."[52]

In an article published in *The New York Times* February 15, 2008, Lizette Alvarez and Deborah Sontag describe Sergeant Erin Edwards being assaulted by her husband, Sergeant William Edwards after their joint return from Iraq. William Edwards hit his wife, choked her, dragged her over a fence and slammed her into the ground. She knew what to do after that because she was an aide to a general at Fort Hood. She pressed charges, got a protection order and arranged

-----------------------------------------------------------------

[51]Patricia Horner." Domestic Violence in the Military: Addressing the Need for Policy Reform." *Law and Society Journal at UCSB,* Volume IV (2005).
[52]Ibid.

for a transfer to New York. In the meantime she sent her children to be with her mother. Her husband's commander assured her that her husband would not be allowed off post unless with another officer. July 22, 2004, Sergeant William Edwards left Fort Hood unescorted, drove to his wife's home in Killeen and when she left the house he shot her in the head and then shot himself. During an investigation the local police said if the protection order had been followed by the military, these deaths could have been avoided.[53]

Dr. Jacquelyn C. Campbell, a professor at Johns Hopkins School of Nursing and a member of the disbanded Pentagon Domestic Violence Task Force, said that deployments to Iraq and Afghanistan increased trauma and the risk of domestic violence. *The New York Times* found 150 cases of reported domestic violence or child abuse by soldiers since the invasion of Afghanistan in 2001. "The Pentagon's Domestic Violence Task Force, appointed in April 2000 and comprising 24 military and civilian experts, met regularly for three years to examine a system where, they found, soldiers rarely faced punishment or prosecution for battering their wives and where they often found shelter from civilian orders of protection."[54] That task force report was scheduled on March 20, 2003, the day we invaded Iraq, which rendered the report irrelevant. A request to reconvene in two years to reevaluate was rejected by Congress. "The Pentagon Task Force had one overarching recommendation: that the military work hard to affect a "culture shift" to zero tolerance for domestic violence by holding offenders accountable and by punishing criminal behavior.

-------------------------------------------------------------------

[53]Lizette Alvarez and Deborah Sontag."When Strains on Military Families Turn Deadly." *The New York Times.* 15 February 2008.

[54]Ibid.

There was, members believed, a core credo that needed to be attacked frontally: This notion that the good soldier either can't be a wife beater or, if they are, that it's a temporary aberration that shouldn't interfere with them doing military service," as Dr. Campbell put it.[55] A higher authority has to break through the military's denial system if that culture of abuse is to be changed. The overall attitude of the military is that they are untouchable and can remain in denial and unaccountable because no one can dispute them. For their sake and our country's sake they must be challenged. They must be forced to change by 'we the people' and a higher authority. If each person who reads this book calls their representatives and senators regularly to ask that they investigate the culture of abuse in our military and insist on accountability, rather than the empty rhetoric of "zero tolerance," which shows up as leadership passivity.

The military acts like a country apart from the rest of us. They cannot be sued and seemingly are not required to be accountable. Judge Liam O'Grady dismissed the class action lawsuit against the DOD filed in February 2011 for not providing protection from sexual assault in the military." In his two page ruling, Judge O'Grady described the sexual assaults detailed in the case as 'troubling' but ruled in favor of Rumsfeld and Gates, citing the military's immunity from external judicial review in cases of injury incurred "incident to service."[56] The issue is the well-known Feres Doctrine that our military hides behind. That doctrine emerged after a 1950 Supreme Court case involving Army Lt. Rudoph Feres, "Who died in a fire allegedly caused by an unsafe heating system in his New York barracks. In this and later opinions,

---

[55]Lizette Alvarez and Deborah Sontag."When Strains on Military Families Turn Deadly." *The New York Times*. 15 February 2008.

[56]*Service Women's Action Network Press Release*. "Sexual Assault Lawsuit Dismissed." 14 December 2011

the Supreme Court interpreted the Federal Tort Claims Act to **effectively bar any tort actions** by service members, even though <u>Congress exempted only 'combat-related' injuries.</u> The court unilaterally decided that even injuries in peacetime that are far removed from any combat-related function are still, incident to service." Because of this doctrine, there is no deterrence for military negligence or even criminal activity. Whether it was failure to diagnose and treat a medical condition appropriately, leaving someone dead or paralyzed or failure to protect women from rape and domestic violence the military need only invoke the Feres Doctrine and walk away, leaving service members and family with no recourse. "If members of Congress truly want the best for our troops, they should start by giving them the same legal protections that the members themselves enjoy. No one is asking for Congress to treat our soldiers as high-value VIPs, but simply full-valued citizens with the same protections as the people they are defending around the world."[57] Both Congress and our President/Commander-in-Chief need to act in concert to remove this impediment to fair treatment of our service members under the law.

A film entitled Semper Fi: Always Faithful and news articles in the Stars and Stripes described yet another example of leadership failure and lack of integrity. This time, the U. S. Marine Corps covered up contaminated drinking water at Camp LeJeune, NC from 1957-1987. Even with repeated reports and warnings given to the leadership at Camp LeJeune, they failed to address the issue or to notify those living and working on base, and continued to deny there was a problem. Even when questioned by the Senate Armed Services

------------------------------------------------------------------

[57]Jonathan Turley. "The Feres Doctrine: What Soldiers Really Need are Lawyers." *www.jonathanturley.org* 18 August 2007.

Committee about why the marine corps did not notify families on base about the contamination and health hazards, the response was empty rhetoric. Documents showed that there was as much as 1.1 million gallons of fuel that may have spilled into the groundwater, in addition to high PCE and TCE levels. (Tetrachloroethylene (PCE) is a nonflammable, liquid solvent widely used in dry cleaning and Trichloroethylene (TCE) is a man-made chemical that does not occur naturally in the environment). This affected over one million people. Both children and adults were getting sick and dying from a variety of conditions including leukemia and breast cancer in men. Again the military is protecting itself and its image and NOT those serving our country.

I saw a Larry King interview with Mary Tillman on August 16, 2010, and The Tillman Story film, where I learned the truth of what happened to Pat Tillman, which was not known, because of a cover-up that extended all the way to President Bush. Evidence of what happened was destroyed and the investigation showed that Pat Tillman was actually killed by men in his platoon. There was a deliberate attempt to cover up what happened. A P-4 memo was sent from General Stanley McCrystal to the entire chain of command on April 29, 2004. The purpose of the memo was to protect the image of the military, the army in this case. President Bush was warned in a memo that it could be embarrassing if the circumstances of Pat Tillman's death became public so his speechwriter specifically avoided any mention of how Tillman died, when Bush gave a speech two days after that memo was sent. All those in the chain of command knew the truth, which was stated in the P-4 memo, yet kept silent about it to protect the army from embarrassment, if the truth of the cover-up became public.

During a House Congressional Oversight Committee in April 2007, Pat Tillman's brother Kevin, who was in the same platoon and on the same road when Pat was murdered, spoke out for the first time since his return from Afghanistan. The entire platoon conspired to keep the truth from Kevin until long after it occurred. Kevin confronted the actions of the military in covering up his brother's death and, in the same hearing, one general after another starting with General Abazaid, and all the way to Donald Rumsfeld hedged and fudged their way through the questions, so as to avoid any and all accountability. Those House Members on the committee also did not follow up and ask the type or number of questions designed to elicit truth. Instead they were complicit in maintaining the cover-up.

This was not an isolated incident. Apparently there are many families like the Tillmans who were lied to, including the Johnsons regarding the rape and murder of LaVena Johnson noted in chapter one. We know that our military does not investigate when it needs to, destroys and taints evidence to suit them and covers up what really happened. Covering up criminal negligence is in itself a crime. When an institution, like the U.S. Military places itself above the law, proclaiming it stands for honor and integrity while being accomplices to criminal activity and cover-ups, it needs to be stopped. When a university like Penn State covers up child sexual abuse for years to protect their image and program, leaders are ultimately, even years later, held to account. Not so with our military. If we do not stand up and call our military to account for the culture of abuse and insist on change, we are as guilty as they for its continuation.

These words also apply to the military: "The instinct is to protect first the institution and its prevailing culture at all costs, minimize the offense and ignore the damage to the children involved. The differences, too, are striking. Penn State University has a board of directors, and it demanded accountability. Within days of Sandusky's arrest, 84-year-old Joe Paterno, one of the most celebrated and revered coaches in modern college football history, was gone. His offense? He didn't do enough."[58]

"In contrast, in the ongoing abuse crisis in the Church, only one bishop who oversaw a cover-up, Cardinal Bernard Law, was removed from a position after public outrage and the outrage of his priests in Boston, reached such a pitch that the Vatican had to do something. That something was to transfer him to a cushy position in Rome...Cardinal Anthony Joseph Bevilacqua, who oversaw the cover-up of hideous crimes against children committed by numerous Philadelphia priests, was able to slip quietly into retirement on the grounds of St. Charles Borromeo Seminary in Overbrook, a suburb of Philadelphia. The Vatican never uttered a word of reprimand for the institutional harm to children that he helped to hide during his tenure and that is detailed in a Philadelphia grand jury report."[59] No Board of Directors exists to demand accountability of the Catholic Bishops. "Penn State's decision was to close the investigation, bring no charges and not call the police or other outside authorities."

That is what our military does when there is a crime against a woman. "Another eerie similarity in all of this is that both institutions — church and university — acted first to protect themselves, the reputations of their programs and the personnel involved."[60] That, too, is what our military does. All of these large institutions are denying accountability. That must stop.

---

[58] Tom Roberts. "Abuse and Cover up: Penn States Catholic like Scandal." *National Catholic Reporter* 10 November 2011
[59] Ibid.
[60] Ibid.

"Enough is enough. How many more of our brave women and men in uniform must experience sexual assault before we truly address this issue," said Representative Louise Slaughter of New York. She also insisted, "We need a change in culture…Sexual assault needs to be viewed as the heinous crime it is and not dismissed as just 'boys being boys.' This change in culture needs to come from the top. It should come from Commander-in-Chief, who needs to insist on real accountability to end sexual violence and rape in the military. The President must gather his generals and admirals and commanders and work out a way to end this treachery in our ranks. Let him say, "Our servicewomen deserve better. And that's an order!"[61]

A Reuters article from January 2012, reported that violent sex crimes increased by ninety percent between 2006-2011 and outpaced the national trend. The top four felony offenses committed were: aggravated assault, rape, aggravated sexual assault and forcible sodomy.[62] One in five military women said they were sexually assaulted, quoted in the Pentagon Health Survey, conducted in 2011. The highest rate of assault was in the marine corps at almost 30% and both the army and navy were 24%.[63] After reading Jane Mayer's book, The Dark Side, and her statement that President G.W. Bush felt entitled to disregard what Congress said. It seems to me that from the top down, men in the military were given the clear message that it is OK to disregard long held American values after 9/11 and perhaps that played a role in the increases of sexual assault toward women serving our country in the military. Our Commander-in-Chief was modeling

------------------------------------------------------------------

[61]Kim Gandy. "Stop Rape and Assault - That is an Order!" *Now News* 6 April 2009.

[62] Mary Slosson." Violent sex crimes by U.S. Army Soldiers rise: report." *Reuters* 19 January 2012.

[63] Gregg Zoroya." More Female Servicemembers Reporting Sexual Abuse." *USA Today* 23 April 2013.

how to deal with a threat by essentially discounting the laws and values we fought hard to achieve and hold.

There are no statistics on the use of drugs used to rape, however it does seem to be on the increase as well. Drugs, such as Rohypnol cause disorientation, muscle relaxation, slowing of psychomotor abilities, blackouts, and temporary memory loss. It seems to add another dimension to the issue when drugs are deliberately used in order to render the woman incapacitated so she cannot fight back. This then makes the rape a deliberate premeditated attack. It also lends credence to so many women who reported that they could not move during the attack.

The movie, *The Invisible War,* had its debut in January 2012, where it won the Sundance Film Festival Audience award. This searing documentary by Kirby Dick, touched audiences everywhere it played, because of the breadth and depth of coverage and the authenticity of the courageous survivors and their spouses who agreed to be included. This film interspersed dramatic emotional personal accounts with facts and information about military sexual assault, rape, issues of reporting, military responses to reports and shows in detail the shame of our military services, lack of leadership and failure of policy in practice. People who see the movie have their own emotional reactions when faced with the realities of the culture of abuse in our military that has been covered up for so long. I spent a weekend with Kirby Dick, Amy Ziering and several of the women being filmed to provide support for them.

Leon Panetta the Secretary of Defense, saw the film in 2012 and called a press conference to begin to institute changes in policy to mitigate the situations depicted in the film. Kirby Dick, the director, said that when he was at the Pentagon half the people he spoke with about the issue who were in positions to do something about it, were not even aware of the results of military studies highlighting the problems. Dick believes the cover up in the military is vast. He is correct. *The Invisible War* was nominated for best documentary at the Academy Awards in 2013.

It is time for action and change. Our military has lost its honor and integrity. It cannot be redeemed but can be transformed. Men in the military who rape ignore the "NOs" of their victims. We can now ignore the "NO" of our military and demand change and justice. I am calling for full, thorough and unbiased congressional investigations into all the military services including every part of military culture from the top down and including the entire Military Justice System. Sweeping change is required and must take place. I ask everyone moved by the stories of these women to call or visit your Congressional Representatives and Senators at home or in Washington, D.C. and insist on their support for FULL UNBIASED CONGRESSIONAL INVESTIGATIONS into all the military services and the Military Justice System to RESTORE THE HONOR AND INTEGRITY of our military, by insisting on positive cultural change. I am also asking that whoever is part of this congressional process be fully committed to seeking the complete truth and being as courageous as the women who serve in the military in carrying out your mission to bring positive change to our military culture. Silence equals support for this despicable behavior.

Military Sexual Trauma changes everything. The woman who is sexually assaulted will never be the same again. Her body, mind, emotions and her sense of self were violated. She may never feel safe or confident again. Depending on how others respond to her after her assault she may be able to heal and move on. If she is not believed, supported, given the care she needs immediately, treated with dignity, respect, compassion, she is likely to be left with serious symptoms that may never go away. The way our military handles sexual assaults is disrespectful, indignant, cold and harsh. Women are shamed, humiliated, denied compassion, medical care, protection, even the kind of investigation that affirms she is believed and that the military values integrity and accountability. Women who are sexually assaulted in the military are denied justice.

The way our military responds to reports of sexual assault re-victimizes the survivor. Even the process of investigating and interviewing the victim is done in unnecessarily hurtful ways. Russell Strand, a military criminal investigator and the Chief of the Family Advocacy Law Enforcement Training Division at the U.S. Army Military Police School at Fort Leonard Wood said, "Military Sexual Trauma takes away everything you are in a minute." He teaches journalists, police, and first responders how NOT to re-victimize survivors. Strand teaches a forensic experimental trauma interview (FETI), based on brain function and memory. He describes how under high stress people experience involuntary fight, flight, freeze responses and the amygdala part of the brain, which reacts to the threat, releases a cascade of chemicals and hormones to prepare the body to react quickly. That reaction starts before the threat is even consciously registered in the brain and people do not react the way they might think because the prefrontal cortex shuts down. The trauma is stuck in the parts of the brain that cannot communicate with thinking or understanding and there is no way to verbalize a coherent description of what took place because the part of the brain that performs that function is shut down.

Another way to understand this, is that the memories are stored in the right side of the brain in pictures and feelings while coherent expression in words require the left side of the brain. These two parts are not communicating when there is a trauma and so what comes out is confused and incoherent. Because of that survivors cannot give a coherent beginning to end narrative account of what happened or the details. The brain under that level of distress notes sounds, smells, tastes, emotions and sensations. In fact, when they are questioned the survivor can literally go back into the traumatic event with a full body reaction including increased heart rate, shortness of breath, shaking, sweating, and have dry mouth.[64]

When asked open-ended empathic questions, survivors are able to give more accurate detailed information. If the survivor feels doubted or disbelieved or experiences being shamed they will shut down.

Representative Jackie Speier is a true champion of women soldier victims of sexual assault in the military. Not only has Congresswoman Speier spoken out repeatedly on the House floor sharing the horrific stories of women who were raped and assaulted, she introduced legislation known as the Sexual Assault Training Oversight and Prevention Act, the STOP Act, H.R. 3435, on Wednesday, November 16, 2011, and then reintroduced it April 17, 2013. This bill would take the reporting, oversight, investigation, and victim care of sexual assaults out of the hands of the military's normal chain of command and place jurisdiction in the newly created, autonomous Sexual Assault Oversight and Response Office comprised of civilian and military experts. By appointing a Director of Military Prosecutions, the bill

-------------------------------------------------------------------

[64] *Dart Society Reports.* "The Narrative Comes Later." 12 November 2012.

addresses the inherent conflicts of interest of those in the immediate chain of command responsible for prosecuting their subordinates, and takes the onerous burden of determining case dispositions off the desk of commanders who can then focus 100% on accomplishing their unit's mission. The STOP Act, also provides oversight of military court decisions to ensure that the punishments given fit the crime. The STOP Act by itself is not enough and never progressed in Congress.

On March 12, 2013, Representatives Jackie Speier (D-San Francisco/San Mateo), Bruce Braley (D-IA), and Patrick Meehan (R-PA) introduced the bipartisan Military Judicial Reform Act to strip military commanders of the unilateral power to overturn convictions or lessen sentences handed down by judges and juries at court martial. The bill amends articles 60 and 63 of the UCMJ (Uniform Code of Military Justice) removing from the convening authority the power "to dismiss, commute, lessen a finding or order a rehearing after a jury or judge has found the accused guilty and delivered a sentence." There is an appeal process in place that is sufficient, and at present no one, not even the Secretary of Defense or the Commander in Chief have the authority to overturn Franklin's decision. (Referring to Lt. Gen. Craig Franklin, who dismissed the case against Lt. Col. James Wilkerson after he was found guilty of aggravated sexual assault and sentenced at Aviano Air Base in Italy). Wilkerson was convicted by an all-male jury and sentenced, yet Franklin overturned all of that in a decision that is not reviewable at any level and essentially granted him a pardon and even recommended him for promotion.

Kirby Dick's sentiments expressed at that same press conference mixed with mine, are essentially that the Pentagon believes they can 'train' their way out of the overall structural and cultural problem in our military and they cannot. As long as victims of military sexual assault must report the crime to their chain of command and ultimate authority for the outcome rests with the chain of command that has demonstrated repeatedly that they will protect their own career, the image of the corps and the perpetrators of sex crimes, the problem will prevail unchecked.

The culture of abuse in the military and its effects on women serving is like a large infected wound. Up until now, Congress and our military have been trying to ignore the infection and cover it up with Band-Aids. We need to go into the wound, (our military), clean it out, (do full thorough investigations into all the services) and treat the infection, (change the system). The military can make itself, through its leaders, look and sound good but that is not enough and hopefully Congress and the public can see through that cover up. Congressional leaders are speaking out more now and offering legislation and my concern is that this culture of abuse will continue, unless a complete overhaul is done. Changing small pieces here and there is not sufficient.

The Sexual Assault Prevention and Response Office announced in May 2013, that unreported rapes and sexual assaults skyrocketed from 19,300 to 26,000 in 2012, a 34.5% increase. Annual sexual assaults for women increased from 4.4% to 6.1% and .9 to 1.2 for males. Only 3,374 cases of the estimated 26,000 sexual assaults were reported, a rate of just fewer than 13%, and perhaps the worst part, 62% of those who reported sexual assaults were retaliated against. The crisis today is worse than ever and has been going on since WWII. In 2012 one in 16 women were sexually assaulted, up from 1 in 23 in 2011. The numbers for the military academies are also worse with 80 cases reported in the 2011-2012 academic year as compared to 65 in the previous year. There are over 70 sexual assaults a day in the U.S. Military. If all that is not enough, only days before the annual report numbers were released, the man the air force put in charge of their Sexual Assault Prevention and Response Office, Lt. Col. Jeffrey Krusinski, was arrested for sexual assault.[65] The time for action is now.

Oversight of our Military resides with Congress and oversight strengthens authority. We need Congress to take their rightful place and DO THE OVERSIGHT. Without oversight there is abuse of power and THAT is what women have experienced over decades. Abuse of power will destroy our military and our country if it is not held in check. I am asking that each person who reads this book call or write your representatives and senators and insist there be full thorough investigations into our military services and how they are dealing with women in their ranks, how they deal with reports of sexual assaults at every level, how women are treated when they report and after they report. Look into all the inappropriate discharges against women who reported and how the cases are investigated or not, and prosecuted or not. Ask them to examine the Uniform Code of Military Justice thoroughly as it pertains to women and sexual assaults and find out how the Feres doctrine can be changed. Ask Congress to start by pulling out the Pentagon Domestic Violence Task Force report from March 2003, and follow the recommendations and go from there. We all know from years of experience that the military will not change unless ordered to do so and with consistent oversight.

Many of the recommendations in that report apply to sexual assault as well: victim advocate program, "ensure the institution, not the victim, is responsible for holding the offender accountable," commanding officer guidelines, law enforcement protocol, primary prevention, commanding officer and senior enlisted training.

---

[65]Molly O'Toole. "Military Sexual Assaults Spike Despite Efforts to Combat Epidemic." *Huffington Post,* 8 May, 2013.

This quote from the report applies: "Encourage commanding officers at every level of command to assert and reinforce, in briefings, public addresses to service members, and other opportune times in an ongoing fashion, that domestic violence [military sexual assault] hurts morale, negatively impacts readiness, and is inconsistent with the core values of the U.S. Military."[66] That particular task force asked for a small independent group to assess the implementation of recommendations in two years and to re-evaluate and the DOD said no. Do not accept their "no" on issues of sexual assault and domestic violence.

Susan Burke said clearly that it is a national disgrace that our service members in uniform are treated as second-class citizens when it comes to justice.

I am grateful for the attention and outrage of our members of Congress and ask that you all consider being methodical in how you go about making changes to the laws. Have legal experts in sexual assault and prosecution participate in developing changes that will provide clarity, protection for victims and accountability to perpetrators. Rather than tinker with parts, look at all the UCMJ as it relates to sexual crimes and write the best possible changes to bring about the justice that has long been missing.

To restore the honor and integrity of our military we need full, thorough, and unbiased congressional investigations and the follow through stated above with the changes listed below.

Each branch of the military needs a true advocate with the authority to challenge inappropriate behavior and a group, council,

-----------------------------------------------------------------------
[66] *Defense Task Force on Domestic Violence Third Year Report* , March, 2003. http://www.ncdsv.org/images/Year3Report2003.pdf

or board a victim can go to that has both the power and authority to demand change from the military. Change in the military must take place at every level from the squad, platoon, company, battalion, brigade, division, and corps leadership. Every level of command must demonstrate appropriate attitude, behavior, communication, demeanor, expectation, and respectful follow through in all interactions with military women. There must not be a double standard for women.

Other change suggestions:

- Allow women who report sexual assault to be seen by a civilian ARNP or doctor immediately and receive the treatment they need.

- Create a designated office/clinic room specifically for confidential examinations that include rape kits with at least two fully trained personnel available on each shift. Any woman seeking this kind of assistance needs to be accompanied by a trained civilian advocate.

- Personnel who are the first to examine a sexual assault victim are trained in the specifics of gathering forensic evidence and empathic interviewing techniques.

- Require counseling for every woman who reports sexual assault of any kind.

- Make counseling outside the military available to women who were raped or have MST.

- Require separate training for men and women returning to a woman's corps with their own chain of command, in order to teach appropriate respect and responsiveness as it was before men and women soldiers were integrated.

- Before separate training is fully implemented, require every male, no matter what rank, to go through basic attitude/respect/response to women educational program developed and executed by women.

- Teach and train every soldier of every rank what is OK and not OK to say and do with one another.

- Provide practical training intervening between people to stop any inappropriate activity or behavior noticed. Begin to reward appropriate behavior and reporting.

- Teach and train every soldier of every rank what domestic violence is and that it is always wrong. Provide resources on how to deal with stress, arguments, and returning from deployment so there is no stigma attached to getting help.

- Provide specific debriefing and retraining for soldiers returning from deployment, so they have a better chance of re-integrating back into their families in healthier ways.

- Teach officers at every level that wives and girlfriends are part of the support system for soldiers and must be respected and kept safe. Set up structures and resources to insure that.

- Complete overhaul of the Military Justice System, by a group to include more civilian authorities in the criminal and judicial field than military.

- CID training programs include civilian instructors familiar with sexual assault.

- Require the highest levels of leadership in all the services to go through testing to determine their attitudes, opinions and judgments toward women and then provide appropriate training in respectful attitudes, behavior and responses to women soldiers, OR take them out of leadership positions that include dealing with female soldiers.

- Anyone found guilty of sexual assault is immediately given a dishonorable discharge.

- Take all decisions regarding investigations and adjudication out of the chain of command and create a separate body to handle reports of sexual assault, protection orders, investigations, and adjudication. That body to include both military and civilians specifically trained in dealing with sexual assault.

The following from the Miles Foundation Testimony in 2004 may also be included. "The decades of indifference to sexual and domestic violence within the Military community warrant the establishment of an Office of the Victim Advocate (Miles et al., 1999; Hansen, 2004)"

The Office of the Victim Advocate would:

- Coordinate programs and activities of the Military departments relative to services and treatment for victims.

- Serve as headquarters program manager for the victim advocates/victim service specialists authorized by Congress (Victims' Advocates Programs in the Department of Defense, 1994).

- Coordinate and navigate services for victims among military and civilian communities.

- Evaluate the prevalence of interpersonal violence among the ranks.

- Evaluate the programs established by the military departments providing services to victims of interpersonal violence.

- Evaluate the delivery of services by the military departments.

- Review the facilities of the military departments providing services to victims.

- Review the hotline programs including command and installation hotlines, National Domestic Violence Hotline project, and Child Care /Child Abuse Hotline.

- Review disciplinary actions.

- Establish system accountability standards.

- Recommend to the Secretaries of the military departments policies, protocols, and programs to enhance accessibility of services.

- Recommend changes to policies and procedures to address sexual misconduct, assault and intimate partner violence.

- Conduct education and training within the military.

- Develop protocols for accountability of commanders in response to incidents of violence.

- Report annually to the Secretary of Defense relative to an assessment of the current state of affairs within the Military departments related to victims, as well as, propose initiatives to enhance the response of the military departments.

- Report annually to Congress relative to an assessment of the current state of affairs within the Military departments related to victims, as well as, to propose initiatives to enhance the response of the military departments.

- Serve or designate a person to serve on the fatality review panel established by the Secretary of Defense.

- Conduct training and provide technical assistance to commands, Family Advocacy Program, victim witness assistance liaison, commissions, medical personnel, law enforcement, security forces and Judge Advocate General Corps.

- Conduct programs of public education.

The staff of the Office of the Victim Advocate would consist of:

- Director-a person with knowledge of victims' rights, advocacy, social services, and justice within state, federal and military systems. The director shall be qualified by training and expertise to perform the responsibilities of the office.

- Victim advocates/victim service specialists-positions authorized by Congress shall be contracted by and assigned to the Office of the Victim Advocate. Personnel shall be qualified by training, certification, and expertise to perform the duties of a victim advocate/victim service specialist within the Military departments.

- Victim witness liaison personnel-shall be assigned to the Office of the Victim Advocate.

- Staff-shall be provided to carry out the responsibilities of the Office of the Victim Advocate including, but not limited to, sexual assault nurse examiners, community liaison, trauma specialist, behavioral specialist, et al.

The Office of the Victim Advocate would have access to:

- Name of a victim receiving services, treatment or other programs under the jurisdiction of the military departments, and the location of the victim if in custody.

- Written reports of sexual harassment, sexual misconduct, sexual assault, spouse abuse, intimate partner violence, child abuse and neglect prepared by military departments.

- Records required to maintain the responsibilities assigned to the Office of the Victim Advocate.

- Records of law enforcement, criminal investigative organizations, health care providers, Command and Family Advocacy Programs as may be necessary to carry out the responsibilities of the Office of the Victim Advocate.

The Office of the Victim Advocate would support and:

- Establish levels of care and services which mirror civilian communities, including sexual assault response teams, sexual assault nurse examiners, domestic violence response teams and enlightened criminal investigators.

- Establish protocols to provide for the safety of victims during administrative and criminal investigations, including protective orders and safe havens.

- Reform the Uniform Code of Military Justice (UCMJ) to expand the definition of rape, beyond reasonable resistance (by force and without consent), and age of consent.

- Reform the UCMJ to encompass the recent Supreme Court ruling relative to sodomy.

- Reform the Manual for Courts-Martial (MCM) to provide privacy for victims of sexual and domestic violence (Rule 513).

- Reform victim preference within the MCM (Rule 306(b)).

- Establish a rape shield for victims of sexual violence within the MCM (Rule 412).

- Reform the MCM to preclude the character and military service of an alleged assailant in cases of domestic and sexual violence as a factor in disciplinary actions by Commanders (Rosenthal and McDonald, 2003).

- Reform the Service Members Civil Relief Act in order to provide sufficient opportunity for the service and enforcement of civilian orders of protection.

- Establish a registry for the reporting of sexual assault and domestic violence incidents, disciplinary actions and military justice outcomes.

- Establish a registry for sexual offenders associated with the military, including notification of federal and state law enforcement officials.

- Adopt a privilege for sexual and domestic violence victims noting that without confidentiality many victims will refuse to report an attack, driving the problem "underground."

- Craft choice for victims when reporting an incident to a victim advocate, psychotherapist or chaplain.

- Provide transportation to a hospital and/or court, and any necessary support, to a victim who chooses to receive a rape kit examination or protection order; and Training (Hansen, 2004).[67]

------------------------------------------------------------------------

[67]*Prepared Statement of Christine Hansen,* Executive Director, The Miles Foundation Personnel Subcommittee, Senate Armed Services Committee, February 25, 2004

# Glossary

AFB –Air Force Base

AG – Adjutant General

AIT – Advanced Individual Training

Article 15 –Administrative Reprimand

Article 32 – Investigation into charges preliminary to court martial.

AWOL – Away without Leave

BOQ – Bachelor Officer Quarters

CID – Criminal Investigation Division

CO – Commanding Officer

CONUS – Continental United States

CQ – Charge of Quarters

DAV – Disabled American Veterans

DOD – Department of Defense

EEO – Equal Employment Opportunity

GWS – Gulf War Syndrome

IED – Improvised Explosive Device

JAG – Judge Advocate General (legal corps)

MOS – Military Occupational Specialty

MP – Military Police

NAS – Naval Air Station

NCIS – Naval Criminal Investigative Service

NCOIC – Non Commissioned Officer in Charge

OCS –Officer Candidate School

OER – Officers Evaluation Report

OIC – Officer in Charge

PT – Physical Training

R & R – Rest and Recreation

SAPRO – Sexual Assault Prevention Office

SJA – Staff Judge Advocate

UCMJ – Uniform Code of Military Justice

VSO – Veteran Service Officer

VA – Veterans Administration

VVA – Vietnam Veterans of America

WAC – Women's Army Corps

# WOMEN UNDER FIRE:Blog

From website www.womenunderfire.net

July 1, 2013

There is a new voice in the world, shining a bright light on the culture of abuse toward women in the U.S. Military. It is mine, Sarah L. Blum, and you are going to be hearing from me often for a while. I am a nurse Vietnam veteran and began this journey in 2006 when I was asked to write about women serving in our military. As I began to interview women veterans from WWII through the different military conflicts and time periods up to and through the current women veterans from Iraq and Afghanistan, I was hearing stories of pride and service, basic training and mustard gas, and then many stories of military sexual trauma. My focus was on all the stories and experiences.

Because I had never tried to write a book before, I was also learning how to write effectively and learning about the publishing industry. In 2008 and 2009 I attended the Pacific Northwest Writer's Association Conferences and learned a great deal. Then in 2009, I asked an editor to look at what I had so far and give me feedback. What he shared was invaluable to me including, narrow the focus of the book to the culture of abuse in the military. I was reluctant to do that because I was very connected to the women who graciously gave me their stories and I did not want to lose those stories that did not fit into a narrow focus on sexual assault. It took me several months to deal with my emotions and understand what to do. When I got clear, I understood that I had two books and the stories that did not fit into either book could go on the website you are now visiting.

The first book, Women Under Fire: Abuse in the Military will be released in early November and Women Under Fire: PTSD and Healing is not yet completed. You may pre-order the first book to ship in early November with this link: https://ec128.infusionsoft.com/app/ orderForms/Women-Under-Fire-Pre-Order-2013

The U.S. Military has been covering up their abusive culture for decades; and now, sexual predators believe they are safe in our military, where they have a target rich environment to prey on. For decades they have gotten away with their violent, despicable behavior, and have been emboldened to continue by the failure of military leadership to hold them accountable. Military predators believe they are entitled to take what they want from their victims and they know, because it has always been true, that they will be protected by their brothers and promoted by their commanders.

Victims, on the other hand, are shamed, humiliated, ostracized, isolated, denied privacy and compassionate care, have their health and self respect destroyed and lose their careers. Sixty-two percent of those who reported sexual assault were retaliated against over this past year.

This pervasive problem has been going on and covered up for decades. It is time for accountability. Our military has avoided it for too long and Congress has been too passive with its oversight. The military has been spouting the meaningless phrase, "Zero Tolerance" ad nauseam; and they have lost credibility. The U.S. Armed Forces habitually ineffective responses to sexual assault toward the women who report it, have demonstrated a consistent failure of leadership; they failed to take ownership of their pervasive and continuing culture of abuse toward women, to address it fully and deal with all of its effects appropriately.

It is time for Congress to take their role in oversight seriously and to call for full investigations into the culture of abuse. The military cannot and must not investigate themselves. It is time to insist that the criminal behavior of sexual predators in our military be investigated and prosecuted independent of the chain of command and with civilian oversight. The military has shown they are incapable of providing justice from within the culture of abuse. Women serving our country have been denied fair and compassionate responses and justice. That must change.

The Pentagon's Domestic Violence Task Force report from March 2003, recommended a "culture shift" by holding offenders accountable and punishing criminal behavior. Many of their specific recommendations apply also to military sexual assault. It seems to me that since the military and congress ignored that report ten years ago, they can start by reviewing it and utilizing what applies right now and move forward from there. We need a comprehensive look at all the services, how they handle a victim from first contact to the last and how they handle the report, follow up, investigations, and court case. We also need a new look at the UCMJ regarding violent sex crimes and determine the changes needed to usher in justice for all. At present it is not providing "uniform justice," but rather cover for the military itself. Lastly, legal experts need to look at the Feres Doctrine and change it so that everyone in our military receives appropriate justice.

Below are some links to Op Eds that I wrote and video's from the news that are current regarding the issue of military sexual assault toward women.

http://truth-out.org/opinion/item/13923-a-target-rich-environment-sex-crimes-continue-to-plague-the-us-military?tmpl=component&print=1#.UPYjMOiTvl8.email

http://seattletimes.nwsource.com/html/opin- ion/2018674273_guest13blum.html

## Sexual assault in the military jumps in 2012

http://video.msnbc.msn.com/all-in-/51811397

Video on msnbc.com: The Pentagon released new numbers today showing an increase in sexual assault in 2012. Chris Hayes talks about the new Pentagon numbers with Congresswoman Louise Slaughter, Goldie Taylor, and Susan Burke.

## How the military fails miserably to address sexual assault

http://video.msnbc.msn.com/all-in-/51811570

Video on msnbc.com: The military doesn't seem to grasp the enormity of its problems with sexual assault. Chris Hayes talks about military culture with Congresswoman Louise Slaughter, Goldie Taylor, and Susan Burke.

## Military sex assault revelations spur calls for accountability

http://video.msnbc.msn.com/the-r...

Video on msnbc.com: Sen. Claire McCaskill, D-Mo., member of the Senate Armed Services Committee, talks with Rachel Mad- dow about the shocking problem of sexual assaults in the U.S. Military and how the system can be restructured to bring accountability to of- fenders as well as negligent leadership.

## Sen. Gillibrand on fighting rise of sexual assualts in military

http://video.msnbc.msn.com/the-last-word/51836119

Video on msnbc.com: Democratic Sen. Kirsten Gillibrand of New York plans to introduce legislation to change the way the military handles allegations of sexual assault. In an exclusive interview on The Last Word, she explained why it should be "more parallel to the civilian system."

## Back-to-back scandals highlight epidemic of sexual misconduct in US military

http://video.msnbc.msn.com/all-in-/51898827

Video on msnbc.com: Chris Hayes talks with Sen. Kirsten Gillibrand, Rachel Maddow, and Anu Bhagwati of the Service Women's Action Network about the barriers to progress in combating sexual assault in the military.

## Military sex abuse scandals spark reform talk in Senate

http://video.msnbc.msn.com/the-r...

Video on msnbc.com: Senator Barbara Boxer talks with Rachel Maddow about yet another high profile sex abuse scandal in the U.S. Military and what can be done legislatively to fix a problem at which military leaders have failed miserably and which is apparently sustained in part by military culture.

## Another sexual assault prevention official is in trouble

http://video.msnbc.msn.com/all-in-/51911913

Video on msnbc.com: Moments after President Obama met with Pentagon leaders to talk about combating the problem of sexual assaults in the military, the manager of the sexual assault response program at Fort Campbell, Ky. was arrested. Chris Hayes talks with Spencer Ackerman, senior writer for Wired'…

# Military brass rejects outside accountability on sexual assaults

http://video.msnbc.msn.com/all-in-/52101577

Video on msnbc.com: Today the women of the Senate Armed Services Committee grilled military leaders about sexual assault in the military. Chris Hayes talks about the hearing with Senator Kirsten Gil- librand, Anu Bhagwati, and Goldie Taylor.

## Rape survivor Zerlina Maxwell to Senator Carl Levin: Who's side are you on?
http://mobile.nytimes.com/2013/06/04/opinion/dont- trust-the-pentagon-to-end-rape.html

Blog Post July 14, 2013

Military Sexual Trauma is any sexual abuse experienced in the military from sexual harassment, sexual assault, to rape. It is a personal and sexual boundary violation, which affects the victim emotionally, physically and spiritually. The victim (I will now refer to as a woman) experiences extreme vulnerability, helplessness, shame, humiliation, a breach in her sense of self and bodily integrity, and a lowered sense of self-esteem and self-confidence. If a fellow soldier, or worse, a superior of higher rank, perpetrated the violation, the woman experiences betrayal. For those who perceive their military unit or the corps as family, the violation equates to incest. One of their own has violated them.

From that moment on she feels unsafe in the military. She has no sense of being protected and safe. She experiences a clear violation and betrayal of the values taught in the military such as honor, respect, accountability, fellowship. She can no longer count on her brother soldiers to 'have her back' in combat. It has been referred to as a grievous psychological injury and is an assault on her as a person, her sense of self and her soul, which leaves her reeling in confusion, shock, shame, dismay, disintegration and dissociation. The woman often be- comes numb from the dissociation and has less access to her internal resources, even the ability to speak, ask for help, or tell what happened.

MST leads to PTSD—the symptoms begin while the assault is happening; the woman becomes numb and often dissociates. The numbness or dissociation is automatic and unconscious. The woman's sense of self and bodily integrity have been so violated, that she is un-able to stay connected fully to her body and the abusive experience, so she unconsciously attempts to cope in the moment by splitting off part of her self, her energy, her personality. This is often what happens in other traumatic experiences such as combat or combat injury. When the psyche is overwhelmed by an extremely painful experience beyond what is ordinary, the self decides, "I am out of here" and will ener-getically lift up from the body and observe what is happening to the body.

The body is fully experiencing but the psyche and sense of self, splits off, along with the emotions. This dynamic occurs to preserve the self and later becomes the problem to be solved therapeutically, to reconnect all parts of the person, body and emotions, for full healthy functioning.

During a trauma, a common response is to freeze. That freeze state makes it impossible to access normally occurring resources, e.g. the ability to move, run, or speak. A person in that state feels and is helpless.

Many rapes in the military are predatory and include the use of drugs. Drugs, such as Rohypnol cause disorientation, muscle re-laxation, slowing of psychomotor abilities, blackouts, and temporary memory loss. Drugs are deliberately used to render the woman inca-pacitated so she cannot fight back. This then makes the rape a deliber-ate premeditated attack. It also lends even more credence to so many women who reported that they could not move during the attack.

Whether from a freeze response or being drugged the victim is indeed unable to fight back. Military Sexual Trauma changes every-thing. Anyone who is sexually assaulted will never be the same again. Their body, mind, emotions and sense of self were violated. They may never feel safe or confident again. If the rape victim is not believed, supported, given the care she needs immediately, treated with dignity, respect, compassion, she is likely to be left with serious symptoms that may never go away. The way our military handles sexual assaults is dis-respectful, indignant, cold and harsh. Women are shamed, humiliated, denied compassion, medical care, protection, even the kind of investi-gation that affirms she is believed and that the military values integrity and accountability. Women who are sexually assaulted in the military are denied justice. The way our military responds to reports of sexual assault re-victimizes the survivor.

Russell Strand, a military criminal investigator and the chief of the Family Advocacy Law Enforcement Training Division at the U.S. Army Military Police School at Fort Leonard Wood said, "Mil-itary Sexual Trauma takes away everything you are in a minute" He teaches journalists, police, and first responders how NOT to re-victim- ize survivors through the use of his forensic experimental trauma inter- view (FETI) based on brain function and memory. He describes how people do not react the way they might think because the prefrontal cortex shuts down. The trauma is stuck in the parts of the brain that cannot communicate with thinking or under-standing and there is no way to verbalize a coherent description of what took place because the part of the brain that performs that function is shut down. Memories are stored in the right side of the brain in pictures and feelings yet co- herent thinking and words require the left side of the brain. These two parts are not communicating when there is a trauma, so what comes out is confused and incoherent. Survivors cannot give a coherent de- tailed beginning to end narrative account of what happened. The brain under that level of distress notes sounds, smells, tastes, emotions and sensations. When questioned the survivor can literally go back into the traumatic event with a full body reaction including increased heart rate, shortness of breath, shaking, sweating, and have dry mouth. (from Dart Society Reports. "The Narrative Comes Later." 12 Novem- ber 2012

# Invisibility of Women Veterans

Blogpost 8/5/13

Women have been serving our country since its earliest beginnings. During the revolutionary war, Margaret Corbin took over her husband's gun position and was wounded and disabled for life. Women were not allowed to be in the military back then.

During the Civil War women took on men's names, cut their hair, and dressed as men in order to serve a military that prohibited their presence as women. About 400 women both white and black served in both the Union and Confederate Armies. Sarah Edwards was a nurse, spy, courier and soldier for the Union Army. Loreta Valesques served the Confederate Army as Lt. Harry T. Buford. She recruited and commanded a troop of soldiers. When she was wounded at the battle of Bull Run her identity was discovered yet she joined again later in the Calvary.

The first woman physician entered the Civil War as a nurse because female doctors were prohibited. In 1964, Mary T. Walker was commissioned as a lieutenant in the Medical Corps and awarded the Congressional Medal of Honor—the first and only woman to receive that honor.

The first female marine was Lucy Brewer who served as George Baker for three years aboard the U.S.S. Constitution during the war of 1812.

During WWII the Women's Air Force Service Pilots (WASPS) flew every aircraft the Air Force had and logged over 300,000 hours of flying but were not given full military status until 1976. During WWII we had eighty-one American women captured along with male troops and were forced into the Bataan Death March from Manila to Corregidor. These brave women stayed side by side with the troops and continued their nursing, dietary, and therapy services under unsanitary conditions and on starvation rations for the three and one half years they were in captivity. For twenty-six years, until 1981, those women were denied VA medical care for service-connected ailments from when they were prisoners of war.

Even today, our women veterans struggle to be acknowledged, recognized and treated with respect both in the military and in the Veteran's Administration. Here is an experience described by a woman veteran from last month. "I was at the local VAMC (VA Medical Center) today ... went to get travel reimbursement ... there was a man being waited on, then another women vet, then me, then another male vet ... the clerk finished with the first man ... the other woman moved to the front of the desk and I was right next to her .... the clerk looked right past us to the male and asked if he was next, as if we weren't even there. Apparently women veterans have the magical capability of being invisible, unable to be seen even when two of them are about two feet from your face ... and male vets are seen even when they are six feet away and behind the women ......arrrrrrgggghhhhh !!!!!"

Kirby Dick the director of The Invisible War movie made a strong statement with his movie that the issue of sexual assault to both women and men needs to be made visible. Military sexual trauma and those who experienced it have been invisible for too long. Military sexual assault, rape and sexual harassment are not acceptable yet have been going on for decades; our military has actively supported it staying invisible. The movie made the problem visible. http://www. notinvisible. org/

Those who saw the movie were outraged and have commented. Here are some of the comments: "Keep in mind being shot or blow up while serving in the military is considered an occupational hazard, military rape is not, it is a crime and should be treated as a crime.

I watched THE INVISIBLE WAR and it shook me to the bone. How can sexual attacks on women AND men be called an "Occupational Hazard?"

I am not invisible. I have MST. I spent the rest of my time in service trying to pretend it didn't matter, it didn't happen, and that I deserved it."

**NOTE TO READER**: If you would like to support the author's work of bringing justice to women in our military you can make a donation on the website www.womenunderfire.net

The money will be used for travel expenses from November 2013 until November 2014 and any money left will be donated to charities working directly with survivors and homeless women veterans.

# APPENDIX

http://www. seattlepi.com/local/219613_crusader11.html

**Vet becomes crusader for victims of Soldier rape**

Monday, April 11, 2005

**By M. L. LYKE,** SEATTLE POST-INTELLIGENCER REPORTER

The Army Vet listens and let's fly. She has zero tolerance for tales of Soldier rape. In the Military, they'll tell you, "Lady, you can't get compensation for having sex," said Susan Avila-Smith, the Puget Sound area's outspoken advocate for sexually assaulted Veterans.

Her client Donna Jean Patee nods from her wheelchair, her service dog asleep at her feet." It happened to me," said the former Navy Petty Officer, who filed a rape claim in 1993. Patee said she was on waterfront watch in San Diego in the 1960s when five Sailors gang-raped her.

Former Army linguist Susan Avila-Smith runs

Women Organizing Women, a non-profit patient- to-patient support group, from her Sammamish home.

The claim was denied. "I've spent years being told it didn't happen, that 'none of my men would do anything like that, "said the disabled 59-year-old, who is working with Avila-Smith on filing government claims for seizures and other disorders. "I thought I had no recourse."

"Then Susan happened."

Susan happens. And all hell may break loose.

Day after day, the outraged, sometimes outrageous housewife from Sammamish battles to get Military discharges, Veteran benefits, Social Security disability pay, medical treatment, Military back pay and counseling for female Vets. At a time when Military Sexual Trauma is in the national spotlight, she's a mama bear on a tear, stirring it up, rattling brass, breaking rules as she decodes Military-speak and spiels off statistics.

The statistics aren't pretty.

In 2003 and 2004, 147 sexual assaults were reported in Iraq, Afghanistan, Kuwait and other active-deployment areas, according to Pentagon figures. But the numbers represent only a small fraction of attacks. A study by the Department of Veterans Affairs shows that 75 percent of assaulted Military women never tell their Commanding Officer.

The reasons are complicated.

Some assaulted female Soldiers express concerns that they won't be "one of the guys" if they tell -- or that higher-ups might use reports as an excuse to cut back on women in the Military, just as they are making gains in combat support roles. And most have heard horror stories of retaliation.

Avila-Smith, 47, cites case after case of clients who reported assaults and were vilified, blamed for the act, grilled on whether they were actually attacked. The former Army linguist said, "Some clients have been threatened with multiple charges: filing a false report, 'conduct unbecoming' and adultery, if they are married."

It makes her blood boil.

"If you want to be a sexual predator, the Military is a great place for you," the laser-focused, dark-eyed crusader said.

In interview after interview, her traumatized Vets -- World War II to Iraq -- sing her praises. She finds them beds to sleep in and couches to surf on, buys them groceries, invites them home for the holidays. She gives them rides to VA appointments and stands in for them when they can't bear to tell their stories again -- can't handle the smell, the sight, the gazes of so many men in one place.

She listens as they vent, blow, break down, describe struggles with drugs, alcohol, homelessness, continued abuse, their inability to hold jobs. A good number have attempted suicide. Their stories are difficult.

"It's like you're lying bleeding in this foxhole for 20 years, and everybody just goes by and ignores you. But Susan stops, says, "Oh, you're injured. Let's get you out of there and get you some help," said a former Air Force squad leader and soft-spoken mother of three. Her life unraveled after she reported an assault by her Supervising Officer in Panama.

"I went for help, but they didn't believe me," said the fragile woman, who has been in intensive psychiatric care for almost two decades. She worries constantly about personal safety and delicately calls her assault, "The blow."

The Colonel said, "It never happened -- or else."

# 'In-the-face kind of gal'

If Avila-Smith comforts the afflicted, she can also rub official nerves raw. That was the crusader from Sammamish interrupting a Colonel's speech on Operation Iraqi Freedom to ask: "So what is your policy on Military sexual trauma?"

Rick Price, a program manager for the Washington State Department of Veterans Affairs, describes Avila-Smith as high-maintenance.

"She's a little obnoxious, a very in-the-face kind of gal. In that way, she's a pain . . . ," he said. "But to get things done, sometimes you need people like her to make it happen."

Eyebrows may go up in VA circles when her name is mentioned. Avila-Smith is neither a therapist nor a sanctioned counselor, some will point out. She is herself, a patient with her own horror tale of service-connected sexual abuse. She is on full disability for post-traumatic stress disorder, which can manifest in anxiety, sleeplessness, flashbacks, irritability, nightmares, and depression.

Her future was determined in 1995, when, during a women's trauma-support group at the Puget Sound VA, she realized how hard it was for some patients to fill out their own disability paperwork, reliving their tales again in writing. "It was too emotional to put this stuff down and hand it over to a stranger, for them to make a decision about your life," Avila-Smith said.

So she began filling out forms for sisters in crisis.

And an advocate was born.

# Insider know-how

PTSD can sharpen nerves to a ragged edge -- as is evident as Avila-Smith talks. She fidgets with her hands, grinds her teeth, works to silence, "The chatter in my head."

Studies indicate that women exposed to trauma are 2 1/2 times more likely than men to develop PTSD. They typically experience more symptoms than men and endure a longer course of illness, often accompanied by physical problems.

If the trauma is sexual, the women's PTSD rates are even higher.

Avila-Smith, who sits on the King County Veterans advisory board, estimates that she has successfully filed more than 200 PTSD claims for her sexually assaulted Vets, Soldiers in a battle they never expected. "The government has a responsibility," she said. "You protect the country. The country protects you. Done."

Her insider know-how is invaluable, those who've watched her in action say. "She knows PTSD inside and out," said Bridget Cantrell, a Bellingham-based licensed mental health counselor contracted with the state Department of Veterans Affairs who has worked with Avila-Smith. **(Editor's Note: Her position was misstated in the original version of this story.)** "She knows the nuances of PTSD, how it affects someone's life. Things that aren't written down in books -- Susan knows these things."

Her manner is manna to women in crisis. "She just nods and understands; she knows. That was so therapeutic after facing so many people who just did not understand, or didn't agree, or hated me," said Audra, a former Fort Lewis Sergeant, now living in Pennsylvania, who asked that her last name not be used.

The former tactical intelligence specialist filed an assault report from Kuwait in 2003 that detailed how she was knocked unconscious, tied up with her hands tied behind her back, gagged with her own underwear and raped. In a sworn statement, she described how her masked assailant whispered, "Be quiet or else," and threatened to cut her genitalia.

When she reported it, Commanders gave her a rape exam, got her treatment for her cuts and took her to another camp, where she was asked to take a lie-detector test. Although the Army denied that she received inadequate care, Audra said she was left alone, with no rape counseling, distraught, and almost overdosed on anxiety medications.

Then Susan happened.

Avila-Smith helped Audra return home, find a trauma counselor, get medical treatment and prepare VA claims. Audra is now on full disability for PTSD and injuries to her head, back and elsewhere. The crusader also took Audra and her husband into her home, fed them and lent them her car and, always, her shoulder. "I'm totally in debt to her," said Audra, who received an honorable discharge last spring.

It's a story heard often in the suburban Sammamish house Avila-Smith shares with her second husband, who works for the Federal Railroad Administration. The town-and-country rambler, dolled up with a pretty palette of paint on the walls, is home base for Women Organizing Women, her non-profit patient-to-patient support group. She is Founder, Director and one-woman hot line. The phone rings constantly.

Yes, the advocate says, picking up the receiver to hear sobs, she can help. No, she doesn't charge anything, only that each female

Vet help three others. "Sometimes you have to fight to be heard, and that's not right," she says into the receiver.

Only a few of Avila-Smith's clients know her own tangled story. After living abroad for years, she joined the Army at age 34, looking for three squares, a cot and, "A wardrobe that's picked out for you. How hard could it be?"

She was soon married to a Soldier husband who, she says, abused, stalked and threatened her in the early 1990s, on a Military base on Oahu, Hawaii. Honolulu police records show a string of domestic violence calls to 911 and a no-contest plea to third-degree assault charges by her ex-husband. Avila-Smith said base Command neither backed her charges nor enforced restraining orders -- complaints she made in formal, sworn statements before her honorable discharge in 1995.

"The Commander told me I was not worthy to be in the Military."

Those were fighting words for the nervy girl from California, who boasts that she, "Bosses the Colonels around now." She's a Soldier on a mission, marching to her own orders.

Her goal is to get 300 Veterans hooked up for Military disability pay, which ranges from $108 to $2,229 monthly. So far, she figures she has helped file about 200 successful claims. She has 150 or more others in the works.

If she is successful, she figures, the claims could cost the Defense Department about $300 million. "It's my way of dealing with my rage and indignation," Avila-Smith said, flashing a fleet smile.

Her time frame is limited. She plans to retire when her husband does, within a year and a half. She is looking for someone to fill her shoes.

It's not going to be easy.

The crusader's shoes are big, heavy and kick hard.

And they aim where it hurts.

# WHERE TO GET HELP

National Sexual Assault Hotline: 800-656-4673

The Puget Sound VA Health Care System: 800-329-8387

VA Health Care Benefits: 877-222-8387

Military One source hot line: 800-342-9647

To contact Susan Avila-Smith at Women Organizing Women, e-mail:smith715@comcast. net

# RELATED ARTICLE

- Assaults in Military go unreported for a variety of reasons

P-I reporter M. L. Lyke can be reached at 206-448-8344 or m.llyke@seattlepi.com

*© 1998-2010 Seattle Post-Intelligencer*

# About The Author

**Sarah L. Blum**, is a decorated nurse Vietnam veteran who earned the Army Commendation Medal serving as an operating room nurse at the 12th Evacuation Hospital Cu Chi, Vietnam during the height of the fighting in 1967. Sarah was awarded the Certificate of Achievement for exemplary service as head nurse of the orthopedic ward at Madigan Army Hospital in 1968, where she was also the assistant director of nursing on evening and night shift in 1970. She received her Bachelor's Degree, Summa Cum Laude, from Seattle University and her Master's, Cum Laude, from U. W. and at age 73, Sarah is still a practicing nurse psychotherapist with over 28 years experience working with PTSD and trauma resolution.

Under her married name Saralee McGoran, she is featured in Myra MacPherson's book Long Time Passing: Vietnam and The Haunted Generation on pages 502-506; and the last chapter of Kathryn Marshall's book In The Combat Zone: An Oral History of American Women in Vietnam. The article "Reseeding The Fields of War" by Sherry Stripling in The Seattle Times, September 29, 1996 featured Sarah prominently.

Sarah was one of the first two women elected to the National Board of Directors of the Vietnam Veterans of America in 1983, and she was active in veterans affairs and successfully lobbied Congress to study the connection between Agents Orange, Blue, White and Purple, and birth defects in the children of women Vietnam veterans. KING and KOMO TV did specials on Sarah's work during 1984-1985.

Sarah obtained her black belt in Aikido at age 68, teaches aikido and is an African Drummer and at age 69 she began sculling. Sarah is full of vitality and loves to dance, drum, sing, and bring people together. Sarah lives in Auburn, WA has two grown children, a daughter who is a well-respected and effective M.S.W., and a son who is a professional musician and college teacher; and she has two gratnddaughters and a grandson on the way.

Sarah's first Op Ed "Sexual Abuse in the Military Needs to be Brought to Light", was published July 12, 2012 in The Seattle Times and her second,"Sex Crimes Continue to Plague the U.S. Military," was published in Truthout on January 15, 2013. Her authentic passionate voice reverberates through the pages of Women Under Fire: Abuse in the Military and the sequel, Women Under Fire: PTSD and Healing.

If you are interested in having Sarah speak at your event please visit
# www.womenunderfire.net